An Active Guide to Education

Jace Hargis
University of North Florida

KENDALL/HUNT PUBLISHING COMPANY
4050 Westmark Drive Dubuque, Iowa 52002

Acknowledgement

I would like to acknowledge Dr. Eugene Todd, who provided an ideal opportunity into the academe and to Dr. John J. Koran whose guidance, mentoring and critical encouragement were nothing short of amazing. May they rest in peace.

The State of Florida Statewide Course Detail indicates that the course EDF1005 Introduction to Education will consist of a survey of the historical, sociological, and philosophical foundations of education and an orientation to professional education, which includes the code of ethics for the teaching profession. This course experience includes a field experience of at least 15 hours. This textbook will address these components as well as other aspect of education, teaching, and learning.

ISBN 0-7575-1693-9

Printed in the United States of America

10 9 8 7 6 5 4 3 2 1

CONTENTS

CHAPTER 2—Is Teaching for Me?

Guest Editorial: *Alison Morris-Shetlar, PhD, Biologist, Professor and Director of the Teaching and Learning Center/University of Central Florida*

CHAPTER 3—How Do I Become a Teacher?

Guest Editorial: *Deryl Bailey, PhD, Associate Professor of Counselor Educator/University of Georgia and Mary Bradbury-Bailey, M.Ed*

CHAPTER 4—Critical Aspects of Teaching and Learning

Guest Editorial: *Scott Lewis, PhD, Science Educator*

CHAPTER 5—Individual Learning Needs

CHAPTER 6—Society and Teaching

CHAPTER 7—School Governance

Guest Editorial: *Gary Senn, PhD, Assistant Professor of Science Education and Director, Dupont Planetarium, University of South Carolina, Aiken*

CHAPTER 8—Legal and Ethical Concerns for Educators

Guest Editorial: *Professor Tim Richardson, Seneca College/University of Toronto, Ontario, Canada*

CHAPTER 9—Historical Aspects of Education in America

Guest Editorial: *William Russell, Doctoral Candidate, Florida State University*

CHAPTER 10—Instructional Technology

CHAPTER 11—Assessment and Measurement

CHAPTER 12—Are You Ready to Teach?

Epilogue

PREFACE

"I hate quotations."

—Ralph Waldo Emerson

Purpose and Audience

The purpose of this text is to provide useful, meaningful information on the profession of teaching and learning to pre-service and in-service teachers. It is ideal for courses introducing students to the career of education as well as a resource guide for current teachers. Although there are many texts available for introducing students to teaching, this text provides an opportunity for students to actively participate in a variety of methods relating to teaching. In addition, this text encourages pre-service teachers to begin processing, planning, and critically evaluating their role as a teacher now, enabling them to capitalize on their transitional situation from one side of the podium to the other.

Description of Text

The book attempts to set the stage for students who are considering the profession of teaching. Six major themes are used to explore education, including perspective, change, communication, opportunity, priority, and attitude. The intent is to inform, but more importantly to question and encourage potential teachers to look inside themselves to realize what they can contribute to society. An initial section provides extensive information addressing the foundational concept of learning. This section includes learning theories, strategies, orientations, and educational philosophies. This section provides the first view of the philosophical underpinnings of teaching and strongly encourages students to begin considering their own professional educational philosophy.

The first chapter allows students to reflect on their own abilities and compare them to those of a qualified teacher. Questioning is highly encouraged, comparing the current requirements and conditions of teaching with the desires of pre-service teachers. The next chapter details the steps to become a teacher, including the education, certification and interview process. The following chapters present a global view on critical aspects of teaching, individual learning needs, society and teaching, school governance, legal and ethical concerns, multicultural and historical aspects of education, assessment and measurement, and educational technology.

No Child Left Behind Literature

Soon after taking office in January 2001, President George W. Bush announced *No Child Left Behind,* his framework for education reform that he described as "the cornerstone of my Administration." The President emphasized his belief in our public schools, but an even greater concern that "too many of our neediest children are being left behind," despite the nearly $200 billion in federal spending since the passage of the Elementary and Secondary Education Act of 1965 (ESEA). The President called for solutions based on accountability, choice, and flexibility in federal education programs. Less than a year later, the President secured passage of the *No Child Left Behind Act of 2001* (NCLB Act). The new law reflects how to improve the performance of America's elementary and secondary schools while at the same time ensuring that no child is trapped in a failing school. The NCLB Act, which reauthorizes the ESEA, incorporates the principles and strategies proposed by the President. These include increased accountability for states, school districts, and schools; greater choice for parents and students, particularly those attending low-performing schools; more flexibility for states and local educational agencies in the use of federal education dollars; and a stronger emphasis on reading.

Think. . . . Really Think

Finally, an overtly global goal of this text is to encourage people to think. Some of the many attributes of thinking are "to use or exercise the mind or one's power of reason in order to make inferences, decisions, or arrive at a solution or judgments; decide by pondering, reasoning, or reflecting; believe, consider, suppose; to visualize; imagine." I prescribe to these and many more and strongly encourage the pre-service and in-service teacher to think, in multiple contexts, diverse methods and beyond traditional, linear precepts. The text encourages the reader to consider more questions than answers—good, high-level questions of evaluation, synthesis, analysis, and application that question prior conceptions, re-evaluate, reconsider, and debate contradictions, that question current ideology, personally, professionally, and historically. And of course, that question the future of education, without bounds, stereotypes, and expectations. Above all, question everything. If a picture is worth a thousand words, a good question is worth a thousand pictures.

INTRODUCTION: SETTING THE STAGE

What Is Education?

Ed saw her from across the counter at the soda shop. He wasn't the forward type, so he did what most young men did. He stared—and dreamed. He dreamed of walking over to young Edna, gallantly introducing himself, then proceeding quickly to stimulating discourse. Upon which, she would gaze into his eyes amazed at how articulately he was able to synthesize current events. He finally gathered the courage to stumble across the shop. He stuttered his name, barely audible, paused awkwardly and looked down. After an eternal two seconds, Ed placed his hands deep into the pockets of his jeans, looked up and he stared again. He tried to swallow, although his Adam's apple only made it half way up his throat, so he tried to relax. But he only sighed and stared, again.

That is love. It is also a method of storytelling, a powerful approach to sharing information in a context that people find interesting and can recall effectively. Some might say that this is the definition of education. But what really is education?

Some people believe in the Greek concept of *paideia,* which indicates the goal of education is not mastery of subject matter, but of one's person. The paideia plan is built on the understanding that education serves to prepare individuals for (a) earning a living, (b) citizenship, and (c) self-development. Others believe that education is the process society uses to improve itself by imparting knowledge and developing skills, both academic and social. Also, that it is important in any modern society, whatever its political or economic forms. But a society such as ours, dedicated to the worth of the individual, committed to the nurture of free, rational, and responsible men and women, has special reasons for valuing education.

Emerson believed that "when a man is pushed, tormented and defeated, he has a chance to learn something." Although teachers new to technology may share this perspective, Mark Twain cautioned that students should "never let formal education get in the way of learning." However, most of us realize that a smooth sea has never made a skilled mariner. Piaget favored an approach of disequilibrium to learning. Only when we are uncomfortable, unsatiated, and out of sorts, can we discover methods to overcome the circumstance and re-equilibrate. Piaget called these ways to make ourselves feel better, acclimate, and accommodate.

There are many people that have shared their thoughts on what education means to them:

- Education is not the filling of a bucket, but the lighting of a fire. —*W. B. Yeats*
- Knowledge is the food of the soul.—*Plato*
- We learn by doing.—*Aristotle*

- Only the educated are free.—*Epicetus*
- Start where the learner is.—*John Dewey*
- As we acquire more knowledge, things do not become more comprehensible, but more mysterious.—*Albert Schweitzer*
- If you treat an individual as he is, he will remain as he is. But if you treat him as if he were what he ought to be and could be, he will become what he ought to be and could be.—*Goethe*
- What wine is so sparkling, so fragrant, so intoxicating, as possibility!—*Soren Kierkegaard*

But what about *quality* education? Is that a different concept?

A quality education is a specialized design that addresses the unique abilities of each student and results in a positive experience. Quality education assesses how the student learns as well as how the teacher teaches. Quality education includes components such as excitement, depth, complex, ownership, creativity, integration, and most of all motivation—maximizing the intrinsic type and minimizing extrinsic motivation. Quality education combines the science of teaching, the art of instruction, and the intuition to identify the best method to help students want to learn.

Above and Beyond

Therefore quality education encourages an "Above and Beyond" environment. One story that exemplifies this in the context of education is the following. Ed was a schoolteacher. At the beginning of each term, he provided an assignment with complete instructions to the students. He asked them to go home, complete the assignment, and return it the next day. The following day, they turned in the work and he graded their papers. He returned the work the following day and every student in the class received a "C" for his or her assignment. Of course, many students were confused and upset at their grade and inquired as to how it was determined. Ed kindly compared one student's paper with the assignment guidelines and indicated, that indeed, the student did everything that was expected of them, so they received a C. Even more upset, now, the student asks, "Well, how could I receive a B, or even an A?" Ed replied, "Now that is simple. To receive a B, all you need to do is to go "Beyond" what I ask of you and to receive an A, you must go "Above Beyond" what is asked of you."

Now, this may seem silly to some people. However, when you compare this scenario to the world in which most of our students will enter someday, it makes sense. In reality, a dishwasher does not receive a raise for washing dishes, but for cleaning up, helping out and going beyond their job duties. The salesperson does not receive awards and bonuses for meeting his quota, and simply doing what he is asked to do. He receives outstanding evaluations for going above and beyond what is expected of him. However, in education, when students simply meet the criteria, we provide an "outstanding" or "excellent" evaluation. Many students could become conditioned that meeting a job description merits promotions and significant pay increases.

Another example of going "Above and Beyond" occurred to Edna as she entered the lobby of an upscale hotel. It was one of those hotels with an enormous breakfast buffet. She was trying to lose a few pounds and did not need the temptation of the large amount and variety of high-fat foods. So, she asked the waiter for a booth in the back facing away from the buffet. He gladly obliged and then offered her a menu. Edna denied the menu and confidently said, "No, I would just like a small bowl of oatmeal, please." With that information, the waiter whisked away. Soon afterward, the waiter reappeared with a bowl of warm oatmeal. Placing it on the table, he confessed, "I was not certain what you like in your oatmeal, so I brought some fruit, including bananas, strawberries, blueberries and raisins. I also was not sure if you liked milk, so I brought some 1 percent, 2 percent, whole milk, half and half, and cream. Then, if you like sugar, I brought some brown sugar, white sugar, Nutrasweet®, and honey."

Before she knew it, there before her was an entire oatmeal breakfast buffet. The waiter went "Above and Beyond"—without a request. This is an alternative definition of *quality.* Possibly, this definition could apply to education one day.

Six Major Themes for Exploring Education

Theme #1: Perspective

Perspective Example 1

Remember Ed from the introductory paragraph. Well, Ed was somewhat of an adventurer. He prided himself in trying different experiences. That being the case and the fact that he had never rode a horse in his life, prompted him to tackle this adventure one summer day. He identified the horse, approached the beast cautiously, and somehow managed to mount. The horse began to move, slowly at first, but then picked up speed quickly. He realized that his main goal was to stay aboard. He teetered left and teetered right. However, within minutes, he found himself out of control and unable to hang on. Ed fell from the horse and unfortunately his foot got caught in the stirrup. There was Ed, head bouncing along the ground, which didn't bother the horse, as the horse kept moving. Before he knew it, Ed found his life flashing in front of his eyes. Just before he lost consciousness, the Wal-Mart® manager came out and unplugged the horse.

Now, I hope this was humorous and we are not as concerned about Ed's health as we were moments ago as we visualized his demise. But the point of perspective is made, since most people will clearly see Ed in distress and even cringe at the possibility of significant harm to another person. The power of our mind's eye is incredible. We are able to visualize practically anything that we find interesting and that catches our attention. Gagne (1973) indicates that the first step in learning and memory is for the learner to attend to a stimulus. This attention and subsequent visualization can be a powerful learning tool. Further support of attention is the generic Information Processing (IP) system commonly referred to as the two-store (dual-memory) model, originally proposed by Atkinson and Shiffrin (1971). The IP theory views learning as the coding of information in long-term memory by creating schema produced by relating new knowledge to existing information in the short-term memory. Short-term memory is the information that you are focusing on at a given moment. The short-term memory is fed by the sensory memory, which is the point of attention in processing.

Perspective Example 2

A second example of the power of perspective occurred when a college friend of Ed's was hospitalized and went into a coma. The man's wife was next to him at all hours of the day. After two months, he finally woke up and she was right there to greet him. She told him how much she loved him and had been there the entire time. The man pondered the thought and paused. Then when he had the strength to talk, he said. "You know you were with me when I went bankrupt in my business. You were there when I was shot and mugged. You were right beside me when they foreclosed on our house. And now you are by my side during this time of my illness." She smiled at her husband's realization and then he spoke again. "You know, I think you're bad luck."

Perspective Example 3

Unfortunately, Ed found himself in a courtroom as a witness for his own small claims lawsuit against the city. The small city hired a large city attorney to fly in and cross-examine the plaintiff. The lawyer began by asking, "Now, when you were at the scene of the accident, did you or did you not tell the police officer who arrived at the scene that you were fine?" Ed looked at the lawyer and replied, "Well, I was loading Betsy, my horse . . ."

"Now, I did not ask you anything about your horse, sir. Simply tell the judge, did you or did you not indicate that you were fine at the scene of the accident?"

Ed looked a bit flustered, but began again, "Well, it was Saturday, which is when I take Betsy . . ."

"Now, sir, I am not asking about the day or your horse, just answer the question!"

Ed looked at the judge and the judge said, "Actually, I am a bit interested in what the horse has to do with this. Please continue."

So, Ed continued, "Well, it was Saturday and Betsy did not really want to get into the trailer, but I finally coaxed her in there. Then I was driving down state road 24 and the fire truck came out of nowhere and I swerved and ran into the ditch. Betsy was thrown out of the trailer and into one ditch and I was thrown into the other ditch. When the policeman arrived, he walked over to Betsy first, since she was making so much noise and in pain and he said that she was hurt really bad and so he took out his gun and he shot her. Then he walked over to me, with his gun still in his hand and asked me how I was doing. Well, I looked at that gun and I said I was just fine."

Are we all just fine? Sometimes it is all about perspective. Is education just fine, or should we shoot it and release it from its misery?

Theme #2: Change

The beginning of a new term is an ideal time to renew our perspective on life, review and refocus our goals, and possibly redirect a few approaches that may have wandered off while we were looking the other way. For some, this is a very scary time of change. One paradigm on change is discussed in the book "Who Moved My Cheese" by Spencer Johnson. Cheese represents what makes us happy and fulfilled, including financial, spiritual, physical, or mental well being. Cheese has many things in common.

- The more important your cheese is, the more you want to hold onto it.
- To keep your cheese, you may need to change.
- The possibility of losing our cheese makes us afraid.
- We should smell our cheese often to know when it's getting old.
- Movement in a new direction helps you to find cheese.
- The quicker you let go of old cheese, the sooner you will find new cheese.
- Old beliefs do not lead you to new cheese.
- So move with the cheese and enjoy it!

Ideally we should try to anticipate change and keep in mind, they will always be moving our cheese, so be ready to change again. It seems a common misperception about education is a lack of change, even from potential pre-service teachers. Once one begins to investigate the daily modifications in a teacher's schedule, a quick awareness to the necessity of change is revealed.

Theme #3: Communication

Communication Example 1

Ed loved his garden. He spent much of his spare time in his garden, tending his vegetables. One day after thirty years of marriage, Ed came into the house to clean up for supper. As soon as he walked in, he knew Edna had made him some of his favorite food. He could smell the Yankee pot roast thick in the air. He could almost see the little cooked carrots; redskin potatoes, green beans, and he just knew she would have made a little strawberry Jell-O® with fruit cocktail in it. He did love that Jell-O®. And Edna had done just that. The same as she had done for many years. After they ate, they retired to the living room. Ed sat at the back of the room in his favorite chair, reading the newspaper and petting his old hound, Tipper. Edna sat much nearer to the television set finishing up her crochet. It was Saturday night and the Lawrence Welk Show was on, one of their favorites. It was up a bit loud, just as they like it. Ed finally set the paper down and looked up at Edna. He realized what a good wife and companion she had been all these years and said, "Edna, I'm kind of proud of you!" Edna turned and quickly turned down the television set.

"Yea, well I'm sick and tired of you, too!"

Communication Example 2

Ed took a drive to pick up a new shovel from the store to plant green beans. While he was gone, there was a news bulletin that came across the television program that Edna was watching. The news report said that someone was driving in the wrong direction on the local highway. She frantically called Ed, who had a new fancy cellular phone in his car. She told him that she saw on the television where someone was driving on the wrong side of the road. Ed quickly replied, "Someone? Every one is driving on the wrong side of the road!"

If you were to ask how effectively people believe their own communication skills are, chances are most would rate their own quite highly. Practically every job description indicates a need for good oral and written communication skills. However, something as simple as a "peanut butter sandwich" activity can demonstrate our limitations to communicate. In the peanut butter sandwich activity, students are asked to prepare written directions on how to prepare a peanut butter sandwich. If the directions are good enough, so that a colleague can take the directions and without assistance successfully prepare the sandwich, then both students can enjoy the product. However, most times, the recipe is incomplete as many times, the students forget the first step—"open the peanut butter jar."

Theme #4: Opportunity

After many years, Ed and Edna finally had the opportunity to take a vacation. They decided to visit the Grand Canyon. Once there, they thought it would be a good idea to rent one of the mules that took visitors down the canyon. Edna approached her mule and it stumbled just as she was about to hoist herself up. Edna looked sternly at the mule, raising her index finger.

"That's one!"

They boarded the mules and began their journey. At about halfway down the canyon, Edna's mule slipped and jerked Edna's head and back. She regained her composure and raised two fingers.

"That's two!"

They progressed and finally reached the bottom of the canyon, when the mule stopped abruptly and Edna fell off. She got up, dusted herself off, walked over to the mule, raised three fingers and yelled, "That's three!"

She then pulled out a pistol and shot the mule. Ed was completely surprised and chastised his wife. "Edna, you didn't have to do that to the poor mule!"

Edna turned to Ed and said very calmly, "That's one!"

Opportunity is a wonderful phenomenon, and one that as teachers we should embrace. In class, this is frequently called a "Teaching Moment," when a student provides a thought or response that opens up an avenue to pursue that integrates the lesson and connects the concepts to something familiar to the student and their colleagues. Sometimes, teachers are hurrying to complete their lesson and overlook this powerful moment in the classroom. It may be better to present less coverage and spend time on ideas that students can connect, process, and extrapolate into other areas.

Theme #5: Priority

Ed won tickets to the Super Bowl, but his seats were too high. He saw one open on the fifty-yard line just thirty rows from the front. He made his way down and asked the man sitting next to it if anyone was sitting there. The man said no. Ed couldn't believe that whoever bought this did not go to the game. After several plays, the man said, "Actually the seat belongs to my wife. We have been going to every game since 1967. But she passed away last week."

Ed was sympathetic, "I'm so sorry. Couldn't you find another friend or relative to come to the game?"

The man said, "No, they are all at the funeral."

Everyone has priorities set in their life. At times, we are able to select our own, other times they are selected for us. As a teacher, the state will prioritize what you teach in the form of content standards. You must select how you are going to teach the concepts and in what priority and with what emphasis. This method of teaching is just as important as what is being taught. Especially when considering which portions of the concepts the student will retain for subsequent retrieval from long-term memory.

Theme #6: Attitude

> "The longer I live, the more I realize the impact of attitude on life. Attitude, to me, is more important than facts. Is it more important than the past, than education, than money, than circumstances, than failures, than successes, than what other people think or say or do. It will make or break a company, a church, and a home. The remarkable thing is we have a choice everyday regarding attitude we will embrace for that day. We cannot change the past, we cannot change the way people will act, and we cannot change the inevitable. The only thing we can do is play on the one string we have and that is our attitude. I am convinced that life is 10% what happens to me and 90% how I react to it. And so it is with you, WE are in charge of our attitudes" (Swindoll, 2004).

Swindoll's (2004) commentary on attitude is exemplified by the academic teacher. There are so many things that we can do with a good attitude and infinitely more that we will prevent ourselves from doing with a poor attitude. Maintaining a good attitude requires an exceptional, mature, professional person, especially in the chaos of a classroom. In most countries, teachers are praised, even idolized because of their knowledge and abilities. A teacher's ability to maintain a positive attitude in the arena of less than ideal conditions allows their abilities to surface and accomplish their goals of caring, teaching, and learning in a positive environment.

References

Atkinson, R. C., & Shiffrin, R. M. (1971). The control of short-term memory. *Scientific American, 225,* 82–90.
Gagne, R. M. (1973). *The conditions of learning.* New York, NY: Holt, Rinehart, and Winston.
Swindoll, C. (2003). Attitude. Retrieved April 2004, from *http://home.xnet.com/~ansible/attitude.html*

1

A Prelude: How Do We Learn?

Learning Theories

"The roots of education are bitter, but the fruit is sweet."

—Aristotle

A theory is often times thought of as an explanation of some aspect of the world, or a belief that guides behavior, or a broad generalization that explains a body of knowledge.

Learning is known as the cognitive process (thinking or conscious mental processing) of acquiring knowledge, skills, or dispositions. There are three criteria needed for learning to take place: behavioral change, or change in the capacity for behavior; the change endures over time; and, it occurs through practice or other forms of experience (Schunk, 1996).

Learning theories are an attempt to explain what learning is and why it may operate in that particular way. They are general principals designed to help us understand more global themes and situations. They are, at times models, or representations, for which we can derive understanding, extrapolate, and expand our understanding. They allow learners to become aware of their processing skills in order that they might capitalize on this process to learn more effectively in a variety of areas.

There are many aspects, derivatives, and interpretations of learning theories and how we learn. There is not a best approach, only a more appropriate one. As an educator, one of your roles will be to understand many of the theories and know when best to apply these in the context of your classroom. This process should be transparent to the students. Although you will be expected to understand the intricacies of the theories, your students will only view the products of your application of them. Many students new to the post-secondary education system may wonder why they must learn the philosophical and psychological orientations of educational learning theories. Especially, in the area of elementary education, students often pursue this career simply because they like children and wish to help young folk. In order to do this, a pre-service teacher candidate must understand the foundational underpinnings of educational theory sufficiently so as to be able to use these models in the classroom when their students require assistance in learning and/or behavior modifications.

The intent of this text is to provide a broad introduction to many learning theories in hopes that subsequent courses will be taken to enhance, clarify, and apply these methods. A brief discussion of the learning theories of information processing, self-regulation, self-efficacy, metacognition, and constructivism will be presented. Their importance and how they might be applied in an education setting will be presented.

In addition, an introduction to other learning approaches and philosophies will be discussed as they will come to the forefront throughout this journey into the educational system. The following is a non-inclusive list, and it should provide a sense of psychological orientations frequently used in the area of education.

- Operant Conditioning (Skinner)
- Social Cognitive (Bandura)
- Cognitive Development (Piaget)
- Contextualist/Social (Vygotsky)

I^3 (I-cubed = Input, Interact, Infer)

Periodically, the text will pause to involve students in a meaningful discussion that will help students make sense, share their thoughts, and encourage higher level, critical thinking, and questioning skills, which are important as teachers. These brief "intermissions" are called **I^3**, which stands for "Input, Interact, and Infer." A question will be posed to the class and each student should consider their thoughts on the item. Students should share their thoughts, listen, and interact with others and then finally make some inferences on what the question and responses mean to teaching and learning.

Here is the first one:

I^3 *When and how did you learn something well?*

Try not to make this too difficult, these activities are intended to create an environment of thought and analysis, there are typically no right or wrong answers. This is the area of gray that exists in reality. Many times, we are enculturated through the K–12 process that there are always absolute answers to every question, where ideas are right and wrong, or black and white. However, even theories mentioned in the beginning of this chapter, are dynamic, changeable, and often rewritten as more empirical data is gathered. For this response, try to think of something as simple as tying your shoe or riding a bike. What type of conditions was present during those times that really made the event easier to learn and learn well?

Since we have warmed up, let us try another I^3:

I^3 *What blocks meaningful learning?*

Can you think of times or conditions when you were unable to or had a difficult time learning something? Try to be as insightful as possible; chances are your colleagues have experienced something similar. When others are responding, try to determine if there is a trend or pattern in the responses. Some possible responses might be that learning was difficult in a sterile environment, such as a classroom with little or no maniputables, stimuli, or graphics, a situation in which only inert knowledge was shared, which had little or no meaning and/or application for you, an environment in which the students were passive learners, simply sitting and listening to the teacher without interaction, a situation with a hurried teacher attempting to complete their objectives and losing sight of "teaching moments"; or a place that holds negative memories for you, such as a science class with specimens or microscopes that you had seen earlier in your career and were intimidated and performed poorly.

After all of the exciting interaction between students, hopefully we can synthesize the information shared and consider the following question. Let us not approach this as an I^3 activity, but try to make some connections from the data gathered earlier and derive some possibly solutions in your mind about the following question.

How are learning and memory connected?

Information Processing

"A teacher affects eternity; he can never tell where his influence stops."

—Henry B. Adams (1838–1918), U.S. Historian

Information processing theories focus on attending, encoding, storing, and retrieving information. One assumption of human information processing (IP) theory is that it is analogous to computer processing, in that it receives information, stores it in memory, and retrieves it as necessary (Schunk, 1996). The generic state of the IP system is commonly referred to as the two-store (dual-memory), originally proposed by Atkinson and Shiffrin (1971) (Figure 1).

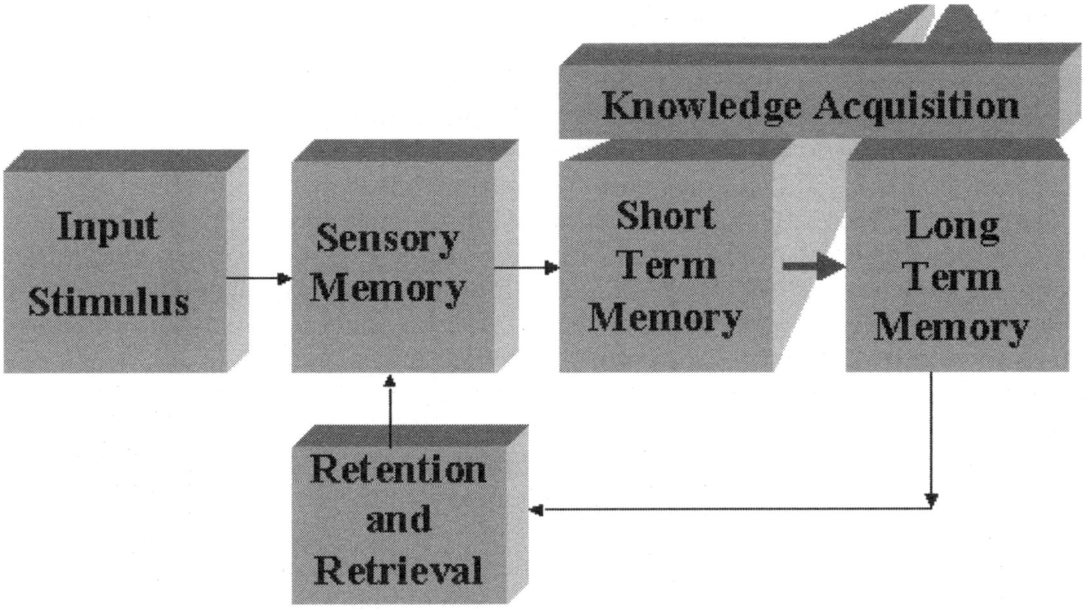

FIGURE 1. IP model.

The first step to processing or learning is to provide an adequate stimulus for students to attend. This may sound sensible and possibly relatively easy. However, the challenge is to offer an appropriate stimulus that will endure and align with the concepts taught. This should be an event, demonstration, activity, and so on that will enable the student to make connections to similar events following the instruction.

Did you know that apples, not caffeine, are more efficient at waking you up in the morning or that diddly-squat actually came from early American carnival lingo, because workers referred to nickels and dimes, the going rate for games of chances, as "diddle-e-squat." Also, no piece of paper can be folded more than seven times, most dust particles in your house are made from dead skin, and Tonto's nickname for the Lone Ranger, *Kemo Sabe,* actually means "soggy shrub" in Navajo. These could be trivial tidbits of useless knowledge or they could be the item that could help your students pay attention to subsequent concepts.

If this is successful, students are able to transfer the information to their Short-Term Memory (STM) or working memory. Here is where students work with the information and determine its value based on previously conceived criteria—much of which you can populate with various activities, thus increasing the power of student connections. Memory can be retained here for up to 20 seconds or more if rehearsed repeatedly. Short-term memory typically can hold up to seven plus or minus two items. STM capacity can be increased many ways especially if the information is meaningful, contextual, relevant, and can be applied. The key transitional stage in this model is the teacher's ability to successfully motivate students to transfer critical content and processing information from STM to Long-Term Memory (LTM). This step is very important as students and teachers. As teachers, we hope to own the small arrow in the diagram, since it governs how students acquire knowledge. The diagram presents several ways in which to own the processing step between STM and LTM. These include mnemonics, chunking, serial positioning, and the learning theories. A brief description of some of these will be presented now and a further description of the learning theories will follow in a subsequent section.

Mnemonics is a method or system, such as a formula or rhyme for improving memory. These are low-level instruments and although can be useful should be carefully examined by the instructor as to their appropriateness for the particular concept. It seems that the most effective use of mnemonics can be recalling the order of things, such as the planets, order of mathematical operations, the metric system, bodily functions, battles, presidents, and so on. An example of a mnemonic would be ROY G. BIV, which is Red, Orange, Yellow, Green, Blue, Indigo, Violet— the colors of the rainbow, in order, or My Very Easy Method-Just Set Up Nine Planets for help remembering the nine planets.

Chunking is a phenomenon, which Microsoft® has used successfully, while gaining great financial earnings as well. Their product PowerPoint® essentially takes this approach by offering slides, which contain five to seven easily digestible bullets of information. Ideally, the presenter or instructor will provide these bullets associated with other information, examples, stories, anecdotes, and so on, to engage the audience and help them recall the information. One of the pitfalls of this method is that students may only write or recall the bullet text, learning only superficial information or simply the words and not their meanings and connections to a concept.

Serial positioning is our ability to recall various items in the order they are presented. For instance, if someone were to verbally describe 10 items that they would like you to purchase for them at the store and you did not write them down and went to the store, chances are you would recall the first several and the last several items. We tend to recall concepts in the order or position we hear them. This extrapolates to teaching and learning in that as an instructor you may wish to place the more complex concepts at the beginning of the lesson or the end of the lesson, or ideally at both ends.

There are many ways to capture the arrow between STM and LTM, one relatively new method is through using technology to enhance teaching and learning. Some students are able to attend and process better using this mode of teaching, while others are not. An entire chapter will be presented later in this text that will describe how technology can be used effectively in instruction.

If transfer from STM to LTM is accomplished, theoretically, the information will remain there forever, with minimal degradation. Long-term memory has unlimited capacity. Some materials are "forced" into LTM by rote memorization and overlearning. Deeper levels of processing and higher cognitive skills such as generating linkages between old and new information are much better for successful retention of material. Then upon appropriate cues and prompts, the student will be able to recall or retrieve the information from their LTM. Besides the arrow between STM and LTM, the portion between LTM and recall is another vital point in which teachers should take responsibility. Measurement and assessment should be highly correlated with instruction and the IP model. The key here is to basically test, either traditionally or authentically in the same manner, the material that was taught. Nothing is more frustrating to a good student who attended, processed, and studied the material than to be assessed on material that was not covered or was presented in a different mode. In this case, internal validity issues arise and confounding variables are typically the reason for poor performance. Simply stated, the instrument may not be measuring what it was intended to measure. This text will provide further information in a later chapter on measurement and assessment.

Remember, curiosity plays a role during the initial step of stimulus by acting as both a response to a stimulus and a factor for influencing further attention. As Koran and Longino (1983) found, the greater the complexity of the object, the higher degree of curiosity it will evoke. They also compared the time spent as a measure of attention to time in the vicinity of the stimulus can be a measure of curiosity. Further, Koran and Koran (1984) demonstrated that curiosity is a response to a novel stimulus, such as manipulatable objects found in informal settings. This stimulus will increase the amount of attention to the object. Koran and Koran (1984) also proposed that static stimuli influence attention for only a short period, thus coding is minimized and information storage and retrieval is low. Likewise, holding power, and engagement time, or the time spent actively learning, will also be limited. So, the bottom line is that for IP to be effective, our instructional techniques would be better served if they provided novel, interesting, and intrinsic ideology and as much student-centered hands on events as possible.

Let us try a few examples to determine how well we are processing.

I^3 *Information Processing Example #1*

- Say the word white.
- Spell the word white. ________________
- Say the word white again.

What do cows drink?

If you said milk, you are in the majority. Many people process the term white and place it in their STM. Then when asked what cows drink, they immediately connect this to the closest idea in their current schema, which results in a response of milk instead of the correct response. There is absolutely nothing wrong with this type of processing. It capitalizes on the concept mapping approach, which will be discussed in later sections. However, it is up to us as teachers to act as quality control managers, when students try to make inappropriate connections in the information processing approach. By the way, cows drink water.

I^3 *Information Processing Example #2*

Please read the following:

> **"Finished files are the result of years of scientific study combined with the experience of years."**

Now count the number of Fs in that sentence.

How many Fs did you count? ________________

There are actually six Fs in the sentence. A person of average intelligence finds **three** of them. If you spotted **four,** you are above average. If you found **five,** you can turn your nose at most anybody. If you caught six, you are a genius. There is no catch to this. Many people forget the OFs. The human brain tends to see them as Vs and not Fs.

Bruner (1966) states that a theory for learning should address four major aspects: (a) predisposition towards learning, (b) structured so that it can be readily grasped by the learner, (c) an effective sequence to present the material, and (d) the nature and pacing of reinforcements. Good methods for structuring knowledge should result in simplifying, generating new propositions, and increasing the manipulation of information. Garner (1990) agrees that strategies enhance learning. However, learners often fail to invoke strategic behaviors due to five reasons, poor cognitive monitoring; primitive routines; meager knowledge base; attributions and classroom goals that do not support strategy use; and minimal transfer. If learners do not notice that they are not learning, they are unlikely to seek a strategic remedy (Glenberg, Wilkinson, & Epstein, 1982). This statement provides substantial support for the need of self-regulated learners.

Self-Regulated Learning

"Even if you're on the right track, you'll get run over if you just sit there."

—WILL ROGERS

"Teachers open the door, but you enter by yourself."

—ANONYMOUS

Self-regulation means regulating your own behavior. This can be accomplished many ways and for various settings. In an educational setting, a self-regulated learner is a person who is able to determine if they were able to learn a concept. This is a very different approach than we typically use in schools whereby teachers are the authorities who determine whether a student learns and understands a concept.

One of the greatest difficulties facing teachers is the question "Is learning taking place?" We have already discussed the idea of what learning is, however just because we know what it is may not be sufficient to determine if it is occurring, how often, and in what quality. The simple answer seems to be "ask the learner." How does the learner know whether they have learned? Traditionalist will quickly respond with data from test scores. However, we know that we are unable to ever determine true scores, because we can only determine observed scores that are inferred from behaviors, typically the behaviors documented from test-taking. More of this and alternative assessments will be discussed in chapter 11. However if the learner is self-regulating, that is, if they are constantly and consciously monitoring their comprehension and correcting comprehension failures, they themselves will have a better idea if they have met the learning goals. How can the teacher know whether the learner is self-regulating? This aspect typically requires additional measures. Because it is a complex cognitive event, which involves numerous activities for the learner, it is difficult to measure a self-regulation learner (Howard-Rose & Winne, 1993).

Self-regulated learners are students whose academic learning abilities and self-discipline make learning easier, thus motivation is maintained. Bandura (1977) defined self-regulation as the ability to control our own behavior and it is the workhorse of human personality. Bandura suggests three steps: (a) self-observation, we look at ourselves, our behavior, and keep tabs on it; (b) judgment, we compare what we see with a standard; (c) self-response, if we did well in comparison with our standard we give ourselves rewarding self-responses. If we did poorly, we give ourselves punishing self-responses.

Zimmerman (1989) defines self-regulated learning strategies as actions and processes directed at acquiring information or skill that involve agency, purpose, and instrumentality perceptions by learners. Strategies include self-evaluation, organizing, and transforming, goal setting and planning, seeking information, keeping records and monitoring, environmental structuring, self consequating, rehearsing, and memorizing, seeking social assistance, and reviewing records. Subskills required to organize a course of action are themselves governed by broader self-regulatory skills, such as knowing how to diagnose task demands or constructing and evaluating alternative strategies. Self-regulated learning is not a mental ability, e.g., intelligence, or an academic skill, e.g., reading proficiency; rather, it is the self-directive process through which learners transform their mental abilities into academic skills (Schunk & Zimmerman, 1998). Possessing these self-regulatory skills can permit students to improve their performances across varied academic activities. Bandura, Zimmerman, Schunk, and others have been instrumental in tracing the relationships of self-regulation for self-efficacy and academic achievement.

Self-Efficacy

"It is one of the most beautiful compensations of this life that no man can sincerely try to help another without helping himself."

—Ralph Waldo Emerson

Self-efficacy is a person's sense of being able to deal effectively with a particular task; a belief about personal competence in a particular situation. If an individual student believes they are capable of learning the concept, then their ability to learn will increase. Therefore, the correlation between self-efficacy and achievement is typically direct. Schunk and Zimmerman (1998) indicate that self-efficacy provides a bridge between the cognitive and the contextual forces, such as informal settings. Informal settings include learning environments such as museums, aquaria, zoological parks, nature centers, and so on. Nearly the whole of our knowledge about the natural world has come from investigators who had direct experiences with phenomena of natural science outside of the formal classroom (Keown, 1986). There is no classroom equivalent to observing a river—clean, clear, and healthy as it enters a city—and later to find it green and oxygen-deficient with the community of pollution organisms as it leaves the city. These informal settings are experiences that engage all of a student's senses.

"More and more of today's children are having to interrupt their learning to go to school."

—William Glasser

Remember, self-efficacy influences the choices we make, the effort we put forth, how long we persist when we confront obstacles, and how we feel. Students with high self-efficacy work harder, persist longer when difficulties are present, and achieve at higher levels. Successes raise and failures lower self-efficacy. Although low self-efficacy can be detrimental, effective self-regulation does not require that it be exceptionally high (Zimmerman, 1998). Self-regulation and self-efficacy requires an insightful, conscious effort of cognitive process that may not typically be inherent for many students, but it can be taught, encouraged, and fostered in every student. This overt internationality of thinking also fosters student's metacognitive abilities.

Metacognition

"What is a weed? A plant whose virtues have not yet been discovered."

—Ralph Waldo Emerson

Metacognition means to understand what you're thinking about. Metacognition is thinking about thinking, knowing "what we know" and "what we don't know." Metacognition is having knowledge (cognition) and having understanding, control over, and appropriate use of that knowledge (Tei & Oran, 1985). Just as an executive's job is management of an organization, a thinker's job is management of thinking. The basic metacognitive strategies are:

- Connecting new information to former knowledge.
- Selecting thinking strategies deliberately.
- Planning, monitoring, and evaluating thinking processes (Dirkes, 1985).

Constructivism

> ***"When I was a boy of 14, my father was so ignorant I could hardly stand to have the old man around. But when I got to be 21, I was astonished at how much the old man had learned in seven years."***
>
> —Mark Twain

A constructivist approach allows the learner to build upon their prior experiences at their own pace and in their own particular direction of interest and perspective. Perhaps the first constructivist philosopher, Giambatista Vico, commented in a treatise in 1710 that one only knows something if one can explain it (Yager, 1991). Immanual Kant (1724–1804) further elaborated this idea by asserting that human beings are not passive recipients of information. Learners actively take knowledge, connect it to previously assimilated knowledge, and make it theirs by constructing their own interpretation (Cheek, 1992). Inferences, elaborations, and relationships between old perceptions and new ideas must be personally drawn by the student in order for the new idea to become an integrated, useful part of their memory. The learner must actively construct new information onto their existing framework for meaningful learning to occur.

Although constructivist theory has become popular in recent years, the idea of constructivism is not new. Aspects of the constructivist theory can be found among the works of Socrates, Plato, and Aristotle (ranging from 470–320 B.C.), all of which speak of the formation of knowledge. Saint Augustine (A.D. mid-300s) taught that in the search for truth, people must depend upon sensory experience. This of course left him out of balance with the church. More recent philosophers such as John Locke (1632–1704) taught that no man's knowledge can go beyond his experience. Kant explained that the logical analysis of actions and objects lead to the growth of knowledge and the view that one's individual experiences generate new knowledge (Brooks & Brooks, 1993). Although the main philosophy of constructivism is generally credited to Jean Piaget (1896–1980), Henrich Pestalozzi (1746–1827), also from Switzerland, came to many similar conclusions over a century earlier.

However, Piaget provided the foundation for modern day constructivism and its hybridization, therefore many believe him to be the father of constructivism. In Piaget's view, intelligence consists of two interrelated processes, organization, and adaptation. People organize their thoughts so that they make sense, separating the more important thoughts from the less important ones, as well as connecting one idea to another. At the same time, people adapt their thinking to include new ideas as new experiences provide additional information. This adaptation occurs in two ways, through assimilation and accommodation. In the former process, new information is simply added to the cognitive organization already there. In the latter, the intellectual organization has to change somewhat to adjust to the new idea (Berger, 1978). Typically, we accommodate or acclimate when disequilibrium is met. This uncomfortable feeling associated with not knowing or confusion is a key element prior to learning. It is this phenomenon that encourages us to regain equilibrium and the best way to do this is to understand the concept that had created the disequilibrium. Therefore, when we feel uncomfortable and frustrated, we are actually on the threshold of success.

BTW

Do you know where the term"threshold" came from? In the 1950s, floors were dirt. Only the wealthy had something other than dirt, hence the saying "dirt poor." The wealthy had slate floors, which would get slippery in the winter when wet. They spread thresh, stalks of ripe corn or a similar crop, on the floor to help keep their footing. As the winter wore on they kept adding more thresh and when they opened the door, the thresh would get tracked outside. A piece of wood was placed at the entryway to keep the thresh in, hence the term "threshold."

The basic idea of constructivism is that the learner must construct knowledge, as the teacher cannot supply it (Bringuier, 1980). This is vividly expressed by the Farsi proverb that a well must produce its own water. The constructivist approach is a view that emphasizes the active role of the learner in building his understanding and thus, making sense of information. Constructivist approaches to learning assume that subjectivity is critical because learners take in information and process it in unique ways that reflect their needs, dispositions, attitudes, beliefs, and feelings. Constructivism espouses creating meaning from experience (Jonassen, 1991). Constructivism stresses the interaction between learner and the environment and learning is embedded in the context in which it occurs. Thereby learners are encouraged to develop their own understanding of knowledge. Brooks and Brooks (1993) state that constructivism is not a theory about teaching. It is a theory about knowledge and learning that believes that process and learning occurs daily and relentlessly in classrooms. It is a philosophy that encompasses knowledge, learning, and thinking. They have compiled a list of characteristics of a constructivist teacher that include encouragement of student autonomy; utilization of manipulative, interactive, and physical materials; use of cognitive terminology such as classify, analyze, and create; inquiry understanding; encourage engagement of dialogue; ask open-ended questions; pursue elaboration of student responses; provide time for students to construct relationships and create metaphors; nurture students through frequent use of the learning cycle method. Inquiry learning is an approach in which the teacher presents a puzzling situation and students solve the problem by gathering data and testing their conclusions.

Learning Strategies

"If you treat an individual as he is, he will remain as he is. But if you treat him as if he were what he ought to be and could be, he will become what he ought to be and could be."

—Goethe

A strategy is a person's approach to learning; how they plan, execute, and evaluate their approach to a task. Students employ learning strategies to assist them in acquiring, interpreting, inferring, broadening, retaining, and utilizing knowledge. These strategies teach students how to learn and apply what they have learned. There are many strategies, which every teacher needs to understand and use appropriately. Throughout a good teacher preparation program, a wide variety of learning strategies should be presented, demonstrated, and modeled for the pre-service teacher candidate. This text will introduce several useful learning strategies, from which the student should understand, expand, and add to throughout their educational experience. The learning strategies which will be discussed are

- Critical thinking
- Active learning
- Conceptual learning
- Collaborative/cooperative learning
- Learning cycles/processes
- Project-based learning

In addition, a brief presentation of learning styles will be briefly shared at the end of this section.

Critical Thinking

"The man who can make hard things easy is the educator."

—Ralph Waldo Emerson

Critical thinking (CT) is reasoned identification and evaluation of evidence to guide decision-making. A critical thinker uses broad in-depth analysis of evidence to make decisions and communicate his/her beliefs clearly and accurately. Characteristics of CT include complexity, commitment to purposeful, self-directed thinking, requiring judgment (no single "right" answer), explicit arguments, and evidence. A critical thinker considers consistency, relevance, and adequacy of evidence. The profile of a critical thinker is one who is habitually inquisitive, well-informed, trustful of reason, faces personal biases, prudent in making judgments, willing to reconsider, clear about issues, orderly in complex matters, diligent in seeking relevant information, reasonable in selection of criteria, and focused on inquiry. CT skills include evaluating information and data; applying and explaining how you arrived at your judgment; and applying thinking to one's own thinking (metacognition); purposeful, self-regulating; and able to distinguish fact, opinion, and judgment. CT dispositions include inquisitiveness, truth-seeking, open-mindedness, analytical, self-confidence, and cognitive maturity.

Critical Thinking Models

General Problem-Solving Model

1. Identify the Problem
2. Represent the Problem
3. Select a Strategy
4. Carry out the Strategy
5. Evaluate the Results
6. Analyze the Process

Center for Research on Evaluation, Standards and Student Testing (CRESST) Problem-Solving Model

1. Content understanding
2. Problem-solving strategies
3. Metacognition
4. Motivation

General CT Model

1. Focus or observation—engagement
2. Question or hypothesis—idea
3. Content and value—data generating

4. Analysis and deliberation component—action component, data, and the value of the question must be scrutinized and evaluate whether the data are valid; use data to make generalizations
5. Decision or description of the solution—choose best solution and should be returned to when new information is available
6. New focus or observation

Other CT Models

1. Bloom's Taxonomy
   Benjamin Bloom created this taxonomy for categorizing the level of abstraction for questions that commonly occur in educational settings. The taxonomy provides a useful structure in which to categorize questions. The following information represents the levels and associated prompts that will assist the teacher in identifying the level of question they are asking.

   a. Knowledge (factual, testing recall)—low level. Who, What, Why, When, Where, How, How Much, Describe, Define, Match, Select, Which One, Choose, Omit.
   b. Comprehension (translate, interpret, and extrapolate)—medium level. State in Your Own Words; What Does This Mean; Give an Example; State in One Word; What Exceptions are There; What are They Saying; Show in a Graph or Table; Classify, Infer, Indicate, Outline, Summarize.
   c. Application (to situations that are new)—low-medium level. Predict, Choose, Select, Explain, Identify, Tell.
   d. Analysis (breaking down into parts)—medium level. Distinguish, What Assumptions; What Conclusions, Make a Distinction, What is the Premise; What ideas Apply; What is the Function of; What Statement is Relevant; State the Point of View; What Ideas Justify the Conclusion; What is the Theme; What is the Relationship Between.
   e. Synthesis (combining elements into a pattern)—medium-high level. Create, How Would you Test; Propose an Alternative; Solve the Following; Plan; Design; Compose; Formulate a Theory, Develop.
   f. Evaluation (according to criteria and state reasons)—high level. Appraise, Judge, Criticize, Defend, Compare.

I³ *Develop two higher level questions on education and write them below.*

1. ____

   ____

2. ____

   ____

Inquiry

"I have no special talents. I am only passionately curious."

—Albert Einstein

"The important thing is to not stop questioning."

—Albert Einstein

"It is not the answer that enlightens, but the question."

—Eugene Ionesco Decouvertes

Inquiry is an instance of intentional questioning and a systematic method of investigation. Inquiry is a dynamic process of being open to wonder and puzzlement and coming to know and understand the world. Inquiry is asking questions, but not any type of questions, but good, high-level, open-ended questions that encourage one to continue asking subsequent questions. One of the more famous users of inquiry was Socrates. Many people use inquiry and the Socratic method of questioning together. The basic steps in the inquiry process are as follows (they are cyclical):

a. Question-asking
b. Planning an approach
c. Gathering and comparing data
d. Determining correlations
e. Communicating findings; and
f. Assessing progress

KWL Approach

A very useful method for organizing thoughts and concepts while teaching is a KWL table. The K represents what the students KNOW, or their prior knowledge; the W is what they WANT to learn or the objectives and the L is what they have LEARNED. At the beginning of every chapter, you will share your thoughts in writing on the KW approach and following every chapter, you will provide your thoughts on what you learned.

Active Learning

"It is possible to store the mind with a million facts and still be entirely uneducated."

—Alec Bourne

Active learning is learning in which the learner constructs meaning (recall constructivism), often working in collaboration (and cooperation, soon to be discussed) with other students. It tends to de-emphasize received knowledge of facts presented in teacher-centered formats such as the lecture and to emphasize active investigation and reflection, such as in hands-on lessons (recall the power of informal settings). Simply stated, active learning is when students are active rather than passive. This means having students "doing" things. There are many, many ways to accomplish active learning, a teachers imagination is their only limitation. The following active-learning ideas and approaches may be helpful.

Think/Pair/Share (TPS)

"What's another word for thesaurus?"

—Steven Wright

Think/Pair/Share (TPS) is a strategy that can be used before introducing new concepts. It gives everyone in the class time to access prior knowledge and provides a chance for them to share their ideas with someone. TPS helps students organize their knowledge, and motivates learning of new topics.

TPS is a cooperative discussion strategy developed by Frank Lyman and his colleagues. The teacher provokes a student's THINKing with a question or a prompt. Students PAIR up to talk about the question. They compare their notes and discuss possible solution, variables, or other questions. After students talk in pairs for a few moments, the teacher calls for pairs to SHARE their thinking with the rest of the class.

A key element of active learning is doing and as such this approach allows students to talk about the concept. TPS structures the discussion and students follow a prescribed process that focuses on-task thinking. Informal/peer-oriented accountability is built in because each must report to a partner, and then partners must report to the class.

When students think, there is wait time, which allows them time to consider their response. Because it is silent thinking, the problem of eager students talking is minimized. This encourages everyone to think instead of only a few students. Students are able to participate collaboratively before having to share with the class. This also allows students to take their thoughts for a test run before they share with the class. Students also are able to reconsider their thoughts and elaborate as they share. This approach is useful because it can be used in large or small classes regardless of the discipline.

The following "quick-thinks" were designed by Johnston & Cooper (1997) for application to a wide range of content areas:

1. Select the best response.
2. Correct the error.
3. Complete a sentence starter.
4. Compare or contrast.
5. Support a statement.
6. Reorder the steps.
7. Reach a conclusion.
8. Paraphrase the idea.

I³ *Select one of these "quick-thinks" and describe how you could use it teaching one of your classes.*

____

____

____

____

Conceptual Learning

"Education is not the filling of a bucket, but the lighting of a fire."

—W. B. Yeats

A concept is an abstract or general idea inferred or derived from specific instances. It is also viewed as something conceived in the mind, a thought or a notion, or a universal entity that serves to designate a category or class of entities, events, or relations. Concepts are the basis of formal education. Principles, generalizations, rules of procedures, and even attitudes are formulated by means of concepts. Conceptual learning means students should be able to

- understand and describe in concrete terms how physical objects, phenomena, systems, or processes behave and how they interact
- understand how mathematical expressions can represent processes, their behavior, and their interactions
- model various reasoning and problem-solving techniques;
- pose and solve paradoxes and dilemmas, and

- transfer material they have learned from the context in which they learned it to other contexts (Dori & Breslow, 2001).

Conceptual teaching is a powerful methodology, which allows students to construct meaning from their prior experiences, categorize these thoughts into their similarities and differences, infer further ideas from these categories, and ultimately predict and connect meaning and understanding to unknown concepts. A popular approach is to map the concepts in order to understand their relational aspects.

Graphic Organizers

Concept mapping is a graphical organizer for assisting and enhancing many of the types of thinking and learning. To develop a concept map, write the main idea in the center of the page, it may be a word, a phrase, a concept, or an idea. Next, place related ideas on branches that radiate from this central idea. This allows the learner to initially brainstorm any ideas that they believe are related to the central concept. The most powerful aspect of concept mapping is when the student makes connections between the central and relational terms. This enables the learner to know more than facts in isolation or memorization of terms, but increases the likelihood of conceptual understanding. Conceptual teaching also capitalizes on analogies. But before using analogies in teaching a concept remember, analogical thinking involves learners using analogies to incorporate concepts into their working knowledge, thus they need to have the prior information already included in their schema. Remember that most of our young students

1. have no recollection of the Reagan era.
2. have only known of one Pope.
3. probably do not recall the Cold War.
4. are too young to remember the first space shuttle accident.
5. have always known about AIDS.
6. have never had a polio shot and do not know what it is.
7. do not remember Atari or vinyl albums.
8. have always seen answering machines, VCRs, microwaves, cable, and remote controls.
9. think the Tonight Show has always been hosted by Jay Leno.
10. have unfortunately never seen Larry Bird play.

I^3 ***Analogical Thinking Activity:*** *Below, prepare a list of 10 "Point of Reference" items that you believe your students may not be aware of.*

1. ______________________________
2. ______________________________
3. ______________________________
4. ______________________________
5. ______________________________
6. ______________________________
7. ______________________________
8. ______________________________
9. ______________________________
10. ______________________________

I[3] ***Concept Mapping Activity***

For practice and to check understanding, review the concept map example below and create one of your own on the concept of "Technology" using the blank page provided.

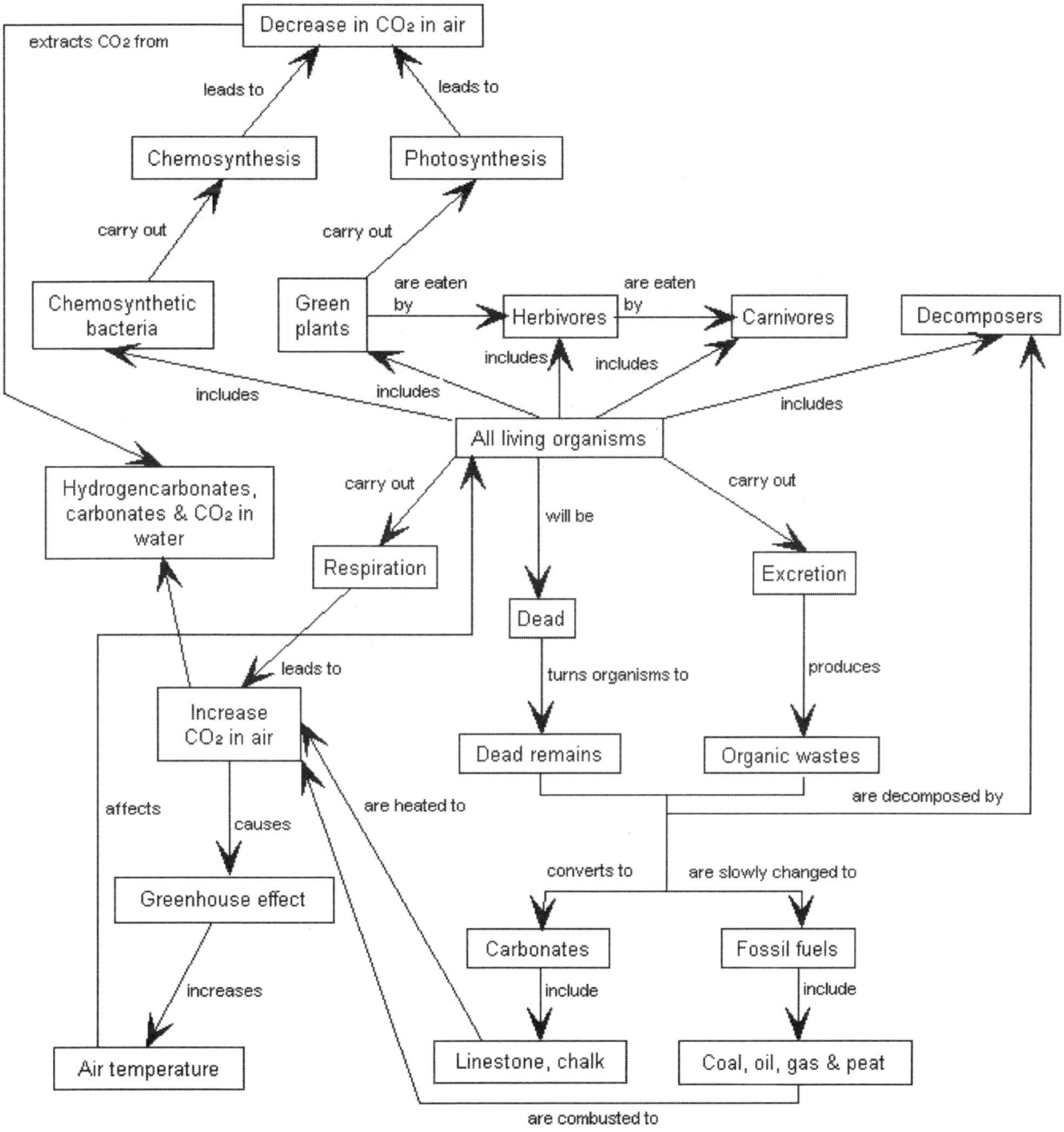

YOUR CONCEPT MAP

TECHNOLOGY

Combing the concept of concept mapping and technology, there are efficient concept mapping software such as Inspiration® and Kidspiration® available that allows the learner to easily create a concept map on the computer. An active method to work with concept maps in class is to divide students into groups of three or four. Have each person write one word on each of their four Post-It® notes. Once everyone is finished, have the students place all of the Post-It® notes in the middle of their table and then rotate to the next table. Once arrived, the students will be asked to generate a concept map using the terms of other students. The Post-It® notes work well as they allow them to work on the wall, moving ideas around and ultimately connecting the notes and writing arrows with the relational terms on the arrows to complete the map. Other graphical organizers include Venn Diagrams, Decision-Making Models, Q/A Charts, Main Idea Pyramids, and so on.

Collaborative/Cooperative Learning

"A professor is one who talks in someone else's sleep."

—W. H. Auden

Collaboration is the act of working jointly, or when two or more people work together to create or achieve the same thing. Collaborative learning involves students working together in some way to aid their learning. There are a number of models and these raise issues and concerns for both the teacher and student and for course design and administration. Collaboration is a philosophy of interaction and personal lifestyle. Collaborative learning is a personal philosophy, not just a classroom technique. In all situations where people come together in groups, it suggests a way of dealing with people, which respects and highlights individual group members' abilities and contributions. There is a sharing of authority and acceptance of responsibility among group members for the actions (Panitz, 1997).

Cooperation is a common effort; the act of working together to achieve a common aim. It is a structure of interaction designed to facilitate the accomplishment of an end product or goal. Cooperative learning is defined by a set of processes that help people interact together in order to accomplish a specific goal or develop an end product, which is usually content specific. It is more directive than a collaborative system of governance and closely controlled by the teacher. While there are many mechanisms for group analysis and introspection, the fundamental approach is teacher-centered whereas collaborative learning is more student-centered (Panitz, 1997).

I^3 *Collaborate with a partner near you and create a list of advantages and disadvantages to working together.*

Advantages: ______________________________

____

____

____

Disadvantages: ______________________________

____

____

____

Learning Cycle

> ***"Only an idiot continues to do the same thing and expects different results."***
>
> —ALBERT EINSTEIN

The traditional learning cycle or the "Five E" method includes engage, explore, explain, elaborate, and evaluate. This methodology allows the teacher to provide students with a process or set of steps, which they can use to learn regardless of the discipline or situation. Using the learning cycle or learning process enables the instructor to teach more about less because the students can step outside of the specific lesson and extrapolate the ideas to other concepts.

Engage: Students are encouraged to make connections between prior knowledge and the topics presented and organize their learning in a framework for understanding. Ideally, students will be asking questions, and identifying a problem to help them focus on the task.

Explore: Students will involve themselves with the concept, especially powerful when using a hands-on approach. This step will be enhanced when coupled with collaborative learning, in which they can share their own ideas and formulate new ones based on each other's prior experiences. It is very important that the teacher act as a facilitator, providing materials, guiding, asking driving questions, and interacting with the students. The students' inquiry process drives the instruction during an exploration.

Explain: Students begin to understand the concept in context. Dialogue between students provides intrinsic motivation for arranging and categorizing ideas into a format that makes sense. Explanations from the facilitator are helpful, but the most powerful, lasting explanations are between students, so the teacher is encouraged to stay as quiet as possible.

Elaborate: Students expand on the concepts they have learned, make connections to other related concepts, and apply their understandings. Observations should lead to further questions, as a cyclical process that can keep students engaged longitudinally. These question asking sessions should be highly encouraged and rewarded.

Evaluate: Students participate in formative assessment that allows the teacher to determine if the learner has attained conceptual understanding. Evaluation and assessment should occur continuously for the teacher and the learner. Several useful instruments for assessment are rubrics, teacher observations, student interviews, portfolios (electronic and traditional), and project- and problem-based learning artifacts. Remember, assessment should be continuous and one should not be able to differentiate where instruction ends and assessment begins. This provides and reinforces a constructivist cyclical structure.

Learning Process

> ***"The object of teaching a child is to enable him to get along without his teacher."***
>
> —ELBERT HUBBARD

The learning cycle asks the student to observe, communicate, measure, classify, infer, and predict.

Observation uses of all our senses—sight, smell, touch, taste, and hearing—to search for patterns and trends. Observations lead to curiosity, questions, and interpretations. These can be generally classified as either qualitative or quantitative. Qualitative observation examples are light green (sight), pungent odor (smell), tastes sour (taste), waxy leaf (touch), and sharp sound (hearing). Quantitative observation examples might be that a leaf is 7 centimeters in length, a rock weighs 5 grams, and the temperature is 22 degrees Celsius. They even include estimates and comparisons such as a plant is as wide as three paper clips.

Communication is in everything we do! Communication can be performed in many ways including graphs, charts, maps, symbols, and diagrams. It must be clear, precise, and unambiguous. For students to improve their communication skills, a useful exercise is for them to describing objects to others or to explain directions. Quickly, they understand the concept of perception. Some may communicate and understand better with pictures, maps, or relative to things of which they have prior knowledge. When communicating with maps or any symbolic representation, the diagrams must include appropriate codes, such as a title, symbols, key, and scale.

Classifying is used to order concepts with respect to similarities and differences. One of the most common classifications is how we are classified by demographics, telephone, address, occupation, and so on. We can classify items from the colors of candy to plant and animal species in order to more easily understand and group them into easily understandable portions from which subsequent inferences can be made.

Measurement is essential in making quantitative observations, comparing and classifying items, and communicating effectively. In science, the metric system is used. For volume, we use liters, for mass, we use grams, and for distance, meter are used. Understanding estimates are very helpful when measuring. For instance a can of soda is about a half of liter and your fingernail is about one centimeter. Also, we combine these measurements at times as 1 cubic centimeter (cc) is equal to 1 milliliter. Engine sizes are measures in cubic centimeters. Other important numbers to remember for temperature are that water boils at 100 and it freezes at zero degree Celsius.

Inferring is an interpretation of an observation. Inference allows us to recognize patterns and by expecting these to reoccur under the same conditions, we can generalize this information to other systems. We form hypotheses based on inferences. Teachers make inferences as to why students behave as they do. Learning is an inference made from observed changes in behavior. Inference examples include "The brass knob is shiny. I infer that the door is used often." Or "Through the window I see the flag waving. It must be windy out." Steps for making good inference include making as many observations as possible. Next, students recall as much relevant material from prior experiences as possible, which can be integrated. State the inference that clearly distinguishes it from an observation or prediction. Monitor and evaluate your statements.

Predicting is a forecast of what a future observation might be. It is the ability, which allows us to determine appropriate behavior—a reasoned statement. Predicting is based on careful observation and inferences made about relationships. "If this happens, what will follow?" "What will happen if I do this?" Prediction examples include "I see it raining and the sun comes out. There could be a rainbow." There are two main types of predictions, interpolation, or predictions made between observed data and extrapolation, predictions made beyond observed data.

I³ *Let's take the learning process for a test drive. In order to set the stage, please complete the quiz below to stimulate your thoughts outside of the classroom.*

Please read the statement and write down the candy that you believe the statement is describing (An answer key is at the end of the chapter.)

1. Famous swashbuckling trio ____________________
2. Indian burial grounds ____________________

3. Galaxy ______________________________
4. Red planet ______________________________
5. Home of the movie stars ______________________________
6. Not laughing out loud ______________________________
7. Can't hold on to anything ______________________________
8. A famous author ______________________________
9. Famous former baseball player ______________________________
10. Famous New York street ______________________________
11. Twin letters ______________________________
12. Superman's other identity ______________________________
13. A sweet sign of affection ______________________________
14. Favorite day for working people ______________________________
15. What bees make ______________________________
16. Nut happiness ______________________________
17. Pleasingly plump ______________________________
18. Two female pronouns ______________________________
19. A feline ______________________________
20. Single women look for him ______________________________

I^3 *Root Beer Experience.*

Have students sit comfortably, close their eyes, and make a cup with their hands in their lap. Indicate to them that you will be placing a small object in their hands. The object will not be alive and if they choose not to participate, ask that they sit quietly and do not disturb the experience for others. The instructor will place an individually wrapped piece of root beer candy in their hands. As the instructor walks around placing the candy, instructions will be provided for the students to walk through the learning process. First they will OBSERVE with all of their senses, feeling the object, smelling (through the wrapper), listening to the wrapper, and so on. Remind them that they are gathering data to ultimately make inferences and predictions. Once they have made the observations, tell them to unwrap the object and place in their mouth if they want to. Remind them, that if they did not enjoy the odor, chances are they will not like the taste and they do not have to place it in their mouth (this will minimize the amount of root beer projectiles across the room). At this point, the teacher should encourage the students to try and name the object. Have them pretend they do not know the name or have not tasted it before (some people may have never tasted root beer before). Also, have them dig deeper, try to detect hints of flavor e.g., earthy, musty, woody, artificial, chemical, and anything that they can gather with their senses. Once they are finished, they can open their eyes and provide characteristics of the object, which the instructor will write on the board.

Please write any observations of the object.

Next the instructor will discuss the derivation of root beer. Begin an inquiry asking students where they believe root beer came from. If the candy was an orange, it would come from an orange, if a grape, it would come from a grape, however, where does root beer come from? Ask the students to provide ideas from their prior knowledge. Typically, very few students know the origin of root beer. Encourage them to walk through the learning process steps. Ask them to break down the parts of the words. Root is the portion of the plant underground, in this case, the root is from the sassafras tree. Ask if anyone recalls their grandparents referring to root beer soda as sarsaparilla? Next discuss the meaning of beer as it relates to fermentation of barley, hops, and so on. Ultimately, share that root beer comes from the fermentation of sassafras tree roots. Now, the ultimate question will be, "Are there fermented sassafras root molecules in your mouth?" After this discussion, many will think so, however, there is not. We have created artificial colors and flavors by recreating the molecular structure, and we now produce it cheaper and more efficiently.

I^3 *Select a concept, which you are familiar with and use either the "Five E" method or the learning process and demonstrate how you would teach this to a student.*

Learning Styles

"The mediocre teacher tells. The good teacher explains. The superior teacher demonstrates. The great teacher inspires."

—William Arthur Ward

There are many types of learning styles and an effective teacher will be able to identify many of these and provide instructional methods that will accommodate each student's learning style.

Left/Right Brain

There are many instruments available to help determine which side of the brain you operate on most of the time.

I³ *Please read the following form, answer the questions, and be ready to provide your responses for an activity in class.*

Right Brain/Left Brain Dominance Quiz. Please read the items below and respond with your first thought by circling the appropriate term.

1. Are you more apt to recall people by their name or by their face? ___________
2. Are you organized or random? ___________
3. Do you read more nonfiction or fiction typically? ___________
4. Do you solve issues in your life using rational steps or your gut? ___________
5. Do you like structure or nonstructure? ___________
6. Do you remember things better by reading words or graphics? ___________
7. Are you artistic or not? ___________
8. Do you joke frequently or are you more serious? ___________
9. Are you detail oriented or are you a big-picture person? ___________
10. Do you learn through recipe-like instructions or trial and error best? ___________

After you are complete, compare your responses with the answers at the end of the chapter and then write down your L/R ratio below.

L : R

___ : ___

Please share your ratio and discuss how it fits your learning style. Compare how you perceive yourself and how you perceive others.

Project-Based Learning (PBL)

"A problem well stated is a problem half solved."

—Charles Kettering

Project-Based Learning (PBL) is a method of teaching that engages children in finding solutions to important questions that are interesting to them and can be carried out through a process of investigation and working with others. PBL engages young learners in exploring authentic, important, and meaningful questions of real concern to students. Through a dynamic process of investigation and collaboration, students work in teams to formulate questions, make predictions, design investigations, collect and analyze data, make products, and share ideas. Students learn fundamental concepts and principles that they apply to their daily lives. PBL helps all students regardless of culture, race, or gender engage in learning. The goal of PBL is to improve the way classes are taught by involving students in finding solutions to authentic questions through extended inquiry, collaboration, and use of technology.

There are several models for PBL. One involves five distinct steps. There are five features associated with PBL.

1. Driving questions organize the activities and concepts and related to project-based instruction.

2. Investigations engage students in asking questions, observing, predicting, designing studies, collecting, and analyzing data, drawing conclusions, and communicating findings over an extended period of time.
3. Collaboration involves students working with members of the community outside the classroom, and with their classmates and teacher, in investigating driving questions.
4. Technology enhances students' ability to retrieve information, gather real-world data, analyze data, and share findings with others.
5. Artifacts consist of reports, displays, models, and other concrete representations of what students have learned during the course of the investigations.

A driving question (DQ) is a well-designed question used in project-based learning that is elaborated, explored, and answered by students and the teacher. It must be feasible, worthwhile, contextualized, meaningful, and sustainable. Typically, an extensive rubric is used to assist the student in this approach to learning and assessing their subsequent artifact. An example of a PBL rubric is provided on pages 26–27.

I³ *Review the example DQ's below and attempt to develop a DQ of your own.*

1. What is in our water?
2. Where does our garbage go?

____

____

____

____

____

____

Teaching, Learning, and Psychological Orientations

"A little nonsense now and then is relished by the wisest men."

—Willie Wonka

There are many philosophies and orientations on learning, education, and teaching. This introductory chapter will attempt to simply open the door to some of these approaches in order to introduce the student to these concepts. The hope is that throughout this course and throughout your pre-service education, they will continually and repeatedly be exposed to these models and philosophies until ultimately they are able to develop their own educational philosophy by synthesizing aspects they have gathered from others.

PBL RUBRIC

Name (s) ____________________

Students will work in groups to apply the framework in creating a project-based resource. Students will address the following parameters. (Each item should be at least one page single-spaced, 12-point font with one-inch margins and each item is worth 1%.)

1. **Summarize** how your DQ meets the five *DQ criteria.* ☐

A. INVESTIGATIVE QUESTION (mini-research paper)

2. **Describe** the sub-DQs you have specified from your DQ. ☐
3. **Describe** your methods of gathering data. ☐
4. Transform data (use at least one graph and one table). ☐
5. **Summarize** analysis of data textually. ☐
6. **Summarize and Reflect** your findings. ☐

B. CONTENT KNOWLEDGE

7. **Summarize** the critical concepts in the content? (check *National Education* or Florida *Sunshine State Standards*). ☐
8. **Summarize** accomplished practices that relate to your DQ. ☐
9. List and **Summarize** the important "facts" of your DQ. ☐
10. **Summarize** the larger themes that are related to the content. ☐
11. **Describe** how the process skills are linked to the DQ. ☐
12. **Summarize** several social ramifications of your sub-DQ. ☐

C. CONTENT MATERIALS

13. Encyclopedia article (**paraphrase,** copy with date, name, and source of encyclopedia—do not use MS Encarta). ☐
14. Reference and **summarize** information of at least two multimedia projects (video, CD, DVD, laserdisc, and so on). ☐
15. List and **describe** at least 10 relevant books, kits, or curricula (name, publisher, and address). ☐
16. List and **describe** at least 10 Internet sites with address and copy of first page. ☐
17. Non-educator, community contact willing to guide and advise. Do not forward entire PBE, simply share notes or ideas and request a **summary** of their feedback (list their name, brief description of their background, phone number, and rationale for selection—should not be a relative). ☐
18. Copy and **paraphrase/summarize** pertinent K–12 education-related article. ☐

PBL RUBRIC *(continued)*

19. Copy and **paraphrase/summarize** pertinent post-secondary education-related article.
20. Educator contact willing to guide and advise. Do not forward entire PBE, simply share notes or ideas and request **summary** of their feedback (name, institution, phone number, area of expertise, and rationale).
21. **Summarize** your thoughts on the educator feedback.

D. PEDAGOGICAL KNOWLEDGE

22. **Summarize** how at least two *learning theories* are useful to the content?
23. **Create/Develop** an *authentic assessment* for the content?
24. **Summarize** how would you integrate at least two other *content areas* into your sub-DQs.

F. OVERALL QUALITY

25. Overall Quality of Report (appearance, organization, grammar, writing level, rubric order).

Subtotal Points (25 possible)

Presentation (creative and innovative) (5 points)

Total Points (30 possible)

Comments:

Operant Conditioning

> ***"We are what we repeatedly do. Excellence, then, is not an act, but a habit."***
>
> —Aristotle

The citrus soda, 7-UP, was created in 1929; "7" was selected because the original containers were 7 ounces. "UP" indicated the direction of the bubbles. Also, around 1929, B. F. Skinner developed a behavioristic theory of reinforcement and conditioning. Conditioning refers to the strengthening of behavior, which results from reinforcement (Skinner, 1965). Skinner's view was that a response to stimuli becomes more likely to occur as a function of the consequences of responding.

Skinner studied how pigeons and white rats learn. His models were based on simple rewards such as food and water, and avoidance of pain. Skinner developed the basic concept of operant conditioning, claiming that this type of learning was not the result of stimulus-response learning. The basic association in operant conditioning was between the operant response and the reinforcer, the discriminative stimulus served to signal when this association would be acted upon. Operant conditioning is used to describe one type of associative learning in which there is a contingency between the response and the presentation of the reinforcer. This situation resembles most closely the classic experiments from Skinner, where he trained rats and pigeons to press a lever in order to obtain a food reward. In such experiments, the subject is able to generate certain motor output, (the *response* R, e.g., running around, cleaning, resting, pressing the lever). The experimentator chooses a suited output (e.g., pressing the lever) to pair it with an *unconditioned stimulus* (US; e.g., a food reward). Often a *discriminative stimulus* (SD; e.g., a light) is present, when the R-US contingency is true. After a training period, the subject will show the *conditioned response* (CS; e.g., touching the trigger) even in absence of the US, if the R-US association has been memorized. Such instrumental or operant conditioning is opposed to Pavlovian or "classical conditioning," in which producing a response has no effect on US presentations.

Social Cognitive Theory

> ***"If we continue on this path, we're likely to end up in the direction we're headed."***
>
> —Chinese proverb

In the 1960s, Albert Bandura developed a model based on social cognition and modeling. He believed by observing others, people acquire knowledge. According to Bandura's social cognitive theory, individuals possess a self-system that enables them to exercise a measure of control over their thoughts, feelings, motivation, and actions. This self-system encompasses one's cognitive and affective structures and provides reference mechanisms and a set of subfunctions for perceiving, regulating, and evaluating behavior, which results from the interplay between the system and environmental sources of influence. As such, it serves a self-regulatory function by providing individuals with the capability to influence their own cognitive processes and actions and thus alter their environments. Individuals engage in self-referent thought that mediates between knowledge and action. Through self-reflection, individuals evaluate their own experiences and thought processes. Bandura (1986) argued that self-reflection is the most uniquely human characteristic. Self-reflective judgments include perceptions of self-efficacy, beliefs in one's capability to organize and execute the courses of action required to manage prospective situations. The higher the sense of efficacy, the greater the effort, persistence, and resilience.

Bandura (1986) wrote that, through the process of self-reflection, individuals are able to evaluate their experiences and thought processes. According to this view, what people know, the skills they possess, or what they have previously accomplished are not always good predictors of subsequent attainments because the beliefs they hold about their capabilities powerfully influence the ways in which they will behave. However, self-perceptions of capabilities help determine what individuals do with the knowledge and skills they currently possess. More importantly, self-beliefs are critical determinants of how well knowledge is acquired initially.

Cognitive Development

> ***"In the middle of difficulty lies opportunity."***
>
> —Albert Einstein

In the 1970s, Jean Piaget developed an approach called cognitive development. Trained as a biologist studying mollusks, his interest turned to how his children were developing. He was a curious person who observed his children and realized that cognition is a constructive process. In development, children assimilate, accommodate, and equilibrate. In Piaget's view, intelligence consists of two interrelated processes—organization and adaptation. People organize their thoughts so that they make sense, separating the more important thoughts from the less important ones as well as connecting one idea to another. At the same time, people adapt their thinking to include new ideas, as new experiences provide additional information. This adaptation occurs in two ways—through assimilation and accommodation. In the former process, new information is simply added to the cognitive organization already there. In the latter, the intellectual organization has to change somewhat to adjust to the new idea (Berger, 1978). Equilibration is the organism's attempt to keep its cognitive structures in balance. This explains the motivation for development.

When a child encounters information that does not match their current schemes, an imbalance or disequilibrium is the result. States of disequilibrium are intrinsically dissatisfying, and there is an attempt to reinstate equilibrium—achieved by altering one's cognitive structures.

There are three tenets of Piaget's theory:

a. development is stage like;
b. development is domain general; and
c. constructivism: (stages; sensorimotor, preoperational, concrete operational, formal operational)

Dialectivism

> ***"To teach well, we need not say all that we know, only what is useful for the pupil to hear."***
>
> —Anonymous

In the 1900s, Vygotsky, a Russian social scientist developed an approach to learning based on dialectivism. Dialectical is examining opinions or ideas logically by question and answer. Vygotsky developed a dialectical process of thesis—one idea or phenomenon, antithesis—an opposing idea or phenomenon, and synthesis—a resolution that produces a higher-level concept. Dialectic constructivism is building behaviors through talking or social interaction (conversation) and dialectic equals constant change toward conflicting and contradicting elements designed to enhance participants' abilities in reasoning and argument, such as in critical thinking.

Using the socially meaningful activity of dialectivism, students can build collaboration skills through communicating or social interaction designed to enhance their abilities in reasoning. Efficient asynchronous collaboration can now more effectively be used through various technology tools such as web logs.

What Is a Web Log or Blog?

A blog is a web page made up of brief, frequently updated entries that are arranged chronologically like a journal. The purposes of blogs vary greatly from links and commentary about other sites, to news, to diaries, photos, poetry, mini-essays, even fiction. Blog posts are similar to instant messages to the web. Many blogs are personal, "what's on my mind" type musings. Others are collaborative efforts based on a specific topic or area of mutual interest. Blogs are also excellent team, department, company, and family communication tools. They help small groups communicate in a way that is simpler and easier to follow than email or discussion forums. A blog can help keep everyone in the loop, promote cohesiveness and create a community culture. Although blogs are relatively new, a significant amount of literature has already been gathered.

Traditionally, educators have encouraged the use of reflective journaling for students to process information. Journaling can be an effective method to assist in the transfer of information from memory or short-term memory to long-term memory. Varner and Peck (2003) indicate that journaling can provide practice in management skills, facilitate comprehension and retention, and can act as an assessment tool. Barlow (2001) identifies how daily journal writing can help students become strong, confident writers.

Duber (2002) in his article on Weblogs identifies SchoolBlog (*http://www.schoolblogs.com/*), a free blogging package and community with the primary aim of providing a forum for children to publish and interact with others over the web. SchoolBlog indicates that teachers and students are motivated to share information because they have ownership of it. Duber (2002) also indicates recent advances in the field include multimedia blogging, such as using audio and video with flash animations. Blogging has been so nicely integrated into education that a site has been created for "Choosing a Blogging Package for Students" at *http://www.oreillynet.com/pub/wlg/1894*. This site states criteria for educational blogs, such as allowing multiple authors, free of charge, allowing searches, and allowing comments. This resulted in the sites called Greymatter (*http://www.noahgrey.com/greysoft/*), Movable Type (*http://movabletype.org/*), Blogger (*http://new.blogger.com/*), Live Journal (*http://www.livejournal.com/*), and Radio UserLand (*http://radio.userland.com/*).

I³ *Please browse some of the blogs found at the Web sites noted above. Then log on and sign up for a free blog site at http://www.blogger.com/start. Write the URL to your blog here:*

____

Humanistic Psychology

> ***"I was awfully curious to find out why I didn't go insane."***
>
> —Abraham Maslow

> ***"Human nature is not nearly as bad as it has been thought to be."***
>
> —Abraham Maslow

In 1950s, Abraham Maslow created what he believed to be a hierarchy of needs that humans exhibited. The levels included physiological, safety, community and love, esteem, to know and understand, aesthetic, and self-actualization. He believed that there were minimal needs required for learning to occur.

"Human life will never be understood unless its highest aspirations are taken into account. Growth, self-actualization, the striving toward health, the quest for identity and autonomy, the yearning for excellence must by now be accepted beyond question as a widespread and perhaps universal human tendency. And yet there are also other regressive, fearful, self-diminishing tendencies as well, and it is very easy to forget them in our intoxication with "personal growth," especially for inexperienced youngsters. . . . We must appreciate that many people choose the worse rather than the better, that growth is often a painful process . . . " (Abraham Maslow, *Motivation and Personality*)

Educational Philosophy

There are four major beliefs about teaching and learning. They include perennialism, essentialism, progressivism, and existentialism.

Perennialists, such as Socrates believe that one should teach the things of everlasting importance to all people everywhere. They believe that the most important topics develop a person. Since details of fact change constantly, these cannot be the most important. Therefore, one should teach principles, not facts. A particular strategy with modern perennialists is to teach scientific reasoning, not facts. This gives the students a human side to the science, and shows the reasoning in action. Most importantly, it shows the uncertainty and false steps of real science. Although perennialism may seem similar to essentialism, perennialism focuses first on personal development, while essentialism focuses first on essential skills.

Essentialism is a theory that states that children should learn the traditional basic subjects and that these should be learned thoroughly and rigorously. An essentialist program normally teaches children progressively, from less complex skills to more complex. An essentialist will usually teach some set subjects similar to reading, writing, literature, foreign languages, history, math, science, art, and music. Essentialist curricula thus tend to be much more vocational and fact-based, and far less liberal and principle-based. William Bagley was an important historical essentialist.

Progressivists believe that education must be based on the fact that humans are social animals who learn best in real-life activities with other people. Progressivists claimed to rely on the best available scientific theories of learning. Most believed that children learned as if they were scientists, following a process similar to John Dewey's model of learning. Given this view of human nature, a progressivist teacher desires to provide not just reading and drill, but also real-world experiences and activities that center around the real life of the students. A typical progressivist slogan is "Learn by Doing!"

Existentalism proposes that we should not accept any predetermined creed or philosophical system and from that try to define who we are. It aims for the progressing of humanity. Existentialists are in favor of independent thinking. Existentialism is not a set of curriular materials. Rather, it is a point of view that influences all that the teacher teaches and how he or she teaches. It engages the student in central questions of defiming life and who we are. It attempts to help the student acknowledge his or her own freedom and accept the responsibility for that freedom. It aims to help the child realize that the answers imposed from the outside may not be real answers. The only real answers are the ones that come from inside each person, that are authentically his or her own. Sartre was a famous existentialist.

What Is YOUR Educational Philosophy?

"Only the educated are free."

—Epictetus

One of the most important things you can do over the next several years is to develop your own educational philosophy. So, consider your educational program a journey, where you will accumulate aspects of what will eventually become your own philosophy on how you believe the best method to teach.

I^3 *Let us begin now. Chances are, this will be difficult, but try to create a framework for your current educational philosophy. Try to write something, worst case is that it may be amusing years from now when you look back and compare.*

Answers to Candy Quiz

1. Famous swashbuckling trio—**Three Musketeers**
2. Indian burial grounds—**Mounds**
3. Galaxy—**Milky Way**
4. Red Planet—**Mars**
5. Home of the movie stars—**Hollywood**
6. Not laughing out loud—**Snickers**
7. Can't hold on to anything—**Butterfinger**
8. A famous author—**O'Henry**
9. Famous former baseball player—**Babe Ruth**
10. Famous New York Street—**5th Avenue**
11. Twin letters—**M&Ms**
12. Superman's other identity—**Clark**
13. A sweet sign of affection—**Kiss**
14. Favorite day for working people—**Payday**
15. What bees make—**Bit-O'Honey**
16. Nut happiness—**Nutrageous or Almond Joy**
17. Pleasingly plump—**Chunky**
18. Two female pronouns—**Hershey**
19. A feline—**Kit Kat**
20. Single women look for him—**Mr. Goodbar or Sugar Daddy**

Right/Left Brain Answers

1.	Are you more apt to recall people by their name or by their face?	**Left = name**
2.	Are you organized or random?	**Left = organized**
3.	Do you read more nonfiction or fiction typically?	**Left = nonfiction**
4.	Do you solve issues in your life using rational steps or your gut?	**Left = rational**
5.	Do you like structure or nonstructure?	**Left = structure**
6.	Do you remember things better by reading words or graphics?	**Left = words**
7.	Are you artistic or not?	**Left = not**
8.	Do you joke frequently or are you more serious?	**Left = serious**
9.	Are you detail oriented or are you a big-picture person?	**Left = detail**
10.	Do you learn through recipe-like instructions or trial and error best?	**Left = recipe**

References

Atkinson, R. C., & Shiffrin, R. M. (1971). The control of short-term memory. *Scientific American, 225,* 82–90.

Bandura, A. (1977). *Social learning theory.* Englewood Cliffs, NJ: Prentice Hall.

Bandura, A. (1986). *Social foundations of thought and action: A social cognitive theory.* Englewood Cliffs, NJ: Prentice Hall.

Barlow, B. (2001). Journaling. *Instructor, 111,* 44.

Berger, Kathleen S. (1978). *The developing person.* New York, NY: Worth Publishers.

Bringuier, J. C. (1980). *Conversations with Jean Piaget.* Chicago, IL: University of Chicago Press.

Brooks, J., & Brooks, M. (1993). *In search of understanding: The case for constructivist classrooms.* Alexandria, VA: Association for Curriculum Development.

Bruner, J. (1966). *Toward a theory of instruction.* Cambridge, MA: Harvard University Press.

Cheek, D. W. (1992). *Thinking constructively about science, technology and society education.* Albany, NY: State University of New York Press.

Dirkes, A. (1985). Metacognition: Students in charge of their thinking. *Roeper Review, 8(2),* 96–100.

Dori, J. & Breslow, L. (2001). What is conceptual learning? *Memorandum to the Microsoft-MIT Assessment Committee.* Retrived from http://216.239.41.104/search?q=cache:eLqTuknChdUJ:www.coe.gatech.edu/eTEE/pdfs/Breslow.pdf+%22wht+is+conceptual+learning&hl=en

Duber, J. (2002). Mad Blogs and Englishmen. *TESL-EJ, 6.*

Garner, R. (1990). When children and adults do not use learning strategies: Toward a theory of settings. *Review of Educational Research, 60(4),* 517–529.

Glenberg, A. M., Wilkinson, A. C., & Epstein, W. (1982). The illusion of knowing: Failure in the self-assessment of comprehension. *Memory and Cognition, 10,* 597–602.

Howard-Rose, D., & Winne, P. H. (1993). Measuring component and sets of cognitive processes in self-regulated learning. *Journal of Educational Psychology, 85(4),* 591–604.

Johnston, S., & Cooper, J. (1997). Quick-thinks: Active-thinking tasks in lecture classes. *Cooperative Learning and College Teaching, 8,(1).*

Jonassen, D. H. (1991). Evaluating constructivistic learning. *Educational Technology, 31(9),* 28–33.

Keown, D. (1986). Teaching science in U.S. schools: A commentary. *Journal of Environmental Education, 18(1),* 30–32.

Koran, J. J., Jr., & Koran, M. L. (1984). The roles of attention and curiosity in museum learning. *Museum Education Anthology, 2,* 205–213.

Koran, J. J., Jr., & Longino, S. J. (1983). *Curiosity behavior in formal and informal setting: What research says. Research Bulletin.* Sanibel, FL: Florida Educational Research and Development Council, Inc.

Panitz, T. (1997). Collaborative versus cooperative learning: Comparing the two definitions helps understand the nature of interactive learning. *Cooperative Learning and College Teaching, 8,(2).*

Schunk, D. H. (1996). *Learning theories.* Englewood Cliffs, NJ: Prentice-Hall.

Schunk, D. H., & Zimmerman, B. J. (1998). *Self-regulated learning: From teaching to self-reflective practice.* New York, NY: The Guilford Press.

Tei, E., & Oran S. (1985). Effective studying from ext. *Forum for Reading, 16(2),* 46–55.

Yager, R. (1991). The constructivist-learning model, towards real reform in science education. *The Science Teacher, 58 (6),* 52–57.

Zimmerman, B. J. (1989). A social cognitive view of self-regulated academic learning. *Journal of Educational Psychology, 81(3),* 329–339.

PowerPoint Outline to Assist In-Class Note-Taking

A. Learning Theories

a. Information Processing

b. Self-Regulated Learning

c. Self-Efficacy

d. Metacognition

e. Constructivism

B. Learning Strategies

a. Critical Thinking

b. Inquiry

c. Active Learning

d. Conceptual Teaching

e. Graphic Organizers

f. Collaborative/Cooperative Learning

g. Learning Cycle

h. Learning Process

i. Learning Styles

j. Project-Based Learning (PBL)

C. Teaching, Learning, and Psychological Orientations

a. Operant Conditioning/Behaviorism (Skinner)

b. Social Cognitive/Modeling (Bandura)

c. Cognitive Development/Constructivism (Piaget)

d. Dialectivism (Vygotsky)

e. Humanistic Psychology (Maslow)

D. Educational Philosophy

a. Perennialism

b. Essentialism

c. Progressivism

d. Existentialism

E. YOUR Education Philosophy

2

Is Teaching for Me?

Guest Editorial: Alison Morris-Shetlar, PhD, Biologist, Professor, and Director of the Teaching and Learning Center/University of Central Florida

Teaching allows you the opportunity to share the passion and excitement that you have for your subject with others. The key to successful teaching is to provide a learning environment that encourages students to take ownership of their learning. By facilitating the exploration of the relevance and application of what your subject means and how it fits into the big picture, the student can bring their own experiences into the classroom. Often we want our students to learn in a traditional manner, yet be able to go beyond standard expectations and develop problem solving and critical thinking skills. While a small class of 10 students would be ideal, and would provide the manageable environment that students need to fulfill these requirements, this is often not possible. The increasing demands from the university system to increase class size, decrease faculty numbers, and ensure that the students receive a good education results in having to face the challenge of creating an environment for successful learning under less than ideal conditions. So how do we develop an environment and curriculum that will support these objectives?

Creating a successful learning environment requires a few major components:

- a clear and comprehensive course design;
- students who are motivated to learn;
- developing teaching methods that engage the students and promote their success in the class;
- discovery learning and reinforcement for long term retention of information; and
- regular formative assessment.

If these components excite you then teaching is for you. If you want to be a part of students discovering the wonders of your discipline then teaching is for you.

There is considerable amount of literature on the ideals of what a successful lecture and laboratory learning environment should be (Randle, 1997; Newby & Fisher, 1997; Lauterbach, White, Liu, Bodner, & Delgass, 1997) but rarely is there a source that gives examples on how to create that environment. In the following few paragraphs you will find suggestions on methods that have been proven, at all educational levels, to facilitate student learning.

When determining your curriculum think first about the goals and objectives that you have for your course. Ask the question, "At the end of the course what is it that I want my student to be able to do?" List the things that are of most importance. Then, think about how you are going to measure the student learning that should occur in the environment that you have created and that will give you the assessment strategies that you can use to find out if the students are indeed learning. Once you have those assessments then you are ready to develop your syllabus.

It really helps student motivation to learn, if you ask your students to apply information regularly. I use the "one-minute paper" (Chemical Engineering Education, 1997) where I ask questions such as, "What were the main themes of the reading you did for today's discussion?" and "What are the three main points from today's lecture?" and "Give an example from your own experience that would show your understanding of the concept discussed today." Ask the students to write these thoughts on a small (4.25- × 5.5-inch—a sheet of paper cut in quarters) piece of paper. Give them 1–2 minutes to write and then collect them in. These could be for credit or just for formative assessment (need to give some kind of feedback, either "Eighty percent of you got three main ideas such as . . ." or "three main points that you should have determined from the reading are . . ."). Either way it gives you information on how your students are doing in the class and will help the student become engaged in the class by seeing the relevance and application of the concepts.

As learners we know that when we see the relevance and application of concepts, especially when we can see how it influences our lives, then we not only learn the concepts but also are able to retain and apply the information more readily. A teaching strategy that can help students retain information is *directed discovery* or *problem-based learning.* With this pedagogy the instructor poses questions that focus the students on the concepts presented then allows the students to think about all aspects of the concept and how they might apply to the problem posed. By being actively involved in the learning process the students engage on a different level than when learning by passive processes.

If these methods, and others available to you (Morrison-Shetlar & Marwitz, 2003), excite you and if you are passionate about others discovering the exciting elements that have turned you on to your discipline then teaching is for you. Just do it!

Remember the KWL table—the K represents what you KNOW about this chapter and the W is what you WANT to learn. Please write in you responses below and at the end of the chapter, you can provide your thoughts on what you LEARNed.

What Do You KNOW? **(prior knowledge)**

What Do You WANT to Know? **(objectives and goals)**

"Teaching is not a lost art, but the regard for it is a lost tradition."

—Jacques Barzun

"It is the supreme art of the teacher to awaken joy in creative expression and knowledge."

— Albert Einstein

Questions from Pre-Service Teachers

Pre-service teacher candidates typically have an ideal perspective on the world of teaching—it is one of wonderment. It seemed one of the best ways to begin a chapter on self-discovery into the teaching field would be to share the many questions gathered from prior students who took this course. Throughout the years, the following represents 100 of the many responses that were collected responding to the question of

"What questions do you have about teaching?"

1. Will the state pay off your student loans if you agree to work in that state?
2. How much does it to take to get nationally accredited?
3. What advice would you give to make the job less stressful?
4. How do you get a job as a teacher?
5. Is the first year of teaching as hard as they say?
6. What are the pros/cons of teaching public versus private?
7. What are the chances I will get the job I want?
8. Do nationally accredited, certified teachers still need state certification?
9. How much leeway are teachers provided in their curriculum?
10. Is experience in secondary education comparable to teaching at a university?
11. To what extent are professors expected to demonstrate teaching qualifications?
12. What is the structure of a school like among teachers, in terms of seniority?
13. How many bosses will I have?
14. What sorts of resources are available to a teacher? (Computers, buses, and so on)
15. Will I have to teach classes I don't want to teach?
16. What, other than a degree and certification, will a school want to see in an applicant for a teaching position (community service, fluency in Spanish, and so on)?
17. Why can't an education major take electives or have a minor?
18. Who decides what is supposed to be taught/learned in each grade level?
19. Why does algebra have to be learned if I will never use it?
20. Why is being nationally certified not a mandatory requirement for all teachers?
21. Why are teachers' salaries not higher since they mold future leaders?
22. How much freedom are teachers given with the way they teach the material?
23. How often are you allowed to teach your own lessons?
24. What do you have to do if you are an elementary teacher and decide to teach secondary?
25. Are you allowed to take field trips?
26. How often are you allowed to take field trips?
27. Are all public schools similar or very different?
28. What does education mean for me in the future?
29. Is an education necessary for me to succeed as a teacher?
30. Will becoming a teacher support my family?
31. When will teachers get paid for the work they do?
32. Am I fit to be a teacher?
33. What makes a person a successful teacher?

BTW

In the Bag means certain to succeed. The term refers to the container in which hunters placed small game, called a "bag" since the 15th century.

34. Do teachers get paid more in a private or public school?
35. What does it take to be a school administrator?
36. Is it easier to teach in an elementary school or a high school?
37. What happens to a school after it receives a letter grade F more than twice?
38. Are we going to learn alternative methods to teach students who do not learn by traditional methods?
39. How does teaching differ from state to state?
40. What are the requirements for keeping your teaching certificate each year?
41. How common is it for teachers to change their profession?
42. What are the most common reason teachers cite for leaving the occupation?
43. Do other countries view and treat teachers differently?
44. How does one become a principal?
45. What's the best way to approach my students as a first-year teacher?
46. How can I have the students learn more about me, without having to tell them personal and intimate details of my life?
47. If I become an elementary teacher, how hard would it be to become a counselor or some other kind of advisor down the road within the same school or district?
48. Are most teachers willing to work with you and help you as a first year teacher?
49. What's the best advice you can give to a first-year teacher?
50. Would you suggest that I should try to teach in the school district that I was schooled in?
51. Would it be easier to get a job in the same school system that I grew up?
52. Am I entering the right field?
53. How much freedom will I have at creating my own lesson plans?
54. How will I know if I have picked the right place to work?
55. What if I am not happy right away?
56. How much of my own money should I expect to spend on classroom supplies?
57. What is the best way to handle a student that will not listen to my directions?
58. Do I have to be careful how attached my students become to me (and vice versa)?
59. What are the best colors to use in the classroom to enhance the student's abilities to learn?
60. Is our society trying to under develop the creative parts of our children's minds so that we are all cookie cutter mathematicians and chemists?
61. Why are the lunches at school so unnutritious?
62. How can one be an effective, yet affectionate teacher?
63. How can I care without crossing certain lines and getting respect from my students?
64. Is the education board made up of people from different backgrounds?
65. What is with the tenure program?
66. Do school districts pay for graduate school?
67. Do students respond to teachers that are more like them?
68. What happens if I become unhappy, will my skills allow me to do something else?
69. If I teach in Florida will my entire curriculum revolve around the FCAT?
70. Are all public schools equal when it comes to having money for the needs of students?

71. Why are there standards that teachers need to follow?
72. What does the school board actually do?
73. What causes teachers to not want to teach anymore?
74. How much of a teacher's life is public?
75. Are there rules about students harassing teachers?
76. Can a teacher date their fellow teachers?
77. Is there a limit on classroom activities that you do with your classes?
78. What does a teacher do when there is no class involvement?
79. What happens when you are asked a question that you don't know the answer to?
80. Can you get in trouble for helping out the students that you tended to favor?
81. What do you do when you have a child with poor hygiene in your class and it is becoming a distraction?

BTW

Did you know that back a couple hundred years ago most people got married in June because they took their yearly bath in May and were still smelling pretty good by June. However, they were starting to smell, so brides carried a bouquet of flowers to hide the body odor.

82. When, where, and by whom was the first school established?
83. How do you find that middle ground between being the "cool teacher" that the students are comfortable with, and the "mean teacher" that all students respect?

BTW

To show your true colors is to be yourself. To sail under false colors was to disguise a pirate ship by flying the flag of a friendly nation.

84. Are there online workshops where I can find advice from teachers?
85. Who decides on the textbook that will be used?
86. Will I be able to provide authentic assessments?
87. Will I retain my vigor and enthusiasm?
88. Why aren't there more people that want to teach?
89. How did we get the standards for education?
90. How does one become a school board official?
91. Do regulations hinder the effectiveness of their classroom techniques?
92. Would the money still be enough after several years?
93. How can you tell, or can you tell, if you're doing a good job teaching?
94. What is the key factor to being a good teacher?
95. If I don't enjoy teaching what else can I do with an education degree?
96. Why there are so many politics behind education?

BTW

To have someone over a barrel means to have the upper hand. In the days before mouth-to-mouth resuscitation, lifeguards placed drowning victims over a barrel, who were rolled back and forth while the lifeguard tried to revive them.

97. Why do we have different standards for every state?
98. How do the states decide on their standards?
99. How much is involved in becoming nationally certified.
100. Can I make my own lesson plans up or are they already made for me?

Why Do You Want to Teach?

"I cannot teach anybody anything, I can only make them think."

—Socrates

The question of why pre-service teacher candidates want to teach is asked early in their collegiate career. Many introduction to education courses explore this issue with students both inside and outside of class in an attempt to determine if their perspective of teaching align with the realities of teaching.

I³ *At this point, early in the book, please take some time and write your responses to this question, "Why do you want to teach?"*

____

____

____

____

____

____

Hopefully, you will share your honest responses with others during class time. Other common responses that people want to teach are:

- A desire to work with children
- They value education in society
- Interest in particular subject
- Influence of own teachers
- Long summer vacation
- Love of teaching
- Desire to serve and help

I³ *Add to this list any new ideas which are discussed in class:*

- ______
- ______
- ______
- ______
- ______

As a pre-service teacher candidate, it is best to prepare as far in advance as possible. Many of the activities that you do (or do not do) during this first year will make your subsequent years both easier and more meaningful. Taking time now to visualize your first year of teaching is a very worthwhile activity. In this venue, here are some typical questions that may be asked of you during your first interview for a teaching position. Addressing these over the next several years, instead of your final year in your studies will serve you well.

- How can you tell students are learning?
- What are your assessment and measurement techniques?
- How would you individualize learning?
- How would you go about setting standards at the beginning of the year?
- How do you get students to do what you want them to do?
- Describe your system of classroom management.
- Compare negative and positive reinforcement and describe effects of each.
- Tell me some ways you would involve parents in your classroom.
- Imagine that you replace a teacher during the year. Describe how you would become acquainted with parents and students.
- What is wrong with education today? What is right?
- What would you say if your first grade student asked if there really was a Santa Claus?
- What were you hoping we would ask you but didn't?
- You have heard students complaining constantly about another teacher. What would you do?
- What are your three most important reasons for wanting to be a teacher?
- How much do you want to know about your students in order to be most helpful to them?
- When you think about your students, in what major ways do you most want to influence their lives?
- What two core teaching strategies do you most use to achieve this result?
- What is your philosophy of education?
- Describe the role of the teacher in the learning process.
- What are some trends, issues, and methodologies in education that relate to your specific curriculum area or grade level?
- What books are you currently reading or have you read recently?
- Tell me how you would spend 500 dollars to enhance your classroom.
- What technology do you need in your classroom to promote a good learning environment?
- What specific technology skills do you possess?

I³ *Please add to this list any questions you believe might be asked or other questions that are developed in class during discussion.*

____

____

____

____

____

Benefits of Teaching

There are many benefits of teaching, although at times, this may not seem the case, especially in the popular media.

I³ *Take a moment and consider all of the possibly benefits, which you believe teaching can provide.*

____

____

____

Some of the common responses to the question of what are the benefits of teaching:

- **Autonomy**—the ability to control much of your own time as opposed to have a direct supervisor monitoring your movements.
- **Enjoyment**—many teacher truly enjoy their jobs. Teaching CAN be a wonderful job if the teacher decides to create an enjoyable environment for themselves and others.
- **Flexibility**—teaching is much more flexible than other professions. Although you will be expected to be at certain places on time and provide material regulated by the state, you have flexibility of how you teach these concepts.
- **Stimulating**—this profession can be very stimulating, although much of this is up to the teacher. Teachers continue to push themselves to learn and question/challenge their students.
- **Collegial**—teachers are encouraged to work closely with colleagues in their discipline to develop ideas, brainstorm, review each other's plans, and so on.
- **Emotive**—exciting, emotional, and stimulating; all of these are possible in any day as a teacher. Students yearn for it and teachers can provide this approach to encourage and provide a contextual environment for sustained learning.
- **Analytical**—for those left-brain individuals, teaching can be a very organized, logical adventure. Concepts can be presented, questions asked, data collected, inferences made and subsequent predictions developed.
- **Keeps Brain Functioning in Diverse Ways**—teaching will continually challenge your mind, perspective, beliefs, and attitudes toward the world, education, and people.
- **Salary**—some believe that a teacher's salary may not be a benefit, however, data indicates that beginning teachers with an undergraduate degree are paid very similarly to most other graduates in other discipline. The discrepancy typically becomes evident after 10 years of low increases in pay.

The following National Average Salaries may help you place salary in perspective.

NATIONAL AVERAGE SALARIES OF PUBLIC SCHOOL TEACHERS, 2000–01

Ranking	State	Salary
1	New Jersey	$53,281*
2	Connecticut	52,693
3	California	52,480
4	New York	52,040
5	Michigan	50,694*
6	Pennsylvania	49,528
7	District of Columbia	48,704
8	Rhode Island	48,474*
9	Alaska	48,123
10	Illinois	47,847
11	Massachusetts	47,789
12	Delaware	47,047
13	Maryland	45,963
	United States	**43,335***
14	Indiana	43,311
15	Ohio	42,764
16	Georgia	42,216
17	Minnesota	42,212
18	Washington	42,137
19	Wisconsin	42,122
20	Oregon	41,711
21	North Carolina	41,151
22	Nevada	40,443 *
23	Virginia	40,197
24	Hawaii	40,052
25	Colorado	39,184
26	Texas	38,361
27	New Hampshire	38,301
28	Vermont	38,254
29	Florida	38,230
30	Alabama	37,956*
31	South Carolina	37,938
32	Tennessee	37,431
33	Missouri	36,722
34	Kentucky	36,589
35	Iowa	36,479
36	Utah	36,441
37	Idaho	36,375
38	Maine	36,373
39	Arizona	36,302*
40	Kansas	35,901
41	West Virginia	35,888
42	Wyoming	34,678
43	Arkansas	34,641
44	Oklahoma	34,499
45	Nebraska	34,175
46	New Mexico	33,785
47	Louisiana	33,615
48	Montana	33,249
49	Mississippi	31,954
50	North Dakota	30,891
51	South Dakota	30,265
	Median	38,361
	Range	23,016

NEA Research, Estimates Database (2002).

* means these states are still estimates.

BTW

In the early days of America, bread was divided according to status. Workers got the burnt bottom of the loaf, the family got the middle, and guests got the top, or the "upper crust."

- **Job Security**—for those who priority is security and securing a job in any town, in the event their spouse or family must relocate, this benefit is very important.
- **Status**—in many cultures, including the United States, teachers are typically valued in society. Although there may be humorous anecdotes in the media or by friends, teaching is still thought of as a respected profession. It will be up to many of you to continue that perspective from others.

BTW

Seedy, meaning somewhat disreputable. During the seasons when rye, barley, oats, and other grains were being planted, a fellow who spent his days in the fields was likely to be covered with seeds. Once the title entered common usage, it came to mean anything run-down, from shacks to individuals.

- **Tenure**—this concept parallels job security, typically after 3 years, a teacher can secure tenure. This allows the teacher to obtain a continuing contract in which they will be employed unless there are legal or ethical rationale for termination.
- **Retirement**—the benefits for teacher retirement are typically very good and most can live a lifestyle similar to that which they have become accustomed to.
- **Quality of Life**—instead of wealth or material possessions, many people, especially in the teaching field concentrate on the issue of quality of life, or enjoying their family, feelings, helping others, caring, and contributing to their community and society.
- **Impact**—many students begin the pre-service teaching program with the idea on their mind of one of their teachers who had a positive impact on their lives. They enter the profession in hopes of returning this impact to other young folk. This may be the number one reason and the most compelling to become a teacher—truly helping others.

I³ *Now take a moment and write down any other benefits that were discussed during class.*

____

____

____

____

____

____

Challenges of Teaching

Yes, there are challenges of teaching, just as there are in any profession. The critical thinking individual will realize that in life there are always multiple sides to a concept. It will be up to you to determine if the benefits outweigh the challenges, or more importantly is the quality of items. There could be only one benefit and numerous challenges, but if the benefit is a top priority for you, then you may have defended your rationale to pursue a career in teaching.

I³ *Take a moment and consider all of the possible challenges, which you believe teaching will place in front of you.*

____

____

____

____

Some of the typical challenges that have been suggested are the following:

- Classroom Management

BTW

When people are stressed, at times they are described as a basket case. The term basket case means an overly anxious or stressed person who can't function normally. This first appeared as a slang term in WWI meaning "a quadruple amputee." Soldiers who had lost all their limbs actually were carried in baskets because if they were carried on stretchers, they'd be too likely to fall out.

- Social problems
- Family and community support
- Long working hours
- Stress
- The unexpected
- Academic pressures
- Administrative workload
- Preparation for standardized tests
- Salary
- Money management
- Time management
- Organization
- Professional development
- Motivation

Frequently, you will hear from supporters of education for young folk to "hang in there" when times are tough.

BTW

Hang in There means to refuse to give up. This hails from the world of boxing where managers exhort exhausted fighters to clinch their opponents or hang on to the ropes to finish a round.

I^3 *Now take a moment and write down any other challenges that were discussed during class.*

____

____

____

____

KWL

What Did You LEARN?

____

____

____

____

____

____

____

____

____

____

____

____

____

References

Randle, I. (1997). The Measure of Success: Integrated Thematic Instruction. *Clearing House,* 71, 85–87.

Newby, M., & Fisher, D. (1997). An Instrument for Assessing the Learning Environment of a Computer Laboratory. *Journal of Educational Computing Research,* 16, 179–190.

Lauterbach, J., White, S., Liu, Z., Bodner, G. M., & Delgass, W. N. (1997). A Novel Laboratory Course on Advanced Chemical Experiments. *Chemical Engineering Education,* 31, 260–265.

Morrison-Shetlar, A. I. & Marwitz, M. R. (2003). In *Teaching Creatively: Ideas in Action.* Minneapolis, Minnesota: Outernet Publishing LLC.

PowerPoint Outline to Assist In-Class Note-Taking

A. Questions from Pre-Service Teachers

B. Why Do You Want to Teach?

C. Benefits of Teaching

a. Autonomy

b. Enjoyment

c. Flexibility

d. Stimulating

e. Collegial

f. Emotive

g. Analytical

h. Keeps Brain Functioning in Diverse Ways

i. Job Security

j. Status

k. Tenure

l. Retirement

m. Quality of Life

n. Impact

D. Challenges of Teaching

a. Classroom Management

b. Social Problems

c. Family and Community Support

d. Long Working Hours

e. Stress

f. The Unexpected

g. Academic Pressures

h. Administrative Workload

i. Preparation for standardized tests

j. Salary

k. Money Management

l. Time Management

m. Organization

n. Professional Development

o. Motivation

3

How Do I Become a Teacher?

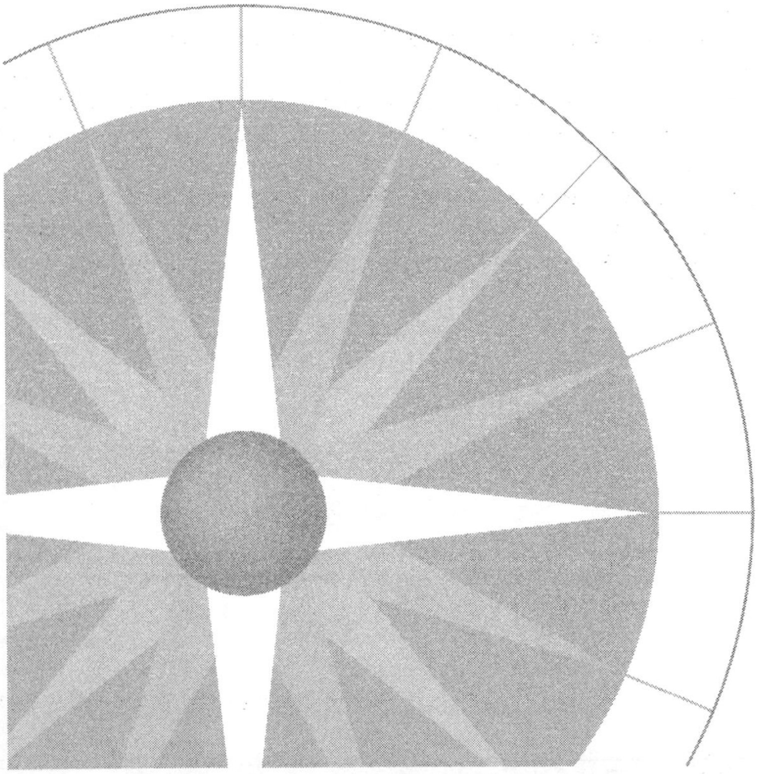

Guest Editorial: Deryl Bailey, PhD, Associate Professor of Counselor Educator/University of Georgia and Mary Bradbury-Bailey, M.Ed

Reflection — Channel — Opportunity — Advocate

If you want to become a teacher, let me rephrase that . . . If you want to become a great teacher, these four words will become an active part of your thinking and your doing, for great teachers they have become second nature.

Reflection

You must first examine your motives as to why you even want to become a teacher. If it is out of love for a particular subject, I applaud your desire to share that knowledge with the next generation, but I can honestly tell you that while it provides a nice start or a good background, it will not be enough. Even in the current standardized test-driven educational environment, great teachers teach students, not curriculum. If the ever trite reply "because I like working with kids" was going to be your answer, you need to rethink your motives. Adolescents are not that "likeable." Remember when you were that age? We all challenged authority, thought we knew everything, and were convinced we were the only generation that knew how to be wild! Great teachers reflect with honesty on their own experiences as adolescents and put that memory into action. Great teachers can have a student a few inches in front of them cussing them out, allow them to finish venting, and then say, "Let's talk as I walk you to the office." Great teachers never take the actions and reactions of their students personally, but instead are able to look inside the student and see the potential and the possibilities. Argumentative students are constantly reminded that once they are lawyers, we expect them to be ethical while those who doodle more than they write are reminded that when their first piece is exhibited you expect an invitation to the showing.

Besides personal reflection, great teachers incorporate professional reflection on a day by day and sometimes moment by moment basis. As you begin planning, you are constantly asking yourself why am I teaching this, how will it impact my students, and how can I get them from point A to point D in their thinking. Even with the best planned units, some students will become easily frustrated and are so willing to share that with you and you have to reflect on what is not connecting for them and orchestrate a "plan B" within minutes of their frustration. Everything we do in the classroom should be very intentional if we want our students to achieve and reflection becomes the tool that can make that a reality rather than a lucky guess.

Channel

Great teachers are able to channel their passion for learning or a particular subject to their students. So you need to ask yourself if you are passionate about learning. Do you take ever opportunity to challenge yourself and learn? If not, then why would you expect students in your class to learn? One thing about students, they can spot a fake a mile away. Are you passionate about the subject or grade level you would like to teach so much so that you are willing to continue learning on a consistent basis until you can see it from many angles and teach it from a variety of perspectives? Young people are being pulled away from education at a frightening rate, especially minority and students from low-income families, and we need teachers who are able to channel these students' energies and focus back into the classroom.

Opportunity

Great teachers take advantage of opportunities. If you want to become a great teacher, take advantage of required service hours before you begin practicum. Don't just sit in someone's class observing them, but get creative and ask if you can participate as a student or work as a "leader" at a local center or become involved in some out of school initiative that focuses on the neediest students. A "teachable moment" happens on a constant basis and you need to begin looking for them. Ask questions; make teachers that are respected explain why they did something a particular way or the order in which they did things.

"Ask. Ask. Ask."

Great teachers borrow ideas and strategies on a consistent basis! They notice how someone else interacts with a particular child or how they present a particular concept and they take it back with them into their classroom, adding their own personal touch. Really great teachers can borrow or steal from teachers in different subjects and different grade levels because they take advantage of the opportunity and have the ability to adapt useful practices and ideas into their own classroom. Great teachers take the opportunity to get to know their students without being too obvious because they are great listeners. Take advantage of any opportunity to get to know students who do not look like you. Tutor on your own time or work with students from an age group you are interested in via church, civic organizations, and community-based initiatives.

Advocate

Most anyone can teach students who have a solid foundation. To be honest, students with a solid educational foundation, regardless of their age, can excel with or without you. Unfortunately, not every child will come to you with such a foundation. As a teacher you must be able to teach every student who sits before you. Meeting them where they are and moving them forward is the key to good teaching. I once asked a teacher who had been awarded the teacher-of-the-year in three different states how she did it. Her reply continues to inspire me. She stated, ". . . some students are easy to teach, others can be challenging. For the students who are a challenge, especially on their worse days . . . and believe you me there are those days. On those days I look the students in their eyes and in that moment I see the student I want them to be and not the student they are presenting." While you prepare to become a good teacher, remember that you cannot be everything to every student, but you can be something for every student. My last piece of advice is to keep in mind that the students you will teach will not need you to be their friend, instead they will need you to be a positive and supportive adult in their lives who is willing to speak on their behalf when they cannot speak for themselves. In closing, I challenge you to be a GREAT TEACHER, one who understands that great teacher is a process and a journey, not an event.

Good luck! (you'll need it)

KWL

What Do You KNOW? **(prior knowledge)**

What Do You WANT to Know **(objectives and goals)**

"Good teaching is one-fourth preparation and three-fourths theater."

—Gail Godwin

I³ *Write down any ideas that come to you after reading this quote.*

"He who can, does. He who cannot do, teaches."

—George Bernard Shaw

I³ *Write down any ideas that come to you after reading this quote.*

I³ *How can you justify that both of these quotes may have merit?*

____

____

First Things First

To become a teacher, you might wish to do your homework first and research historical aspects of teaching. Perhaps your perspective of teaching is like most, as a student viewing their teachers for 12 years. Or possibly your parents, relative, neighbor, or friend is a teacher and has provided some insight. In any case, teaching is the type of activity that one cannot truly understand until they are in front of the classroom. Although it may be sometime before you are able to do this, we hope to provide some indicators of what teaching is like and specific information on how to become a teacher. Maintaining your sense of humor is one common word of wisdom that you will hear many times. In this regard, consider the following rules for teachers in the United States in 1872:

- Teachers each day will fill lamps, clean chimneys.
- Each teacher will bring a bucket of water and a scuttle of coal for the day's session.
- Make your pens carefully. You many whittle nibs to the individual taste of the pupils.
- Men teachers may take one evening each week for courting purposes, or two evenings a week if they go to church regularly.
- After ten hours in school, the teachers may spend the remaining time reading the Bible or other good books.
- Women teachers who marry or engage in unseemly conduct will be dismissed.
- Every teacher should lay aside from each pay a goodly sum of his earnings for his benefit during his declining years so that he will not become a burden to society.
- Any teacher who smokes, uses liquor in any form, frequents pool or public halls, or gets shaved in a barber shop will given reason to suspect his worth, intention, integrity, and honesty.
- The teacher who performs his labor faithfully and without fault for five years will be given an increase of twenty-five cents per week in his pay, providing the Board of Education approves.

Do you find it hard to believe this story? Good, because it is an urban legend. This was written in an attempt to demonstrate how difficult things were in the past and how well we have it now. There has not been any credible evidence authenticating this document. Although it is humorous and somewhat enjoyable to read, as educators, we need to view everything with a critical eye. We will speak at length later in this text about critical thinking and how you can foster these techniques in your approach. As Henry Ford said, "Thinking must be hard work since so few people do it."

In 1915, the *Golden Rules for Teachers Handbook* (Mahoney, 2000) provided the following rules for teachers:

1. You will not marry during the term of your contract.
2. You are not to keep company with men.
3. You must be home between the hours of 8 P.M. and 6 A.M. unless attending a school function.
4. You must not loiter downtown in any of the ice cream stores.
5. You may not travel beyond the city limits unless you have the permission of the chairman of the board.

6. You may not ride in a carriage or an automobile with any man unless he is your father or brother.
7. You may not smoke cigarettes.
8. You may not dress in bright colors.
9. You may under no circumstances dye your hair.
10. You must wear at least two petticoats.
11. Your dresses may not be any shorter than two inches above the ankle.
12. To keep the schoolroom neat and clean you must:
    - sweep the floor at least once daily.
    - scrub the floor at least once a week with hot, soapy water.
    - clean the blackboards at least once a day.
    - start the fire at 7 A.M. so the room will be warm by 8 A.M.

Believable? Yes, this one has been found to be true, sometimes fact is stranger than fiction.

Education

"Start where the learner is."

—JOHN DEWEY

I³ *Write down any ideas that come to you after reading this quote.*

____

____

"For every person who wants to teach there are approximately 30 who don't want to learn."

—W. C. SELLAR AND R. J. YEATMAN

I³ *Write down any ideas that come to you after reading this quote.*

____

____

I³ *How can you justify that both of these quotes may have merit?*

____

____

Typically, the first question anyone asks after they determine what it is they wish to be when they grow up is, "how do they become that person"? There are many steps, aspects, variables, and individual challenges in becoming any professional and teaching is no exception. This chapter will attempt to describe some of the major steps, which a pre-service candidate might wish to consider as they take the journey in becoming a teacher. There are many types of content that you can teach. Some of them include elementary, primary, English, science, mathematics, social science, drama, journalism, biology, chemistry, earth-space science, physics, art, computer science, dance, English to speakers of other languages, health, humanities, music, physical education, world languages, exceptional student education, hearing impaired, speech-language impaired, educational media specialist, guidance and counseling, school psychologist, school social worker, driver education, agriculture, business education, industrial arts—technology education. In addition, a good resource on the web, which will help you understand and determine your aptitude for teaching is located at *http://www.timetoteach.org/*.

There are several approaches to becoming a certified teacher. You may wish to check the Department of Education in the particular state that you wish to teach in, as the requirements differ from state to state. However, most require at a minimum, an undergraduate bachelor's degree.

I³ *How Do You Think You Become a Teacher? Try to outline some of the steps that you believe will be required of you to become a teacher. Do not be apprehensive to write your thoughts; at this point, it is perfectly fine NOT to know the answer, that is why you are in this class.*

____

____

____

____

____

Undergraduate Degree

In addition to a K–12 education, to become a certified teacher, a person requires an undergraduate bachelor's degree. In order to obtain this degree, a person will need to achieve a high school diploma or GED, secure acceptable SAT or ACT scores and GPA, apply to the institution, and be accepted as a student. Once this occurs, the student then begins taking their general education courses. Typically this consists of 60 credit hours of classes, which include English, mathematics, humanities, and the natural sciences. After this course sequence, the student may be eligible to enter their major college and become a pre-teacher candidate. At this point, students begin to take courses specific to their major course of study, such as elementary education, secondary education, early childhood education, special education, and so on. Some examples of courses for an elementary education major might include the following courses:

- Understanding the Learner
- Conceptual Learning
- Literacy
- Teachers of English Speakers of Other Languages (TESOL) Methods
- Art/Music Methods
- History Methods
- Mathematic Methods
- Science Methods
- Assessment and Measurement
- Classroom Management
- Learning and Behavior

In the area of education, field experiences have become very important. Some programs include several levels of opportunities for students to interact with students and a K–12 educational environment. These might include an early experience where students observe an elementary and a secondary environment. Next, the student will participate in a Field I and/or II event where they will be working with teachers in the field. Finally, the pre-service candidate will engage in a full semester's internship where they will be in charge of teaching and learning.

Setting Yourself Apart

"I always wanted to be somebody. I realize now I should have been more specific."

—Lily Tomlin

I^3 *Write down any ideas that come to you after reading this quote.*

____

____

"My best teacher was my dog; the world is my classroom."

—Jane Goodall

I^3 *Write down any ideas that come to you after reading this quote.*

____

____

I^3 *How can you justify that both of these quotes may have merit?*

____

____

As a student, you may wish to try to think into the near future in order to gauge present activities. As a young college student, one metaphor to use is your collegiate career is similar to a large boat. It requires advance warning and planning in order to make turns and change direction. By organizing your plans early, you will have more doors open to you, which are suitable to your background, training and aptitude. It is strongly encouraged that you identify a way to set yourself apart from your colleagues. In a few short years, all of you will be competing for a teaching position. If you wish to secure a particular position or a position at a particular school, you may need to be competitive. Some of the areas where you can build a niche are in technology, action research, English speakers of other languages (ESOL), bilingualism, writing, and special education.

I^3 *Which of these do you believe might be one of your strengths? If not one of these, can you think of others that you might pursue?*

____

____

____

Be Prepared

> ***"To teach well, we need not say all that we know, only what is useful for the pupil to hear."***
>
> —Anonymous

I³ *Write down any ideas that come to you after reading this quote.*

____

____

To be the most efficient at navigating your vessel, here are a few characteristics you may wish to work on:

1. **Time Management.** There is no real secret to time management—if you are not naturally able to efficiently complete your tasks, then you will want to get some help. There are many, many ways to do this. Most universities offer student assistance, tutoring, and so on. Also, there are free sites online, books to purchase, day timers and even electronic gadgets such as Personal Digital Assistants. Do not underestimate this skill, it can save you in times of trouble and it can also impress your teachers and future employers beyond your imagination. Also in managing your time wisely, there will less anxiety and need to be "saved by the bell," if your assignment is incomplete.

> **BTW**
>
> In the 1950s, England started running out of places to bury people. So they would dig up coffins and reuse the graves. In reopening these coffins, about one in 25 were found to have scratch marks on the inside and they realized they had been burying people alive. So they tied a string on the deceased's wrist, ran it through the coffin and up through the ground, and tied it to a bell. Someone would have to sit out in the graveyard all night to listen for the bell. Hence on the "graveyard shift" they would know that someone was "saved by the bell" or he was a "dead ringer."

2. **Organization.** A close cousin to time management and just as essential is organization. Again, if somehow you did not pick this up sometime earlier in your life, all is not lost, however, get help quick, as if you do not resolve this soon, it could become one of your personal characteristics. As a teacher, there is no such thing as being overly organized. Color-coded, numbered, thematic—whatever it takes, identify a method that you can keep track of everything and access it when you need it. Your classes will be demanding enough, you do not need additional frustrations of not finding something important. Also, some of the concepts in one course will be used in another. You will not be able to use the same documents, however, research performed in one course will help in another if you can access it efficiently. Also organization can keep you from feeling like everything is falling on you at once, or as they say, "raining cats and dogs."

BTW

In old England, houses had thatched roofs made of thick straw and piled high with no wood underneath. It was the only place for animals to get warm, so all the pets (dogs and cats) and other small animals (mice, rats, and bugs) lived in the roof. When it rained it became slippery and sometimes the animals would slip and fall off the roof. Hence the saying, "It's raining cats and dogs."

3. **Scheduling.** Try to know yourself and then schedule appropriately. Are you a morning person, a night person, or a procrastinator (definitely seek professional help for this one—otherwise it will haunt you forever), then know who you are and schedule appropriately. Do not try to force a schedule, it will typically result in poor work and you will be unhappy and frustrated. Sometimes, stepping back, exercising, taking a nap, eating, or watching one TV program (only one) will enable you to get back on track.
4. **Networking.** This is a very important skill and many times overlooked by young students, especially networking with professors. Ideally, you can find multiple professors as a possible mentor and several more as a reference and to provide guidance, both during your undergraduate experience and beyond. Your professors are the ones with contacts and can possibly get you and interview at the school of your choice. Or, if you did not impress them, or possibly offended them, they can ensure that you do not get that interview. Be savvy—if you do not have these skills, then find a way to learn them and become comfortable "chewing the fat" with colleagues.

BTW

In the 1950s, many people in England could not afford expensive meat. Sometimes they could obtain pork and would feel really special when that happened. When company came over, they would bring out some bacon and hang it from the rafters to show it off. It was a sign of wealth that a man "could bring home the bacon." They would cut off a little to share with guest and would all sit around and "chew the fat." Those with money had plates made of pewter. Food with a high acid content caused some of the lead to leach onto the food. This happened most often with tomatoes, so they stopped eating tomatoes—for 400 years. Most people didn't have pewter plates, but had trenchers—a piece of wood with the middle scooped out like a bowl. Trenchers were never washed and a lot of times worms got into the wood. After eating off wormy trenchers, they would get "trench mouth."

5. **People skills.** You are entering a people-business, in which you will be expected to have these skills. If you currently do not, but would like to, then you can work on these. If you do not have these and do not want them, then you should probably look for another career. People skills are more than being a good salesman. People skills include genuine listening skills, good communication skills, and are able to empathize.

6. **Money management.** A definitely must as a teacher. Teaching salaries are not high, however, with appropriate money management skills, you can retire comfortably and enjoy your later years in life. Most state systems have very good benefit programs including matching your retirement plan—IF—you elect to participate in these. Many times, young teachers do not know about these or do not try to find out about these. The most important thing to do about this is participate early—time will make you the most money. You can easily set aside 3 percent of your earnings, typically tax-deferred, which can earn you over 1 million dollars by retirement. By addressing your management of funds, you can avoid having to live by "hook or crook."

BTW

By hook or by crook means to obtain something one way or another. In 1100, William Rufus, king of England, was slain by an arrow while out hunting in the New Forest. A charcoal burner named Purkiss found the king's body and took it by cart to Winchester. As a reward, Purkiss was allowed to gather wood from the New Forest—all that could be reached by a shepherd's crook and cut down with a billhook.

7. **Study skills and note-taking.** This is essential for any student, but especially a student who hopes to be a teacher someday. Once again, if somehow you escaped K–12 without these skills, get them now. Most universities offer good programs to assist you with acquiring these skills. One note of advice is that I find students typically "reading" over the notes prior to a test. If the directions of the test ask you to "read," then chances are that person will perform well. However, most tests ask you to "do" something, so I advise students to "do" while studying—practice writing.
8. **Test-taking.** Everyone knows someone who is not a good test-taker—for pre-service teacher candidates, this is not an option. If you feel you are not a good test-taker, you should set your goals to become one. Again, there are services, techniques, and so on, which will help you do this.
9. **Motivation.** Incredibly important and many times will get you through the day and help you return the next day. Please do not underestimate this—if you have no experience in this area, there are many resources on the web, but the best place is most likely securing a mentor, either a colleague or a professor to assist with this.

Graduate Degree

"Your learning is useless to you till you have lost your text-books, burnt your lecture notes, and forgotten the minutiae which you learnt by heart for the examination."

—Alfred North Whitehead

I³ *Write down any ideas that come to you after reading this quote.*

Ideally, you will want to pursue higher education and obtain a graduate degree. Although one is not required to teach, it is advisable. This can be accomplished while teaching and many times it is the best way to approach both teaching and graduate work. They can work symbiotically—that is your projects for graduate work typically involve developing plans, assessments, and so on, which you can use in your own class. And when teaching, you are searching for new methods, ideas, and reforms, which you should be learning in your graduate classes. Yes, going to school and teaching is very demanding, but rewarding and the younger you do this, the easier it will be. To be selected for graduate school, you will need to posses an undergraduate degree, take the Graduate Record Exam (GRE), secure an acceptable score, along with an acceptable GPA and then be accepted into a program. Most programs require 36–40 credit hours and some require a thesis. A thesis will require a research design, collecting/analyzing data, literature review, discussing your results, and citing your references. Although this may seem difficult, if you apply yourself in the undergraduate experience, challenging yourself to become one of the educators who populate the literature pool may be interesting.

Doctorate Degree

"Perhaps half of all learning ability was squelched in the earliest elementary grades, where children found out that there exist predetermined and unyielding "right answers" for everything, that following instructions is what really counts and, most surprisingly, that the whole business of education is mostly dull and painful."

—George B. Leonard

I³ *Write down any ideas that come to you after reading this quote.*

____

____

Some teachers elect to obtain a doctoral degree and continue teaching in the K–12 system, while others opt to enter the post-secondary system. To enter a doctoral program, one needs a graduate degree with an acceptable GPA and then acceptance into a college program. The student completes about 30 hours of courses, qualifying examinations, writes and defends a dissertation. Once again, as a new student, a doctoral degree may seem daunting, however, at one point in your life, so did riding a bike. Everything will be manageable in its due time and if you appropriately prepare along the journey.

College of Education Programs

Secondary

Depending on the discipline, some students elect to pursue a Bachelors of Arts undergraduate degree in an accredited College of Education secondary education program. There are degrees for secondary science, math, English, social sciences, art, music, and so on. Students taking this direction will still have to meet the required discipline specific core courses, however, they will have the opportunity to participate in methods, assessment and other pedagogically-oriented courses. Many people believe that these courses enable the teacher to maintain a better classroom management, teaching environment and identify student needs for learning.

Elementary

Completing a Bachelors of Arts undergraduate degree in an accredited College of Education elementary education program is the primary method for securing the qualifications to teach. These programs specifically prepare the student to work in a K–5 environment. Typical courses include literacy, math, music, art, and science methods for teaching young children.

Non-College of Education Degrees

To teach at the secondary level, some students elect to pursue a degree in their discipline, such as chemistry and then interview for a position teaching high school chemistry. Some believe that learning the content and understanding it thoroughly is the best approach and that teaching methods can be acquired through experience.

I³ *"What do you think?" Which is more important? Content/Discipline Knowledge or Professional Teaching Knowledge?*

____

____

____

____

____

State Certification

"It's fun to have fun but you've got to know how!"

—Dr. Seuss

I³ *Write down any ideas that come to you after reading this quote.*

____

____

After securing an undergraduate degree from an accredited college, a graduate can apply for a state certification to become a professionally licensed teacher. In the state of Florida, for instance, this requires a degree and passing several content and teaching examinations. If a person wishes to move to another state, many times, a teaching license can be transferred or a state specific license secured by taking another series of tests. Some states initially grant provisional certification and expect candidates to undertake a paid internship, working with a master teacher in a school for at least a year. Most states require teacher candidates to pass competency examinations. Each state's education department or licensing office is the most reliable source for information about teacher licensure. Information for the state of Florida can be found at *http://www.fldoe.org/edcert/* and another example, for the state of Wisconsin information can be found at *http://www.dpi.state.wi.us/*.

The authority for licensing teachers is up to each state. The normal route for licensing teachers is through an accredited College of Education teacher education program. A college submits a plan for a teacher preparation program for each discipline, following state-established guidelines, which the state then approves. A candidate for a teaching license applies directly to a college, takes the required courses and meets other specified requirements, such as student teaching, passage of tests, etc. Upon completion of the program, the candidate is granted a standard license to teach.

National Certification

There is a relatively new approach to a national certification called the National Board for Professional Teacher Standards (NBPTS). The mission of the NBPTS is to advance the quality of teaching and learning by maintaining high and rigorous standards for what accomplished teachers should know and be able to do, providing a national voluntary system certifying teachers who meet these standards, and advocating related education reforms to integrate National Board Certification (NBC) in education and to capitalize on the expertise of NBC Teachers. The NBC concentrates education reform in the classroom—where teaching and learning takes place. NBC is a demonstration of a teacher's practice as measured against high and rigorous standards. Offered on a voluntary basis and valid for 10 years, the advanced system of National Board Certification complements, but does not replace state licensing. Each state, school district, and school decides how best to capitalize on the NBC process and the expertise of NBC Teachers as it designs instructional arrangements to promote student learning and support professional practice. All National Board assessments consist of two major parts, the portfolio entries and the assessment center exercises. Teachers prepare their portfolios by videotaping their teaching, gathering student learning products and other teaching artifacts, and providing detailed analyses of their practice. At the assessment center, teachers write answers to questions that relate to content specific to their fields. Incentives for teachers who secure an NBC vary from state to state. For instance, in Florida, the state pays the $2,300 certification fee, a 10% salary increase for the 10-year life of the certificate and 10% to those who provide 12 days of mentoring and related services and $150 incentive to help defray costs for portfolio preparation.

Continuing Certification

In order to maintain your teaching certification license, you must continue your professional development in the area of teaching. There are several methods to accomplish this task. Most schools offer in-house, in-service workshops or seminars, which provide the teacher with points. Criteria are set for the number of points required to maintain certification. Another way to maintain certification is to complete graduate courses at the university. Many recommend this route and to plan a set of these courses to be able to earn a graduate degree in three to four years.

The following topics are typical for renewing a teaching certificate:

- Content specific to the subject
- Methods or education strategies
- Computer education
- Exceptional student education
- ESOL (English for Speakers of Other Languages)
- Drug abuse, child abuse and neglect, or student dropout prevention

Alternative Certifications

Due to the high need of teachers, there is an increasing interest in alternative certifications to teach. Alternative certification programs provide professional education preparation and experience required for a teaching certificate to individuals who already possess a bachelor's degree. Some states offer a competency-based program, which provides on-the-job training for newly hired instructional staff who have not completed a traditional university teacher preparation program.

Findings of National Center for Education Information's 1997 survey of the states regarding alternative teacher certification:

- Interest in alternative teacher certification continues to escalate. Thirty-five states report that interest in alternative teacher certification from "people wanting to get licensed to teach" has increased in the last five years. Only one state (Missouri) reported this year that interest from this group had decreased.
- Twenty-four states reported that state legislators have shown greater interest in alternative teacher certification.
- The biggest increase in interest from a year ago is from higher education officials in schools, colleges or departments of education. Nineteen states, compared with 15 a year ago, reported in 1997 that interest among these individuals had increased. More states are reporting that colleges are developing alternative teacher preparation programs.
- Half the states (25) report that the number of individuals getting licensed to teach through alternative routes has increased in the last five years.
- Fully certified science, mathematics, and special education teachers stand the best chance of finding teaching jobs now (Feistritzer, 1988).

I³ *List and describe other professions that require certifications or a professional license?*

____

____

____

____

____

How Do I Become an Administrator?

"Blessed are they who can laugh at themselves for they shall never cease to be amused."

—Anonymous

I³ *Write down any ideas that come to you after reading this quote.*

____

____

Educational administrators hold positions as curriculum developers, school principals, and district superintendents. They also work in state and federal education agencies. Some students know that they would like to ultimately become a principal or vice principal after they obtain acceptable years in the classroom. The best way to achieve this goal is to prepare in advance. First of all, the teacher candidate will have to obtain an undergraduate bachelor's degree and complete certification exams, teacher training, and graduate courses. Complete a master's and/or doctoral program in education, with an emphasis on educational administration or educational leadership. Complete your required supervised administrative experience. Pass certification exams on both the state and national level for your specific area of educational administration. Along the way, network with colleagues and then identify several school districts, which you believe your skills align with their mission and pursue employment opportunities.

KWL

What Did You LEARN?

References

Feistritzer, C. (1988). *Alternate teacher certification: An overview.* The National Center for Education Information. Accessed on May 27, 2004, from *http://www.ncei.com/Alt-Teacher-Cert.htm*

Mahoney, J. (2000). Golden Rules for Teachers, 1915; Admonitons from a teachers magazine. Accessed June 2004, from *http://www.tomifobia.com/teacher_rules.html*

PowerPoint Outline to Assist In-Class Note-Taking

A. **First Things First**

B. **Education**

   a. Undergraduate Degree

   b. Graduate Degree

   c. Doctorate Degree

   d. College of Education Programs

   e. Non-College of Education Degrees

C. **State Certification**

D. **National Certification**

E. **Continuing Certification**

F. **Alternative Certifications**

G. **How Do I Become an Administrator?**

4

Critical Aspects of Teaching and Learning

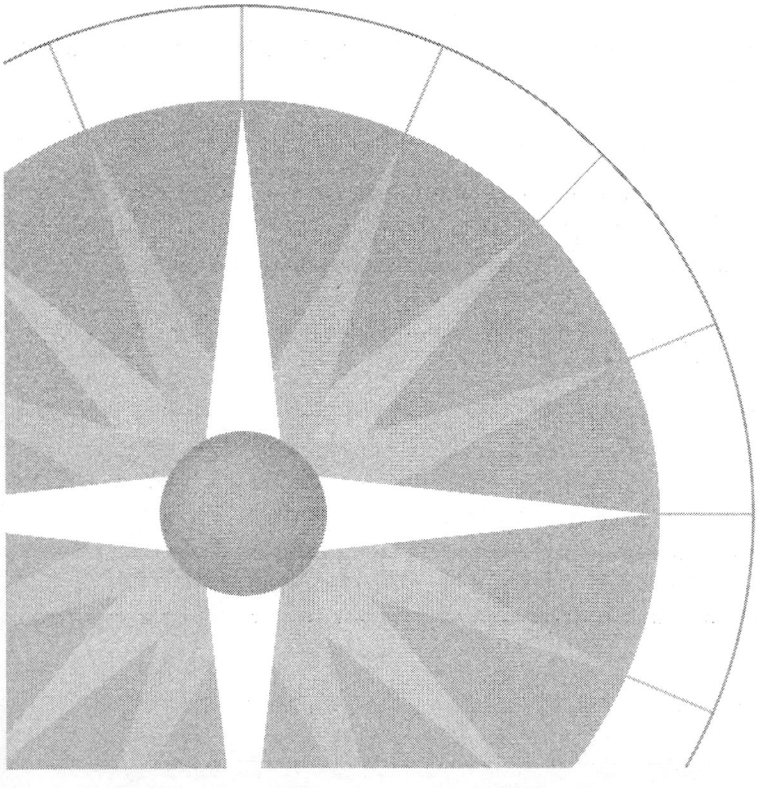

Guest Editorial: Scott Lewis, PhD, Science Educator

Dilemma in student assessment: The tension between using assessments based on a view of learning as in the head of an individual student and assessments based on views of learning as distributed across people and tools.

For many administrators, teachers, and parents, learning in the classroom should be evaluated by giving each student an assessment for which he or she is allowed to use only pencil and paper to answer the questions without assistance from others. This practice is based on the assumption that the knowledge needed to solve problems resides in the head of the individual and that the use of external tools somehow interferes with showing what a person really knows. While pencil and paper tests may allow students to demonstrate knowledge of certain facts and procedures, such assessments do little to inform teachers about the higher levels of learning that students may accomplish, especially when such learning is mediated through the use of tools and working with others. It is akin to judging a high school athlete to be a great basketball player because she is an excellent free-throw shooter—demonstration of great skill in this one area may not be a good indicator of what it takes to play the game at full speed with nine other players on a court.

Recent views of thinking and working call into question the assumptions behind this view of how we learn and how learning is demonstrated. Many researchers now refer to intelligence as "distributed" across people, tools, and settings rather than residing in the head of a single learner (Pea, 1993). In many job contexts, individuals must work cooperatively with others to accomplish a task, where each person brings particular competencies to bear while completing a specific part of the task. In most cases tools such as computers are used in this effort as group members coordinate their actions with each other. Hutchins (1990), for example, describes the critical nature of teamwork and tools needed by a crew of six in steering a Naval ship out of its harbor.

This perspective owes much to the insights of Vygotsky who developed the idea of a "zone of proximal development" in which learners show their potential by working with peers or adults to achieve goals they couldn't have achieved by themselves (Vygotsky, 1978). In support of this view, educators have begun to look to establishing "communities of learners" in the classroom to encourage students to work in groups and with a variety of tools to find answers to higher-level problems. Ann Brown and her colleagues extended the notion of the zone of proximal development to describe classroom communities where students learn to adopt scholarly practices, ways of knowing, and talk while using such artifacts as books, videos, and computers (Brown, Ash, Rutherford, Nakagawa, Gordon, & Campione, 1993). In such classrooms, Brown and her colleagues showed that individual students can become experts on particular topics, can utilize a variety of technologies for learning, and can teach each other and share knowledge as a regular part of their classroom work.

For educators who believe that knowledge is best gained and demonstrated in such distributed environments, assessments should be crafted to match how students perform in such settings. For example, we might want to judge how effectively students can be evaluated as they work with others in finding out the answer to a question—did the student contribute an idea, take responsibility for an action, communicate effectively with others, and so on. We might want to assess whether the students used a tool such as the Internet appropriately to find relevant information—did they specify appropriate key words when using a search engine, were they able to find from reliable Web sites? We might want to note how readily students are using newly learned concepts in other study domains. Evaluating student processes and products must become a regular part of the way we find out about our students' learning. Such assessments are not easy to develop, but may be necessary if we want to have a better sense of whether students are gaining higher levels of learning in the classroom as identified by the distributed learning position.

Teachers who view learning as distributed in the classroom among students and their tools can face a great conflict when asked to administer types of assessments that are built on the assumption that the most important knowledge and learning reside in the head of a learner. The Florida Comprehensive Assessment Test (FCAT), for example, is a high-stakes test that puts significant preparation pressure on schools and teachers, but this test is currently created in a way that minimizes the use of peers and tools as essential parts of learning. Because this test is so politically important, many teachers spend significant time preparing students for this test in ways which run counter to the view that learning as distributed. Teachers should consider whether this jeopardizes their own classroom teaching priorities. In the current environment which puts so much weight on assessing skills, which only show part of what a student is capable of learning, it will be critical for teachers to identify additional means of demonstrating what students can do and to communicate the importance of these methods to colleagues, parents, and administrators. The additional information gathered by teachers using assessments based on a distributed learning view can provide a much more complete picture of student achievement and ability.

"There are three criteria for learning to take place: behavioral change, or change in the capacity for behavior; the change endures over time; and, it occurs through practice or other forms of experience"

—Dale Schunk

I³ *Write down any ideas that come to you after reading this quote.*

___

___

"Who can blame people for not learning what they haven't been taught?"

—William Raspberry

I³ *Write down any ideas that come to you after reading this quote.*

___

___

I³ *How can you justify that both of these quotes may have merit?*

___

___

___

___

KWL

What Do You KNOW? **(prior knowledge)**

____

What Do You WANT to Know? **(objectives and goals)**

____

“It is possible to fly without motors, but not without knowledge and skill.”

—Wilbur Wright

I^3 *Write down any ideas that come to you after reading this quote.*

____

“Here’s a bumper sticker I’d like to see: ‘We are the Proud Parents of a Child who has resisted his teacher’s attempts to bend him to the will of his corporate masters.’”

—George Carlin

I³ *Write down any ideas that come to you after reading this quote.*

I³ *How can you justify that both of these quotes may have merit?*

Learning to Teach

Teaching is an unusual profession in that it seems most of us have been around teaching all of our lives. In this context, some pre-service teachers believe they know more about teaching than they would other professions. In some cases, this may be true. Although observing teaching is a great start, there are many critical aspects of teaching that occur behind the scenes. The perspective and performance distinctly change when one steps from the student desk to the front (or side, or middle) of the room. This chapter will share some of the parameters which teachers must know, be able to use and apply when they are teaching. Many times when I share this information with new pre-service teachers, they are confused by the breadth and depth of theoretical underpinnings, which a teacher must know and know well enough to use the theories and keep unseen to the student. As we discussed in the previous chapter, becoming a teacher does require an undergraduate degree. This degree indicates that the student has undergone a rigorous undertaking studying the philosophical foundations of teaching and learning. In that, they can understand how people learn, behave, and process so that they can modify their teaching approach accordingly. When studying this chapter, the best approach is not to memorize or to view the information as "must know," but more like adding tools to your toolbox. You will have many different types of students in your classroom, each with their own unique characteristics and background—this is an asset, not a problem. The more diversity and cultural ideology, cultures and opportunities to expand perspectives, and perspectives you have, the more powerful of a learning environment. However, in order to capture these benefits, the teacher must be able to quickly understand that the observation of a student's behavior is an indicator of thoughts and perceptions. In this chapter, we will share many methods in which to understand what students are thinking, and how to assist each of them using one of the foundational learning theories (tools).

Standards-Based Education (National, State, District)

> ***"The simplest schoolboy is now familiar with facts for which Archimedes would have sacrificed his life."***
>
> —Ernest Renan

I³ *Write down any ideas that come to you after reading this quote.*

First of all, we must understand that in this country, through many reforms, we have developed a process for teaching. This process will inform the teacher "what" to teach and with their education and skills developed will determine "how" to teach it. The "what" to teach is globally developed by the national government as they provide national standards for each discipline to the state governments. Each state government interprets the standards and can make them more rigorous if they choose, but cannot decrease the amount or substance of the standard. Each state then shares the standards with the school districts, who follow the same pattern as the state in developing an appropriate approach for their students. So, the baseline, which the federal government mandates will be the minimum required standards for the students. Most districts develop their own methods to address the state standards. For instance the state standards for Florida are the Sunshine State Standards (*http://www.firn.edu/doe/menu/sss.htm*).

"Does your school have high academic standards (Percent saying "yes")?

—71% of principals
—60% of teachers
—38% of students

(Education News, 2002)"

I³ *Write down any ideas that come to you after reading this.*

____

____

____

Florida Sunshine State Standards

The Sunshine State Standards were approved by the Florida State Board of Education in 1996 to provide expectations for student achievement in Florida. The Standards were written in seven subject areas, each divided into four separate grade clusters (PreK–2, 3–5, 6–8, and 9–12). This format was chosen to provide flexibility to school districts in designing curriculum based on local needs. The subject areas are language arts, mathematics, science, social studies, physical education and health, the arts, and foreign language. Each concept taught by a teacher must align with at least one standard, although typically a teacher cannot avoid teaching more than one standard at a time and repeating critical standards. The standards are available online or as a CD from the Florida State Department of Education. In addition, the state of Florida has developed a lesson planning software program, which includes the standards in a database, which a teacher can easily view and attach a standard to their lesson. The software is called the Curriculum Planning Tool (CPT) v. 2.1 and a free copy of this software can be downloaded at *http://www.firn.edu/doe/curric/prek12/ecpt.htm.*

"They're called lessons because they lessen from day to day."

—Lewis Carroll

I³ *Write down any ideas that come to you after reading this quote.*

____

____

____

I³ *Can you name a standard? Give this a try. List below your thoughts on what might constitute a standard. At this point, there is no right or wrong answer, but this will enable you to review at a later time and possibly gain a sense of your perspective.*

____

____

____

Methods of Teaching

As indicated earlier, the teacher will use the standards to determine what to teach and they will decide the best way or method to teach it. There are various pedagogical (principles and methods of instruction) methods, which have been developed throughout the history of educating. Like many cyclical parallels, teaching is continually developing, redeveloping, moving forward, possibly backward—all in an attempt to determine the best methodology for teaching and learning. A cycle is a recurring sequence of events. In this context, an example of a cyclical parallel is what has occurred in historical teaching and learning methods and what is currently happening with those practices today. A spring is a visual model of a cyclical parallel. As one moves down the path of the spring, there is a continuance of patterns, or cycles located at adjacent positions. The distance between any two positions on the spring is variable and the direction should be toward greater understanding. Many cycles have been identified in the area of teaching, such as the learning cycle, self-regulation and assessment. Martin and colleagues (2002) describe the traditional learning cycle uses the "Five E" model, which includes engagement, exploration, explanation, extension, and evaluation. Each of these steps can lead to the next step and upon completion they should begin again for another concept or further application of the current concept. We will address these methods of teaching along with others throughout this course, however, you will also take specific courses on teaching methodology in mathematics, science, language arts, music, art, etc.

Learning Theories and Strategies ("Tool")

In the introductory section, general material was presented on learning theories. This section will build upon that information, providing research citations and at times intentionally repeating important information. This intended redundancy should key students into realizing the importance of these concepts.

Bruner (1966) states that a theory for learning should address four major aspects: (a) predisposition towards learning, (b) structured so that it can be readily grasped by the learner, (c) an effective sequence to present the material, and (d) the nature and pacing of reinforcements. Good methods for structuring knowledge should result in simplifying, generating new propositions, and increasing the manipulation of information. Garner (1970) agrees that strategies enhance learning. However, learners often fail to invoke strategic behaviors due to five reasons, poor cognitive monitoring; primitive routines; meager knowledge base; attributions and classroom goals that do not support strategy use; and minimal transfer.

We will be discussing many types of learning theories. I highly recommend that you try your best to befriend these theories, as they can serve you well. Or, you can try to memorize them for the short term and they will haunt you throughout your collegial experience and ultimately every day that you teach. As with the Methods courses, you will have multiple opportunities to interface with learning theories in other courses. However, I strongly urge you to take this time and begin to build your foundation of these concepts now. The theories which we will discuss and use in this course are:

- Information Processing
- Self-Regulation
- Self-Efficacy
- Metacognition
- Constructivism

Information Processing

"The first step in a sequence of learning and memory events is for the learner to attend to a stimulus and attention is the focus on a stimulus"

—R. M Gagne, 1973

I³ *Write down any ideas that come to you after reading this quote.*

____

____

One assumption of human information processing (IP) theory is that it is analogous to computer processing, in that it receives information, stores it in memory, and retrieves it as necessary (Schunk, 1996). The IP theory is referred to as the learning and memory model, which has been used to describe learning in informal settings by Koran, Longino, and Shafer (1983). The generic state of the IP system is commonly referred to as the two-store (dual-memory), originally proposed by Atkinson and Shiffrin (1971). Figure 4.1 should look familiar as it represents a modified version of this model emphasizing the attention, learning acquisition and retention facets. The IP theory views learning as the coding of information in long term memory by creating schema produced by relating new knowledge to existing information in the short term or working memory. Short-term memory, or working memory, is the information that you are focusing on at a given moment. A part of the working memory, the sensory memory is a system of receptors holding sensory information very briefly. Long-term memory is where knowledge is permanently stored. Procedural memory is long-term memory for how to do things or processes.

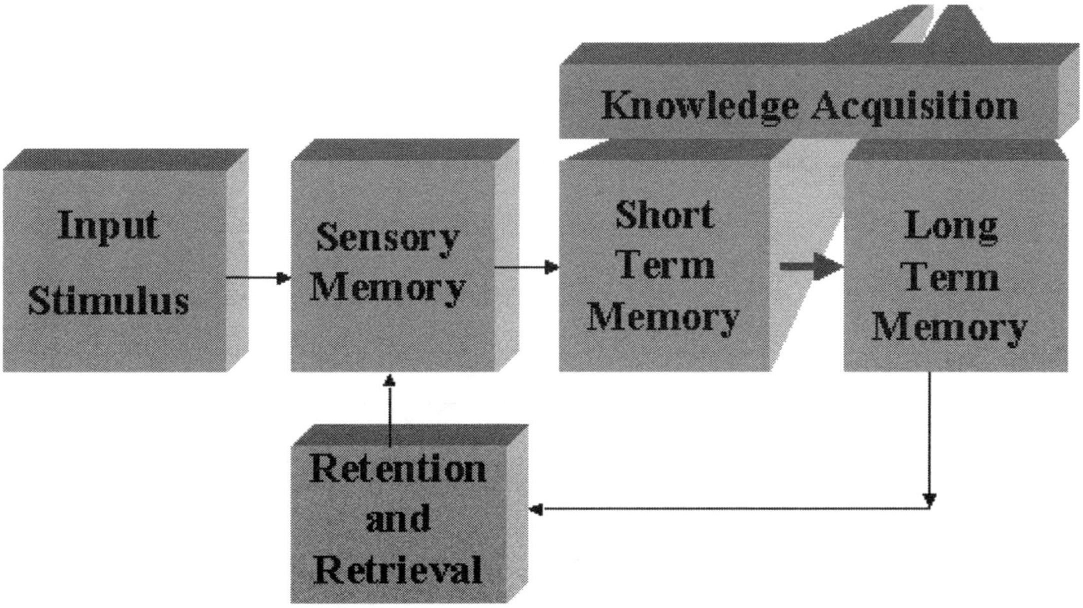

FIGURE 4.1

A critical aspect of this model is attention. Attention is the focus on a stimulus. People's attentional capabilities are limited; they can only attend to a few stimuli at a given moment. A stimulus is an event that activates behavior. To initiate a learning activity, one must first provide a suitable stimulus to attract the attention and arouse the curiosity of the learner, thus attention is a necessary prerequisite of learning.

I³ *Consider some possibilities, which you could use to gain students' attention. Please share some of these below. Try to provide both general approaches and then challenge yourself to list a few from each of the disciplines, e.g., science, math, language arts, and so on.*

____

____

____

____

____

____

Curiosity plays a role at this point by acting as both a response to a stimulus and a factor for influencing further attention. As Koran and Longino (1983) found, the greater the complexity of the object, the higher degree of curiosity it will evoke. They also compared the time spent as a measure of attention to time in the vicinity of the stimulus can be a measure of curiosity. Further, Koran and Koran (1984) demonstrated that curiosity is a response to a novel stimulus, such as manipulatable objects found in informal settings. This stimulus will increase the amount of attention to the object.

"Not to know is bad, not to wish to know is worse."

—Nigerian Proverb

I³ *Write down any ideas that come to you after reading this quote.*

____

____

"The cure for boredom is curiosity. There is no cure for curiosity."

—Ellen Parr

I³ *Write down any ideas that come to you after reading this quote.*

____

____

I³ *How can you justify that both of these quotes may have merit?*

____

____

I^3 *What is curiosity? Why is this important? Are you a curious person? Why and how has it served you? Can you think of a famous quote about curiosity?*

____

____

____

I^3 *What are informal settings? Which informal settings have you visited?*

____

____

____

____

____

I^3 *What are manipulatables? Can you give some examples?*

____

____

____

____

____

Another aspect of attention is perception. Perception, which precedes coding, is the use of all of the senses to acquire information about the stimulus. It is also the mental grasp, awareness, and decoding information and thereby depends on objective characteristics and prior experiences. Information in this instance could be anything from visual questions, pictures, or sensory stimuli. It is an active process and one that is an intrinsic part of learned behavior. Relevance in visual processing is all about being able to discriminate relevant features of an object, structure, image, and through combining these features, deciphering an idea of the whole. Perception is an active process, not merely a passive response to visual input but the result of hypothesis formation and testing conditioned by our expectations (Bodecker, 1995). Good graphics usually means linking perceptual cues to important information, which means both identifying and capturing what are important, and guiding the reader with appropriate cues (Petre, 1995).

I^3 *An unavoidable aspect of perceptions are "misperceptions." Can you give some examples of misperceptions (or non-examples of perception)?*

____

____

____

____

____

Self-Regulation

"Self-regulatory learners (a) tend to learn better under learner control; (b) are able to monitor, evaluate, or manage their learning effectively; (c) reduce instructional time required to complete the lesson; and (d) manage their learning and time efficiently."

—Y. C. YANG, 1993

I³ *Write down any ideas that come to you after reading this quote.*

____

____

Self-regulated learning is a dualistic construct with properties of an aptitude and an event (Winne, 1997). Self-regulated learners are students whose academic learning abilities and self-discipline make learning easier so motivation is maintained. Albert Bandura (1977) studied observational learning and self-regulation. Bandura defined self-regulation as the ability to control our own behavior and it is the workhorse of human personality. Bandura suggests three steps: (a) self-observation, we look at ourselves, our behavior, and keep tabs on it; (b) judgment, we compare what we see with a standard; (c) self-response, if we did well in comparison with our standard, we give ourselves rewarding self-responses. If we did poorly, we give ourselves punishing self-responses.

Zimmerman (1989) defines self-regulated learning strategies as actions and processes directed at acquiring information or skill that involve agency, purpose, and instrumentality perceptions by learners. Strategies include self-evaluation, organizing and transforming, goal-setting and planning, seeking information, keeping records and monitoring, environmental structuring, self-consequating, rehearsing and memorizing, seeking social assistance, and reviewing records. Subskills required to organize a course of action are themselves governed by broader self-regulatory skills such as knowing how to diagnose task demands or constructing and evaluating alternative strategies. Self-regulated learning is not a mental ability, such as intelligence, or an academic skill, such as reading proficiency; rather, it is the self-directive process through which learners transform their mental abilities into academic skills (Schunk & Zimmerman, 1998). Possessing these self-regulatory skills can permit students to improve their performances across varied academic activities. He has also developed a cyclic model, which represents the behaviors of a self-regulated learner (Figure 4.2).

FIGURE 4.2. Cyclic Model of Self-Regulated Learning (Zimmerman, Bonner, & Kovach, 1996).

1. Self-evaluation and monitoring occur when students judge their personal effectiveness, often from observations and recordings of prior performances and outcomes.
2. Goal setting and strategic planning occur when students analyze the learning task, set specific learning goals, and plan or refine the strategy to attain the goal.
3. Strategy-implementation monitoring occurs when students try to execute a strategy in structured contexts to monitor their accuracy in implementing it.
4. Strategic-outcome monitoring occurs when students focus their attention on links between learning outcomes and strategic process to determine effectiveness.

The model is cyclical because self-monitoring on each learning trial provides information that can change subsequent goals, strategies, or performance efforts. So, instead of the teaching nagging you to complete your assignments, through effective self-regulating you can nag yourself.

BTW

To nag is to annoy by constant urging or fault finding. European households of the early Middle Ages had a problem—rats infested every nook and corner, squirrels nested in the roofs; the noise of gnawing was disturbing. The Germans developed the word *nagen,* from an old Scandinavian term meaning to gnaw. Eventually a person who gnawed at another was said to nag.

According to Bandura's social cognitive theory, individuals possess a self-system that enables them to exercise a measure of control over their thoughts, feelings, motivations, and actions. This self-system encompasses one's cognitive and affective structures and provides reference mechanisms and a set of subfunctions for perceiving, regulating, and evaluating behavior, which results from the interplay between the system and environmental sources of influence. As such, it serves a self-regulatory function by providing individuals with the capability to influence their own cognitive processes and actions and thus alter their environments. Individuals engage in self-referent thought that mediates between knowledge and action. Through self-reflection, individuals evaluate their own experiences and thought processes. Bandura argued that self-reflection is the most uniquely human characteristic. Self-reflective judgments include perceptions of self-efficacy, beliefs in one's capability to organize and execute the courses of action required to manage prospective situations. The higher the sense of efficacy, the greater the effort, persistence, and resilience.

"Study without reflection is a waste of time; reflection without study is dangerous."

—Confucius

I³ *Do you self-regulate? If so, list some of the steps you process, either mentally or on paper. If not, share some thoughts on why you do not and how you could begin to work on this process.*

____

____

____

____

____

Self-Efficacy

"Self-efficacy is the belief concerning one's own capabilities to organize and implement actions necessary to attain designated performance levels."

—Albert Bandura, 1986.

I³ *Write down any ideas that come to you after reading this quote.*

Self-efficacy is a critical component of self-regulated learning theory. Self-efficacy is a person's sense of being able to deal effectively with a particular task; a belief about personal competence in a particular situation. If an individual student believes they are capable of learning the concept or regulating their own acquisition of the knowledge, then their ability to learn will increase. Schunk and Zimmerman (1998) indicate that this factor provides a bridge between the cognitive and the contextual forces, by way of increasing self-regulatory learning. Academic self-efficacy influenced achievement directly as well as indirectly by raising students' grade goals. Results of these investigations demonstrate that acquisition of cognitive skills, modeling effects, attributional feedback, and goal setting influence the development of self-efficacy beliefs and that these beliefs, in turn, influence academic performances.

I³ *In what areas do you believe you possess a high level of self-efficacy? Are there other areas where you believe you are low in efficacy? Why do you believe this is so? What can you do to possibly change this perception?*

Metacognition

"Metacognition is 'thinking about thinking.'"

—Steve Yussen, 1985

I³ *Write down any ideas that come to you after reading this quote.*

"In the field of observation, chance favors the prepared mind."

—Louis Pasteur

I³ *Write down any ideas that come to you after reading this quote.*

____

____

I³ *How can you justify that both of these quotes may have merit?*

____

____

One of the most powerful tools we have for learning and enhancing our metacognitive abilities is observation. You will recall that observation is the first step in the learning process method, which includes observation, communication, measurement, classification, inference, and prediction. Observation can be both qualitative and quantitative and should use all of your human senses—taste, touch, smell, sight, and hearing. In attempt to determine how well your current metacognitive abilities are and how well you can address the most critical first step of the learning process, try the following experiment.

Find a partner and have them collect an unusual edible object (the edible portion is important). Ask them not to tell you what it is and then you sit with your eyes closed and have them place the object in your hands. Then walk through your five senses, collecting data on the object mentally. This will be very difficult for many people, because we typically have a significant amount of prior knowledge and our training will be to quickly collect superficial characteristics, name the object, and then proceed. The challenge here will be to find something that you cannot place a label on and therefore force you to proceed through the process. It is also important that you truly collect data in your head because you will be using this information to describe the object later. Please resist the temptation to label the object—you can classify with respect to its components, but the goal is not to name it. Continue through the process by measuring it with your hands qualitatively, and ultimately making inferences of what it could be or where it could be from and predictions. If you are able to complete this process, there is a chance that you may have learned something about how you learn as well as how your students may experience learning something new for a first time. This is important.

If you would like to do this in class with your students, a good object to select is a small piece of root beer candy because it has some good lessons to include in the debriefing. For instance, once they have identified it, you can ask, "What is root beer?" If you gave them a piece of orange or grape candy, they would be able to infer they came from the fruits, but what is root beer?

You can share with them that root beer ingredients include unrefined cane sugar, brown rice syrup, honey, barley malt, root and spice brew, sassafras root bark, and anise. A major component of root beer flavoring is sassafras. Sassafras is a native tree of the southern United States and grows in swampy woods and thickets. It has three differently shaped leaves, one which is unarmed, one elliptical-ovate, and one cuspidate. The derivation of root therefore is that the flavor comes from the root of a sassafras tree; some folks have traditionally called root beer soda, sarsaparilla. The roots are then boiled and fermented to extract the flavor. The fermentation process is similar to how beer is brewed, hence the name beer, although there is insufficient sugar content in the root to produce alcohol.

Ultimately, you will wish to ask your students, "So, now how many of you believe that you currently have molecules of a sassafras root in your mouth?" This may confuse (disequilibrate) some students and they may naturally want to believe they do, since you just spent time sharing the derivation. However, they do not have root molecules in their mouth. They have what is called artificial flavoring of root beer, which is typically used in commercial products since it is less expensive, easier to control the quality of the flavor, and ultimately cheaper to the consumer.

I³ *Refer back to the Introduction and review the concept of metacognition. What were you thinking about? Were you able to connect this learning approach to any contextual portion of your life? Why/why not?*

____

____

____

____

Constructivism

"A well must produce its own water."

—Farsi proverb

I³ *Write down any ideas that come to you after reading this quote.*

____

____

"Piaget's constructivism has left a mark on our schools. Will such educational theories ever give way to more serene and better optimized teaching methods, based on a genuine understanding of how the human mind works?"

—Stanislas Dehaene

I³ *Write down any ideas that come to you after reading this quote.*

____

____

I³ *How can you justify that both of these quotes may have merit?*

____

____

Free choice learning places the responsibility for learning on the learner. They are typically considered to be synonymous to informal learning settings such as museums, aquariums and science centers. Basically, a free choice environment allows the learner to select what and how they are to attend and acquire information. Potential positive attributes are similar to benefits from learning in an informal setting, in addition to possible increase in longer concept retention due to increased learner control. A free choice learning setting resembles a constructivist approach in that it allows the learner to build upon their prior experiences at their own pace and in their own particular direction of interest and perspective.

Perhaps the first constructivist philosopher, Giambatista Vico commented in a treatise in 1710 that one only knows something if one can explain it (Yager, 1991). Immanual Kant (1724–1804) further elaborated this idea by asserting that human beings are not passive recipients of information.

Learners actively take knowledge, connect it to previously assimilated knowledge and make it theirs by constructing their own interpretation (Cheek, 1992). Inferences, elaborations, and relationships between old perceptions and new ideas must be personally drawn by the student in order for the new idea to become an integrated, useful part of their memory. The learner must actively construct new information onto their existing framework for meaningful learning to occur.

Although constructivist theory has become popular in recent years, the idea of constructivism is not new. Aspects of the constructivist theory can be found among the works of Socrates, Plato, and Aristotle (ranging from 470–320 B.C.), all of which speak of the formation of knowledge. Saint Augustine (A.D. mid-300s) taught that in the search for truth, people must depend upon sensory experience. This of course left him out of balance with the church. More recent philosophers such as John Locke (1632–1704) taught that no man's knowledge can go beyond his experience. Kant (1724–1804) explained that the logical analysis of actions and objects lead to the growth of knowledge and the view that one's individual experiences generate new knowledge (Brooks & Brooks, 1993). Although the main philosophy of constructivism is generally credited to Jean Piaget (1896–1980), Henrich Pestalozzi (1746–1827), also from Switzerland, came to many similar conclusions over a century earlier.

Pestalozzi maintained that the educational process should be based on the natural development of the child and his or her sensory influences. Pestalozzi's basic pedagogical innovation was his insistence that children learn through the senses rather than with words. He labeled rote learning as mindless, and he emphasized instead linking the curriculum to children's experiences in their homes and family lives (Fabricius, 1983). Manges and Wigle (1997) believe that through constructivist teaching, students can tap into their natural learning potential because their experiences, their prior knowledge, and their personal interpretations become essential components of all classroom activities.

However, Piaget provided the foundation for modern day constructivism and its hybridization. In Piaget's view, intelligence consists of two interrelated processes, organization and adaptation. People organize their thoughts so that they make sense, separating the more important thoughts from the less important ones, as well as connecting one idea to another. At the same time, people adapt their thinking to include new ideas, as new experiences provide additional information. This adaptation occurs in two ways, through assimilation and accommodation. In the former process, new information is simply added to the cognitive organization already there. In the latter, the intellectual organization has to change somewhat to adjust to the new idea (Berger, 1978).

The basic idea of constructivism is that the learner must construct knowledge, the teacher cannot supply it (Bringuier, 1980). The constructivist approach is a view that emphasizes the active role of the learner in building understanding and making sense of information. Constructivist approaches to learning assume that subjectivity is critical because learners take in information and process it in unique ways that reflect their needs, dispositions, attitudes, beliefs, and feelings. Constructivism espouses creating meaning from experience (Jonassen, 1991). Constructivism stresses the interaction between learner and the environment and learning is embedded in the context in which it occurs. Thereby learners are encouraged to develop their own understanding of knowledge. Brooks and Brooks (1993) state that constructivism is not a theory about teaching. It is a theory about knowledge and learning that process and learning occurs daily and relentlessly in classrooms. It is a philosophy that encompasses knowledge, learning, and thinking. They have compiled a list of characteristics of a constructivist teacher that include encouragement of student autonomy; utilization of manipulative, interactive and physical materials; use of cognitive terminology such as classify, analyze, and create; inquiry understanding; encourage engagement of dialogue; ask open-ended questions; pursue elaboration of student responses; provide time for students to construct relationships and create metaphors; nurture students through frequent use of the learning cycle method. Inquiry learning is an approach in which the teacher presents a puzzling situation and students solve the problem by gathering data and testing their conclusions.

Brandt (1992) has determined a similar list for a constructivist approach: engage students in authentic tasks; assist students with producing knowledge bases that promote the application of information, and diversity of thought; and build learning communities linking students and promote substantial, applicable learning rather than mere credentialing. Students who plan to get through a course by regurgitating content also resist learning independently; they are probably not interested in developing critical thinking or problem-solving skills.

"The empty vessel makes the greatest sound."

—William Shakespeare

I³ *Write down any ideas that come to you after reading this quote.*

____

____

I³ *Please provide several examples of how you have "constructed" information throughout your lifetime. Try to be specific and insightful as to how building upon prior knowledge assisted in true knowledge acquisition or the ability to process information.*

____

____

____

____

____

Psychological Orientations and Educational Philosophy

"Never ignore a gut feeling, but never believe that it's enough."

—Kermit the Frog

I³ *Write down any ideas that come to you after reading this quote.*

____

____

"I studied geography in the fifth grade, and I remember that instead of just TELLING us where things were, the teacher insisted that we make relief maps of the United States by mixing flour and water into a paste and smearing it on a shirt cardboard so as to form important geographical features such as the Rocky Mountains, the Great Plains, Disneyland, etc. . . . As a direct result, I grew up, like most Americans, with a poor grasp of geography."

—Dave Barry

I³ *Write down any ideas that come to you after reading this quote.*

____

____

I³ *How can you justify that both of these quotes may have merit?*

____

____

There are many ways to view education and how we teach and learn. This section will introduce the pre-service teacher candidate to a few of the orientations to teaching. This section is especially important to pre-service teachers in developing their own educational philosophy. Please view these as potential aspects that you might wish to consider adding to your repertoire of skills.

Behaviorism (Watson/Skinner)

John Watson originally developed the concept of behaviorism. Watson believed that psychology was concerned with behavior and therefore, humans could be studied objectively, like rats. Watson's work followed Pavlov's dog studies to conditioning, where he rang a bell as he fed the dog. When the dog heard the bell, he knew a meal was on its way and would begin to salivate. Pavlov then rang the bell without food, and the dog still salivated. They had been "conditioned" to salivate at the sound of a bell. Pavlov and Watson believed that humans react to stimuli in the same way.

Today, B. F. Skinner is most associated with behaviorism, who examined Watson's theories. Skinner rejected Watson's idea on conditioning. He believed that people operate on the environment to produce certain consequences. He developed his theory of "operant conditioning," which indicated that our behavior has had certain consequences in the past, which control how we operate now. For example, if you receive an A every time you read, understand, follow the directions, check your work and submit your work on time, then when you want an A, you will repeat these behaviors. So whatever behavior is reinforced drives our action. Although behaviorism originated in psychology, its concepts are used in the field of education.

Of course, there are many views on behaviorism, please read a few of the following viewpoints:

"Of course, Behaviorism 'works.' So does torture. Give me a no-nonsense, down-to-earth behaviorist, a few drugs, and simple electrical appliances, and in six months I will have him reciting the Athanasian Creed in public."

—W. H. Auden

I³ *Write down any ideas that come to you after reading this quote.*

____

____

"If we ever do end up acting just like rats or Pavlov's dogs, it will be largely because behaviorism has conditioned us to do so."

—Richard Dean Rosen

I³ *Write down any ideas that come to you after reading this quote.*

"Our schools have become vast factories for the manufacture of robots. We no longer send our young to them primarily to be taught and given the tools of thought, no longer primarily to be informed and acquire knowledge; but to be 'socialized'—which in the current semantic means to be regimented and made to conform."

—Robert Lindner

I³ *Write down any ideas that come to you after reading this quote.*

"Using behaviorism to control learning is like using an umbrella to control the weather."

—Steve Nordby

I³ *Write down any ideas that come to you after reading this quote.*

I³ *As you can see, there are many opinions on behaviorism, some which would make others roll over in their grave. Now, please try to critically evaluate the prior information and prepare a few statements on your beliefs of the value of behaviorism in the classroom. Please try to use some of the higher level skills we have discussed and truly critique these approaches.*

BTW

Rolling over in one's grave or the action of a dead person as if appalled by something that has happened. The first known reference to this is in Mark Twain's 1894 novel, "The Tragedy of Pudd 'nhead Wilson."

Essential Knowledge to Teach

"The first educational question will not be 'what knowledge is of the most worth?' but 'what kind of humans beings do we want to produce?'"

—John Goodlad

I³ *Write down any ideas that come to you after reading this quote.*

____

____

"Give me six hours to chop down a tree and I will spend the first four sharpening the axe."

—Abraham Lincoln

I³ *Write down any ideas that come to you after reading this quote.*

____

____

I³ *How can you justify that both of these quotes may have merit?*

____

____

There are many responses to the question of what is the essential knowledge required to teach. Hopefully, in a short time, you will have your own well-organized, rational thought to this question. This section will provide a foundation of options for you to consider and integrate into your own schema of possibilities. Please attend to these ideas critically, either embracing or discarding with appropriate justifications.

Knowledge of Self (Self-efficacy)

"Know thyself."

—Socrates

I³ *Write down any ideas that come to you after reading this quote.*

____

____

"Emancipate yourselves from mental slavery. None but yourselves can free your minds."

—Bob Marley

I^3 *Write down any ideas that come to you after reading this quote.*

I^3 *How can you justify that both of these quotes may have merit?*

Many believe the first step in any profession is to know one's self. This is apparent in the diagnostic tools many secondary students take to guide them into a program or profession. Whenever I think of this concept, the first thought that comes to mind is before a flight, an airline employee gives information about plane safety. An important safety item is loss of cabin air pressure. The airline employee indicates that adults must first get their oxygen masks on and then help their children. It seems that a maternal or paternal reflex would be to assist your child first, however unless you are healthy and free from danger, it may soon be difficult for you to perform. Likewise, you may wish to understand and take care of yourself before you attempt to help your students.

"It is one of the most beautiful compensations of this life that no man can sincerely try to help another without helping himself."

—Ralph Waldo Emerson

I^3 *Write down any ideas that come to you after reading this quote.*

Hopefully, you recall we gave this a name earlier, which was self-efficacy. Knowing yourself, including your capabilities will assist you as a teacher. There are various tools and diagnostic methods which you can easily take to gather data in knowing yourself, how you function and what approaches to teaching and learning are best suited for how you process.

I^3 *At this point, please describe some of your attributes and characteristics. Do not judge these, simply try to be objective and indicate any data that would help determine knowledge of yourself.*

Knowledge of Students

"We busted out of class. Had to get away from those fools. We learned more from a three minute record than we'd ever learned in school."

—Bruce Springsteen

I³ *Write down any ideas that come to you after reading this quote.*

____

____

Typically, many pre-service teachers wish to address this type of knowledge first. Many folks who wish to be teachers are very caring, nurturing people-people. However, as indicated above, the best pre-requisite is to know yourself first and possibly various methods on how to assist your students as well. Then, you will wish to understand how your student processes, think, believe, behave, etc. in order to help them learn, grown and achieve. One question you may wish to keep in your mind is

"What is my product?"

Knowing your product or your end goal may help you understand what your students needs. Unlike a factory with a tangible product, yours will most likely be measured in other ways— affective, behavioral, and what the student can do after they spend time in your classroom. Keeping these aspects in mind, you may approach students and your knowledge of them differently.

Knowledge of Subject (Content)

"One had to cram all of this stuff into one's mind, whether one liked it or not. This coercion had such a deterring effect that, after I had passed the final examination, I found the consideration of any scientific problems distasteful to me for an entire year. . . . It is in fact nothing short of a miracle that the modern methods of instruction have not entirely strangled the holy spirit of inquiry."

—Albert Einstein

I³ *Write down any ideas that come to you after reading this quote.*

____

____

The knowledge of your subject is very important. The content of discipline would be what you teach—chemistry, biology, English, mathematics, and so on. I am sure that we have all had good and not-so-good teachers in the past. And even some were good teachers to some of us and the very same teacher in the same classroom may have been perceived as not-so-good by a colleague sitting next to you. What makes a teacher "good" is highly subjective. However, simply knowing the content may be an insufficient means by which to teach. Especially common in the natural sciences are the teachers who have a degree in the area and then attempt to teach the material. Some of these teachers are able to be successful. Others may find themselves "sharing" the material as opposed to "teaching" the material. Hopefully when you complete this course, you will easily know the difference between these two approaches.

I^3 *Please share your experiences with each type of the teachers described above. Do you believe you will be a "sharing" teacher or a "teaching" teacher? Why?*

Knowledge of Methods (Learning to Learn)

The knowledge of your teaching methods is very important. This is also called professional knowledge or pedagogical knowledge. This course will present material so that you will understand the foundation of this approach. Very possibly, you have had teachers in the past that you considered good, but were unsure of exactly why they were good. Possibly, they could have been a natural teacher, a caring person, or someone you simply connected with in your own thoughts. The knowledge of teaching methods has been covered in this text already in many ways. We will address others such as assessment, classroom management, critical thinking, and processing skills. You may wish to consider how important you believe these aspects to be in becoming a successful teacher who enjoys their career.

I^3 *What type of academic degrees do you believe your professors have to be able to teach at a university? What type of teaching courses have they taken in order to teach and assess your achievements?*

Subject versus Professional Knowledge

A major debate typically occurs when the topic of importance between content and pedagogy. At times, the debate line is drawn between levels, some indicate that content knowledge is more important in secondary education, where professional knowledge is more important in elementary education.

I^3 *So, which do you believe is more important—Subject Knowledge or Professional Knowledge—please support your response with sound, well-thought rationale.*

Knowledge of Technology

The knowledge of technology and its use in the classroom is increasing as we speak, even though cost and effect are still debatable issues. Many schools have argued that they simply cannot afford appropriate technology as their finances are already on skid row. A brief synopsis will be provided here, however detailed attention is provided on this topic in a subsequent chapter.

BTW

Skid Row means a run-down part of town. In the mid-19th century a logging road in Seattle where logs were skidded (drug on the ground) led from the forest to the mill. The Skid Road became a road populated by lumberjacks, sailors, prostitutes, and panhandlers.

Technology has gained attention in education today because of its prevalence; its promise to provide low cost education; and it may help some people to participate more easily, to learn more effectively, and to enjoy learning more (Palmieri, 1997). Given adequate access to technology can provide both teachers and students with an ever-growing resource of information. Teachers can introduce and use information for instruction and supplementing almost any subject matter. Used effectively, this environment has the potential to level the playing field for education in rural communities that typically lack the resources found in major metropolitan areas.

> "Imagine the student sits at a classroom computer grazing the Internet—a global network linking the student with vast databases. Schools are rushing to install networks and Internet nodes so that all classrooms might sit down to sample the electronic feast. How might we take advantage of the Internet to raise a generation of free-range students? The rich information resources to be found in cyberspace are both a blessing and a curse. Unless students have a toolkit of thinking and problem-solving skills, which match the feasts of information, they may emerge from their meals bloated with techno-garbage, information junk food or info-fat. We must teach students to graze and digest the offerings thoughtfully in order to achieve insight. For the computer to bring about a revolution in higher education, its introduction must be accompanied by improvements in our understanding of learning and teaching" (Simon, 1996, p. 23).

Three issues of particular concern to educators emerge in using the seemingly infinite resources available through technology. The first concern relates to information overload and lack of useful instructional format, the second concern relates to identifying the necessary skills and attitudes to enable users to critically evaluate and use the resources, and the third is to effectively design and evaluate different learning formats. Access to technology has the potential to change how educators think of themselves, their roles, and their instructional techniques. Learning through technology provides the flexibility and efficiency of computer instruction as well as individual attention of traditional instruction (Huang, 1997). Instructors could be more than knowledge providers, as technology could allow them to devote attention to a more global facilitation of learning such as appropriate presentation formats. McDonald and Ingvarson (1995) found that technology may have the potential to free teachers from the moment-by-moment demands of whole class teaching, enabling them to concentrate on challenging students and catering to students as individuals. Electronic media can move beyond didactic instruction to model directly the modes of inquiry made easier with computers. Also, by including technology in classrooms, teachers can assist students in becoming active participants in the construction of their own knowledge.

One note of caution—some educators are demonstrating academic anxiety about the information age. Novek's (1996) study suggests that the expansion of the information economy is a cause for deep concern in higher education. If educators are to take full advantage of the interactive characteristics of new technology then we must do more than simply adapt the technology to old styles of pedagogy.

I³ *What are your thoughts about technology? Are you a technophobe or technophile? Do you plan on using technology in your classroom? Why/why not?*

Knowledge of the Future

It seems this knowledge might be the most interesting and enjoyable to discuss, since its limits are boundless. It does not take much for us to look back a few years and view how different education has become. However, many aspects such as desks, straight rows, and teacher in the front of the room has remained the same for decades. We spoke of progressivism, constructivism, and various educational reforms. You have been encouraged to develop your own educational philosophy—does it include thoughts for the future?

I³ *What are some of your thoughts about education in the future? Try to take any limits off and really stretch yourself to imagine what teaching and learning could be like in the near and distant future.*

KWL

What Did You LEARN?

References

Atkinson, R. C., & Shiffrin, R. M. (1971). The control of short-term memory. *Scientific American, 225,* 82–90.

Bandura, A. (1977). *Social learning theory.* Englewood Cliffs, NJ: Prentice Hall Publishers.

Bandura, A. (1986). *Social foundations of thought and action: A social cognitive theory.* Englewood Cliffs, NJ: Prentice Hall.

Berger, Kathleen S. (1978). *The developing person.* New York, NY: Worth Publishers.

Bodecker, B. (1995). *A conceptual approach to multivariate data.* University of Ulster: University Press.

Brandt, R. (1992). A more ambitious agenda. *Educational Leadership, (49)*7, 3.

Bringuier, J. C. (1980). Conversations with Jean Piaget. Chicago, IL: The University of Chicago Press.

Brooks, J., & Brooks, M. (1993). *In search of understanding: The case for constructivist classrooms.* Alexandria, VA: Association for Curriculum Development.

Brown, A., Ash, D., Rutherford, M., Nakagawa, K., Gordon, A., & Campione, J. (1993). Distributed expertise in the classroom. In G. Solomon, (ed.). *Distributed cognitions: Psychological and educational considerations.* New York: Cambridge University Press, pp. 188–228.

Bruner, J. (1966). *Toward a theory of instruction.* Cambridge, MA: Harvard University Press.

Cheek, D. W. (1992). *Thinking constructively about science, technology and society education.* Albany, NY: State University of New York Press.

Fabricius, W. V. (1983). Piaget's theory of knowledge: Its philosophical context. *Human Development, 26,* 325–334.

Gagne, R. M. (1970). Some new views of learning and instruction. *Phi Delta Kappa, 51,* 468–472.

Gagne, R. M. (1973). *The conditions of learning.* New York, NY: Holt, Rinehart, and Winston.

Huang, A. H. (1997). Challenges and opportunities of online education. *Journal of Educational Technology Systems, 25(3),* 229–247.

Hutchins, E. (1990). The technology of team navigation. In J. Galegher, R. Kraut, & C. Egido (Eds.), *Intellectual teamwork: Social and technological foundations of cooperative work.* Hillsdale, NJ: Erlbaum, pp. 191–220.

Jonassen, D. H. (1991). Objectivism vs. Constructivism. *Educational Technology Research and Development, 39(3),* 5–14.
Koran, M. L. & Koran, J. J., Jr. (1984). Aptitude-treatment interaction research in science education. *Journal of Research in Science Teaching, 21(8),* 793–808.
Koran, J. J., Jr., Logino, S. J., & Shafer, L. D. (1983). A framework for conceptualizing research in natural history museum and science centers. *Journal of Research in Science Teaching, 20(4),* 325–339.
Manges, C. D., & Wigle, S. E. (1997). Quality schools and constructivist teaching, *Journal of Reality Therapy, 16(2),* 45–51.
Martin, Ralph, Sexton, Collen, & Gerlovich, Jack. (2002). *Science for All Children: Methods for Constructing Understanding.* Boston: Allyn and Bacon.
McDonald, H., & Ingvarson, L. (1995). *Free at last? Teachers, computers and independent learning.* Paper presented at the annual meeting of the American Educational Research Association, April, 1995, San Francisco, CA.
Novek, E. M. (1996). *Do professors dream of electric sheep? Academic anxiety about the information age.* Paper presented at the annual meeting of the Association for Education in Journalism and Mass Communication, Anaheim, CA.
Palmieri, P. (1997). Technology in education . . . Do we need it? *ARIS Bulletin, 8(2),* 1–5.
Pea, R. (1993). Practices of distributed intelligence and designs for education. In G. Solomon, (Ed.), *Distributed cognitions: Psychological and educational considerations.* New York: Cambridge University Press, pp. 47–87.
Petre, P. H. (1995). *Organization overviews and role management: Inspiration for future desktop environments.* Paper presented at the annual meeting of the American Educational Research Association, Chicago, IL.
Schunk, D. H. (1996). *Learning theories.* Englewood Cliffs, NJ: Prentice-Hall, Inc.
Schunk, D. H., & Zimmerman, B. J. (1998). *Self-regulated learning: From teaching to self-reflective practice.* New York, NY: The Guilford Press.
Simon, A. (1996). Consumers and Cyberspace: Inequitable distribution of information. *Consumer Interests Annual, 42,* 1–4.
Vygotsky, L. (1978). *Mind in society.* Cambridge, MA: Harvard University Press.
Winne, P. H. (1997). Experimenting to bootstrap self-regulated learning. *Journal of Educational Psychology, 89(3),* 397–410.
Yager, R. (1991). The constructivist learning model, towards real reform in science education. *The Science Teacher, 58(6),* 52–57.
Yang, Y. C. (1993). The effects of self-regulatory skills and type of instructional control on learning from computer-based instruction. *International Journal of Instructional Media, 20(3),* 225–241.
Yussen, S. (1985). The Role of Metacognition in Contemporary Theories of Cognitive Development. In D. L. Forrest-Pressley, G. E. MacKinnon, & T. G. Waller (Eds.), *Metacognition, Cognition and Human Performance,* Vol. 1. Orlando, FL: Academic Press, pp. 253–283.
Zimmerman, B. J. (1989). A social cognitive view of self-regulated academic learning. *Journal of educational psychology, 81(3),* 329–339.
Zimmerman, B. J., Bonner, S., & Kovach, R. (1996). *Developing self-regulated learners: Beyond achievement to self-efficacy.* Washington, DC: American Psychological Association.

PowerPoint Outline to Assist In-Class Note-Taking

A. **Learning to Teach**

   a. Standards-Based Education (national, state, local)

   b. Methods of Teaching

      i. Learning Theories and Strategies

      ii. Psychological Orientations and Educational Philosophy

B. **Essential Knowledge to Teach**

   a. Knowledge of Self (Self-efficacy)

   b. Knowledge of Students

   c. Knowledge of Subject (Content)

   d. Knowledge of Methods (Learning to Learn)

   e. Subject vs. Professional Knowledge

f. Knowledge of Technology

g. Knowledge of the Future

5

Individual Learning Needs

Guest Editorial: Nick Hudyma, PhD, Engineer, Assistant Professor, College of Computing, Engineering and Construction/UNF

What distinguishes a great educator from a good educator? For great educators, teaching appears very easy but in reality it is very difficult, requiring a great deal of thought and effort. A great educator realizes they cannot simply present material to students and assume that they will immediately grasp it. Instead, they understand that teaching involves two-way communication: interaction between the teacher and students, as well as between students and teacher. Even more importantly, great educators understand that students learn or grasp the subject matter in a number of different ways and structure their lectures and assignments so that each of the learning styles is implemented so they can hold the attention of their students.

As an engineering educator, I am mostly aware of the research in engineering education that has been conducted by Dr. Richard Felder at North Carolina State University. He has identified four learning styles that are bound by two extreme characteristics. Every student learns by using each of the four learning styles but differs by where their individual learning tendencies fall between the two extreme characteristics. The learning styles described below have been summarized from Dr. Felder's website (*http://www.ncsu.edu/felder-public/ILSdir/styles.htm*).

Visual and Verbal Learners—This category of learning styles is perhaps the easiest to understand. Visual learners tend to understand and retain material presented visually— such as diagrams, pictures, films, and demonstrations. Verbal learners retain material best by listening and by reading.

Active and Reflective Learners—Active learners tend to understand and retain material by doing something with it, like performing a calculation, discussing it, or explaining it to others. On the other hand, reflective learners would rather first think about the material and then do something with it. The easiest way to distinguish between active and reflective learners is that active learners prefer working in groups whereas reflective learners prefer working alone.

Sensing and Intuitive Learners—Sensing learners prefer facts, they are patient with details, and are comfortable with laboratory type work. Intuitive learners prefer discovering possibilities and relationships, and are more comfortable with abstractions and mathematical formulations. The easiest way to distinguish between sensing and intuitive learners is by course preference; sensing learners prefer courses that have a connection to the real world while intuitive learners prefer courses without a lot of memorization or routine calculations.

Sequential and Global Learners—This category of learning style is perhaps the most difficult to understand. Sequential learners tend to understand material presented in a logical order whereas global learners tend to absorb a lot of material to try and understand the whole picture rather than retaining information in a step-wise fashion. The easiest way to distinguish these two types of learners is by the students' ability to solve problems. Sequential learners can typically solve simple problems because the solution often requires a step-by-step solution however, they may have difficulty solving complex problems because they often have trouble relating what they know to different situations. Global learners who tend to have difficulty solving simple problems until they see the whole picture. Once they see the whole picture, they can often apply what they know to new or complex situations and develop innovative solutions to problems.

It is easy to see that the typical university lecture is taught in a verbal and sequential manner, is aimed at intuitive learners, and has little or no active learning component. If an educator follows this format, they are not tapping the full potential of their students' ability to learn.

There is one more important aspect, besides understanding how students learn, to becoming a great educator. Most, if not all students follow a sequence of courses during their university studies because they are interested in a certain subject. This means the educator already has an audience that wants to learn. I feel the best way to captivate and hold the attention of the audience is to use edutainment—make learning fun. This does not mean an educator has to be a stand-up comedian, this means inject some humor into the class, use interesting examples, have interesting assignments, be upbeat in delivering lectures, and perhaps incorporating some of the non-traditional learning styles into lectures.

While good educators may incorporate some of the non-traditional learning styles, most typically visual learning, into their lectures, great educators successfully incorporate all of the learning styles and use aspects of edutainment in their pedagogical strategy.

Learners' Individual Needs

"And how is education supposed to make me feel smarter?"

—Homer Simpson

I^3 *Write down any ideas that come to you after reading this quote.*

____

____

"Ignorance more frequently begets confidence than does knowledge."

—Charles Darwin

I^3 *Write down any ideas that come to you after reading this quote.*

____

____

I^3 *How can you justify that both of these quotes may have merit?*

____

____

____

____

KWL

What Do You KNOW? **(prior knowledge)**

___

___

___

___

___

___

___

What Do You WANT to Know? **(objectives and goals)**

___

___

___

___

___

___

___

"School-days, I believe, are the unhappiest in the whole span of human existence. They are full of dull, unintelligible tasks, new and unpleasant ordinances, brutal violations of common sense and common decency. It doesn't take a reasonably bright boy long to discover that most of what is rammed into him is nonsense, and that no one really cares very much whether he learns it or not."

—H. L. Mencken

I^3 *Write down any ideas that come to you after reading this quote.*

___

___

"Everyone desires to learn, it is only a question of what and when. Without desire there can be no achievement."

—UNKNOWN

I^3 *Write down any ideas that come to you after reading this quote.*

____

____

I^3 *How can you justify that both of these quotes may have merit?*

____

____

Piaget's Model of Cognitive Development

Jean Piaget (1896–1980) made significant contributions in several areas of education, including addressing individual students and their needs. Piaget, also the father of constructivism, created a chronologic model for development, which many theorist and students use to understand student behaviors. Piaget was originally trained as a biologist, specifically studying mollusks. He was concerned with how students come to know thinks and believed that what distinguishes us from other animals is our ability to do reason with abstract symbols. Piaget derived some of his perspective from Vygotsky (1896–1934), who emphasized social interaction as a key to cognition and behavior. Additional information will be provided later on Vygotsky's dialectivism, which focused on the social resolution of dialogue. Piaget was interested in how children think—a worthwhile venture for us in the area of teaching and learning. He observed that younger students' responses were different than older students and concluded it was because they thought differently. This is an important distinction to educators. Realizing where our students are is essential in taking them where we would like them to be. The idea that students are thinking differently at different ages provides us a framework to generalize our approaches in instructional strategies.

As a biologist, Piaget was interested in how an organism adapts to its environment. This adaptation is a biological drive to obtain balance between schemes and the environment (equilibration). Equilibration is a very important concept and oddly enough it is a teacher's objective to cause disequilibrium amongst students. Only then can they categorize, organize and reform the concepts into meaningful ways for understanding. This disequilibrium is typically frustrating for many students. However, a teacher should encourage this healthy frustration as a necessary step towards understanding. Piaget described two processes used to re-equilibrate, which are assimilation and accommodation. Assimilation occurs when a student adds a new thought or concept to their current database. For example if they know how to add, then teaching them how to subtract, they will increase their ability to perform mathematical computations. Accommodation occurs when ideas are replaced or accommodated for previous ideas, which may have been misconceptions. Some young people believe that venous blood is blue because they have seen it this color in diagrams used to represent the difference between arterial and venous blood. In actuality, all blood is red, so the student will have to accommodate and replace their prior ideas with new ones.

Students will behave differently in addressing equilibrium as they age. Piaget created a model to represent what we might typically find in children's behaviors as they age. Remember, the following cognitive model is a simplification of a theory—every student is different and will process differently. This model provides the instructor with baseline behaviors, which students may exhibit. If they operate differently, teachers will need to accommodate.

I^3 *Let us try to represent Piaget's assimilation and accommodation visually, so that your students can possibly understand how they process.*

Piaget Accommodation—Space and Matter

Materials: Glass quart jar, large mouth with lid, small ball, 2 cups uncooked rice.

Procedure: Fill the quart jar with uncooked rice; put the ball inside the jar and close the lid. Hold the jar upright, then turn it over to cover the ball. Shake the jar back and forth vigorously until the ball surfaces—do not shake up and down. The ball comes to the surface.

Lesson: There are spaces between the grains of rice. As the jar is shaken, the rice gets closer together. This is referred to as settling. As the rice moves together, it pushes the ball upward. Two pieces of matter cannot occupy the same spaces at the same time; thus the packing together of rice grains moves the ball.

Piaget's Assimilation—Molecules

Materials: Dark food coloring, tall, one-half pint jar of water.

Procedure: Place the jar of water where it will not be moved or touched for 24 hours. Hold the food coloring container above the water and allow 2 drops to fall into the water. Observe immediately and then again in 24 hours. The drops sink to the bottom forming colored streaks as they fall. After 24 hours, the water is evenly colored.

Lesson: The atoms and molecules that make up matter are in constant motion. Though not seen by the naked eye, water molecules are moving. The small particles of food coloring are being pushed and shoved around by the moving water molecules. Given enough time, the colored particles will evenly spread throughout the jar of vibrating water. The movement is called diffusion.

I^3 *Describe the analogies between these two activities and Piaget's concepts? Why do you believe it may be important for teaching and learning to provide alternate perspectives of this concept in the form of kinesthetic or graphical representations?*

____

____

____

Additional Disequilibrium concepts . . . can you answer any of these:

1. What is the relationship between each of the subatomic particles.
2. Justify the disequilibria between world hunger and overpopulation.
3. Theoretically, what is the relationship between post-secondary education and reality?
4. What assumptions can you make concerning a Neo-Piagetian model to education?
5. Make a distinction between "edu-tainment" and "engaging education."
6. What is the premise behind the kinetics of a microwave?
7. State the point of view, which your state government has on business development.

8. How would you test the fact that flamingo's are not naturally pink.
9. Compose a redundancy, such as "merge together" or "baby calf."
10. Formulate a theory to determine attitudes towards quality life.
11. Develop a three part plan to pay off the national debt.
12. Appraise the economic status of any of the Central American countries.
13. Criticize the concept of "good."
14. Compare the authors persona from the last two novels you have read.
15. If a cow laughed, would milk come out of her nose?
16. Is fiberglass really made of glass?
17. What makes stainless steel stainless?
18. What do you really do for a living—not your vocation?
19. What are two behaviors that are owned by teachers who are instructional leaders?
20. How old would you be, if you did not know how old you are?

Piaget's Stages of Cognitive Development

1. **Sensorimotor stage** (birth to 2 years). Since this course targets students from age five and above, we do not address this stage. Basically, in this stage intelligence is demonstrated through motor activity without the use of symbols. Knowledge of the world is limited because its based on physical interactions.
2. **Pre-operational stage** (age 2–7). In this period, intelligence is demonstrated through the use of symbols, language use matures, and memory and imagination are developed, but thinking is done in a nonlogical, nonreversable manner. Egocentric thinking is predominant.
3. **Concrete operational stage** (age 7–11). In this stage, intelligence is demonstrated through logical and systematic manipulation of symbols related to concrete objects. Operational thinking develops.
4. **Formal operational stage** (age 11–15). In this stage, intelligence is demonstrated through the logical use of symbols related to abstract concepts. About a third of high school graduates are able to obtain formal operations—most people are not able to think formally during adulthood.

I³ *What do you think of Piaget? Do you agree with his work? Provide some support as well as differences that you might see in his approach. Also, visit the Internet and view a few of the many web pages on Piaget and add one other idea about his philosophy, which was not covered in this text.*

____

____

____

Another perspective on development stages is to correlate it with another parameter, such as a learning theory. In this case, let us combine Piaget's developmental stages with Vygotsky's theory of relativism. Relativism in its simplest form is the approach that everything we know and are able to learn is relative to something else, typically our prior knowledge and experiences. Some people believe others might be close-minded, when most of the time, they simply do not have the experiences that allow them to fully explore their ideas.

Please read the following scenarios and respond to the questions, which follow them. Be prepared, some students have indicated they are "doozies."

BTW

Doozie means something wonderful. The word comes from Duesenburg, an eminently desirable motorcar of the 1920s.

Scenario #1

Your next door neighbor is a family of four. Over the last year you have become good friends. Your neighbors agree to have a foreign exchange student live with them for a year. You are surprised when the student is only 13 years old. You are even more surprised when your neighbor explains the following problem. The young lady living with them has been openly talking about the fact that she has had a number of sexual experiences since arriving. After one month, she has been with seven young men ranging from 13 years old to 22 years old. Before telling the girl their feelings on the subject, your neighbors actually spoke with someone from the student exchange program. This person said that the young lady's culture encourages teenage girls and boys to have sex with a number of people as soon as they enter puberty. Apparently this is how people find the person they want to marry. Despite this explanation, your neighbors are still very uneasy about the girl's actions. They think that she should not be behaving in this manner. They think she is too young and is bound to get hurt by the experience. They still have not spoken with the guest however. They want to know if you think they should honor the young lady's cultural practices or if they should explain why they think she should not do this. Only they are very worried for the young lady and they say they think they just could not stand back and watch her continue this behavior. After sharing all of this, they turn to you and ask what you think they should do?

____

____

____

____

Scenario #2

You are married and have three sons. Your spouse convinces you to try to live in another country. Your family ends up living in a small village with only 60 people. After a month, you discover that there is a common practice in this country's culture. Apparently, families castrate every son except their oldest. When you learn that your family is expected to do the same, your spouse tries to explain that you are not sure if you will be living here for longer than one year, but the community does not seem to think that is important. They are so used to their practice that they see it as selfish to want all of your sons to remain uncastrated. In fact, just as we have laws against adults having sex with minors, this culture has laws against not castrating your sons. You are being pressured to decide in the next couple of days. Suddenly after thinking about it, your spouse says that they think you should go along with this culture's norms. What do you do?

Scenario #3

Your new neighbor has just moved to this country. Apparently they lived on a relatively small island in the Pacific Ocean. You are curious when you learn that they were witch doctors in their homeland. One day a friend visits your home with her cocker spaniel, Colby. When she knocks on the door, Colby, as she usually does, starts to bark. Only the dog usually stops barking once inside. This time, Colby does not stop barking and starts to scratch your wall. When your friend walks over to the wall she makes a face, and says, "Oh my goodness, what is that smell?" Realizing it is coming from your neighbor's home you step over and knock on their door. Once he opens the door, you see two dead cats hanging in the kitchen. Apparently, the cats were getting into his yard. He says the best way to stop cats from entering your yard is to skin them and put them in yard. It is the only way to train the other cats to be polite and stay out of the yard. What would you do?

Let us try an activity, which could provide some information on our reaction time. There has been debate about physical and mental reaction time. Let us collect some data and try to make some correlations and inferences about these two parameters.

Have a colleague hold a meter stick from the top so that it is upright and several decimeters above the floor. Your colleague may have to stand on a chair to do this. You hold your fingers around the stick at the 45-centimeter mark, close to but not touching the meter stick. Without warning your colleagues will release the meter stick, and you will attempt to catch it with your fingers. Notice what centimeter mark your fingers are touching. Subtract this number from 45 or subtract 45 from the number to see how many centimeters the stick fell before you caught it. Try this at least three times and average your results. Then switch places with your colleague and determine their data.

Calculate each of your reaction times from the table:

Distance (cm)	Reaction Time (seconds)
5	0.10
10	0.14
15	0.18
20	0.20
25	0.23
30	0.25
35	0.27
40	0.29
45	0.31

I³ *How would you correlate these results with Piaget's stages of cognitive development? Devise a procedure that you would do to make sense of this data.*

____

____

____

____

____

____

Erikson's Psychosocial Development

Erik Erikson's (1902–1994) theory is unique in that it encompasses the entire life cycle and recognizes the impact of society, history, and culture on personality. Erikson is best known for his concept of the identity crisis. He studied and expanded on Freud's psychosexual theory. Although instead of a biological driven approach, he believed the most important force driving human behavior and the development was social interaction. A brief summary of Erikson's eight stages of development are provided in Table 5.1.

TABLE 5.1. ERIKSON'S EIGHT STAGES OF DEVELOPMENT

Stage	Age (year)	Conflict	Critical Event	Synopsis
1. Oral Sensory	0–1	Trust and Mistrust	Feeding	Either forms a loving, trusting relationship or develops a sense of mistrust.
2. Muscular-Anal	1–3	Autonomy and	Toilet training	Energy directed to development of physical skills, learns control but may develop shame.
3. Locomotor	3–6	Initiative and Guilt	Independence	Continues to assert, but may be too forceful, leading to guilt feelings.
4. Latency	6–12	Industry and Inferiority	School	Deal with demand to learn new skills or risk a sense of inferiority.
5. Adolescence	13–18	Identity and Role Confusion	Identity	This is the time when we ask ourselves "Who am I?"
6. Young Adulthood	19–40	Intimacy and Isolation	Love relationships	Develop intimate relationships or suffer feelings of isolation.
7. Middle Adulthood	40–65	Generativity and Stagnation	Parenting	Find way to satisfy and support next generation.
8. Maturity	65–death	Integrity and Despair	Reflection, acceptance of life.	Sense of oneself as one is fulfilled.

I³ *So where are you on this table? Can you recall passing through the prior stages? What are some specific events in your life that occurred that you can connect to some of the stages?*

____

____

____

____

____

____

____

____

Kohlberg's Model of Moral Development

Lawrence Kohlberg (1927–) is a moral philosopher and student of child development. He is director of Harvard's Center for Moral Education. His area of interest is the moral development of children and how they develop a sense of right, wrong, and justice. Kohlberg (1963) observed that children develop through stages of moral decision-making similar to their progression through Piaget's stages of cognitive development.

Kohlberg's Stages of Moral Development

A. *Pre-moral Stages:* *Behavior motivated by anticipation of pleasure or pain.*

Stage 1: Punishment and Obedience—Avoidance of physical punishment and deference to power. Punishment is an automatic response of physical retaliation. The immediate physical consequences of an action determine its goodness or badness.

Stage 2: Instrumental Exchange—Marketplace exchange of favors or blows. "You scratch my back, I'll scratch yours." Justice is: "Do unto others as they do unto you." Individual does what is necessary, makes concessions only as necessary to satisfy his own needs.

B. *Conventional Morality:* *Acceptance of the rules and standards of one's group.*

Stage 3: Interpersonal Conformity—Right is conformity to the behavioral expectations of one's society or peers. Individual acts to gain approval of others. Good behavior is that which pleases or helps others within the group. "Everybody is doing it."

Stage 4: Law and Order—Respect for rules, laws, and properly constituted authority. Defense of the given social and institutional order for its own sake. Responsibility toward the welfare of others in the society. "Justice" normally refers to criminal or forensic justice. Justice demands that the wrongdoer be punished, that he "pay his debt to society," and that law abiders be rewarded. "A good day's pay for a good day's work."

C. *Postconventional Morality:* *Ethical principles.*

Stage 5: Prior Rights and Social Contract—Moral action in a specific situation is not defined by reference to a checklist of rules, but from logical application of universal, abstract, moral principles. Individuals have natural or inalienable rights and liberties that are prior to society and must be protected by society. Retributive justice repudiated. Justice distributed proportionate to circumstances and need.

Stage 6: Universal Ethical Principles—An individual who reaches this stage acts out of universal principles based upon the equality and worth of all human beings. Persons are never means to an end, but are ends in themselves. Having rights means more than individual liberties. It means that every individual is due consideration of his interests in every situation, those interests being of equal importance with ones own.

I[3] *Please read the following Kohlberg Dilemmas (Kohlberg, 1963) and respond to each below each item.*

Dilemma I

Joe is a 14-year-old boy who wanted to go to camp very much. His father promised him he could go if he saved up the money for it himself. So Joe worked hard at his paper route and saved up the 40 dollars it cost to go to camp, and a little more besides. But just before camp was going to start, his father changed his mind. Some of his friends decided to go on a special fishing trip, and Joe's father was short of the money it would cost. So he told Joe to give him the money he had saved from the paper route. Joe didn't want to give up going to camp, so he thinks of refusing to give his father the money.

1. Should Joe refuse to give his father the money? Why or why not? ________________

   ____

   ____

2. Does the father have the right to tell Joe to give him the money? ________________

   Why or why not? ________________________________

   ____

   ____

3. Does giving the money have anything to do with being a good son? ______________

   Why or why not? ________________________________

   ____

   ____

4. Is the fact that Joe earned the money himself important in this situation? _________

   Why or why not? ________________________________

   ____

   ____

5. The father promised Joe he could go to camp if he earned the money. Is the fact that the father promised the most important thing in the situation? ________________

   Why or why not? ________________________________

   ____

   ____

6. In general, why should a promise be kept? Is it important to keep a promise to someone you don't know well and probably won't see again? ______

   Why or why not? ______

   ______

   ______

7. What do you think is the most important thing a father should be concerned about in his relationship to his son? ______

   Why is that the most important thing? ______

   ______

   ______

   In general, what should be the authority of a father over his son?

   ______

   Why? ______

   ______

   ______

8. What do you think is the most important thing a son should be concerned about in his relationship to his father? ______

   ______

   ______

   Why is that the most important thing? ______

   ______

   ______

   ______

9. In thinking back over the dilemma, what would you say is the most responsible thing for Joe to do in this situation? ______

   Why? ______

   ______

   ______

   ______

Dilemma II

Judy was a 12-year-old girl. Her mother promised her that she could go to a special rock concert coming to their town if she saved up from baby-sitting and lunch money to buy a ticket to the concert. She managed to save up the 15 dollars the ticket cost plus another 5 dollars. But then her mother changed her mind and told Judy that she had to spend the money on new clothes for school. Judy was disappointed and decided to go to the concert anyway. She bought a ticket and told her mother that she had only been able to save

5 dollars. That Saturday she went to the performance and told her mother that she was spending the day with a friend. A week passed without her mother finding out. Judy then told her older sister, Louise, that she had gone to the performance and had lied to her mother about it. Louise wonders whether to tell their mother what Judy did.

1. Should Louise, the older sister, tell their mother that Judy lied about the money or should she keep quiet? ______________________

   Why? ______________________

   ____

   ____

   ____

2. In wondering whether to tell, Louise thinks of the fact that Judy is her sister. Should that make a difference in Louise's decision? ______________________

   ____

   ____

   ____

   Why or why not? ______________________

   ____

   ____

   ____

3. Does telling have anything to do with being a good daughter? ______________________

   Why or why not? ______________________

   ____

   ____

   ____

4. Is the fact that Judy earned the money herself important in this situation? ____________

   Why or why not? ______________________

   ____

   ____

   ____

5. The mother promised Judy she could go to the concert if she earned the money. Is the fact that the mother promised the most important thing in the situation? ____________

   Why or why not? ______________________

   ____

   ____

   ____

6. Why in general should a promise be kept? Is it important to keep a promise to someone you don't know well and probably won't see again? ______

   Why or why not? ______

7. What do you think is the most important thing a mother should be concerned about in her relationship to her daughter? ______

   Why is that the most important thing? ______

8. In general, what should be the authority of a mother over her daughter? ______

   Why? ______

9. What do you think is the most important thing a daughter should be concerned about in her relationship to her mother? ______

   Why is that the most important thing? ______

10. In thinking back over the dilemma, what would you say is the most responsible thing for Louise to do in this situation? ________________________________

____

____

____

Why? ________________________________

____

____

____

Dilemma III

In Europe, a woman was near death from a special kind of cancer. There was one drug that the doctors thought might save her. It was a form of radium that a druggist in the same town had recently discovered. The drug was expensive to make, but the druggist was charging ten times what the drug cost him to make. He paid $400 for the radium and charged $4,000 for a small dose of the drug. The sick woman's husband, Heinz, went to everyone he knew to borrow the money and tried every legal means, but he could only get together about $2,000, which is half of what it cost. He told the druggist that his wife was dying, and asked him to sell it cheaper or let him pay later. But the druggist said, "No, I discovered the drug and I'm going to make money from it." So, having tried every legal means, Heinz gets desperate and considers breaking into the man's store to steal the drug for his wife (Kohlberg, 1963, p. 19).

1. Should Heinz steal the drug? ________________________________

   Why or why not? ________________________________

   ____

   ____

   ____

2. Is it actually right or wrong for him to steal the drug? ________________________________

   Why is it right or wrong? ________________________________

   ____

   ____

   ____

3. Does Heinz have a duty or obligation to steal the drug? ________________________________

   Why or why not? ________________________________

   ____

   ____

   ____

4. If Heinz doesn't love his wife, should he steal the drug for her? ______________________

____

____

Does it make a difference in what Heinz should do whether or not he loves his wife?

____

Why or why not? ____

____

____

____

5. Suppose the person dying is not his wife but a stranger. Should Heinz steal the drug for the stranger? ____

Why or why not? ____

____

____

____

6. Suppose it's a pet animal he loves. Should Heinz steal to save the pet animal? ________

Why or why not? ____

____

____

____

7. Is it important for people to do everything they can to save another's life? __________

Why or why not? ____

____

____

____

8. It is against the law for Heinz to steal? ____

Does that make it morally wrong? ______________________________________

Why or why not? ____

____

____

____

9. In general, should people try to do everything they can to obey the law? ___________

Why or why not? ____

____

____

____

How does this apply to what Heinz should do? ____________________

____

____

____

____

10. In thinking back over the dilemma, what would you say is the most responsible thing for Heinz to do? ____________________

____

____

____

____

Why? ____________________

____

____

____

____

BTW

Kohlberg is not really interested in whether the participant says "yes" or "no" to this dilemma but in the reasoning behind the answer.

Dilemma IV

Two young men, brothers, had got into serious trouble. They were secretly leaving town in a hurry and needed money. Karl, the older one, broke into a store and stole 1,000 dollars. Bob, the younger one, went to a retired old man who was known to help people in town. He told the man that he was very sick and that he needed 1,000 dollars to pay for an operation. Bob asked the old man to lend him the money and promised that he would pay him back when he recovered. Really Bob wasn't sick at all, and he had no intention of paying the man back. Although the old man didn't know Bob very well, he lent him the money. So Bob and Karl skipped town, each with 1,000 dollars.

1. Which is worse, stealing like Karl or cheating like Bob? ____________________

____

Why is that worse? ____________________

____

____

____

____

2. What do you think is the worst thing about cheating the old man? ______

Why is that the worst thing? ______

3. In general, why should a promise be kept? ______

4. Is it important to keep a promise to someone you don't know well or will never see again? ______

   Why or why not? ______

5. Why shouldn't someone steal from a store? ______

6. What is the value or importance of property rights? ______

7. Should people do everything they can to obey the law? ____________________

   Why or why not? ____________________

   ____

   ____

   ____

   ____

8. Was the old man being irresponsible by lending Bob the money? ____________________

   Why or why not? ____________________

   ____

   ____

   ____

   ____

Maslow's Model of a Hierarchy of Needs

In 1943, Abraham Maslow developed a needs-oriented hierarchy of human needs based upon experiences with humans, rather than animals such as Freud and Skinner had accomplished. According to Maslow, there are general types of needs (physiological, safety, love, and esteem) that must be satisfied before a person can act unselfishly. He called these needs "deficiency needs." As long as we are motivated to satisfy these cravings, we are moving towards growth and self-actualization. Searching for ways in which to satisfy needs is natural. We all will direct ourselves to meet these needs similar to Piaget re-equilibration approach.

Physiological needs are the very basic needs such as air, water, food, sleep and shelter. When these are not satisfied we may feel imbalanced, which motivate us to resolve these ill feelings. Once they are addressed, we can consider other endeavors, such as safety. Safety needs, such as security and well-being are taken for granted by some people, however, when these are not met such as in a dysfunctional or abusive home, it is difficult to elevate to the next level. This is especially important as a teacher, whom wishes teach students. However, if students arrive to class and they have not met the first two levels, it will be very difficult for them to attend, process, and ultimately achieve. Even the students who can accomplish the first two levels will search for the next level of love, or an acceptance of others. Humans need this feeling and if they cannot find this in the schools through clubs, organizations, athletic endeavors, and so on, they will be unable to proceed further in the step of needs. There are two esteem needs—self-esteem and recognition esteem. At times, pre-service teachers confuse self-esteem with self-efficacy. To clarify, self-esteem is what one believes of themselves, where self-efficacy is what one believes of their abilities. The further need for recognition is for people who have gained all the prior needs and are searching for recognition of their accomplishments. Lastly, is self-actualization or the desire to become everything that one is capable of becoming. They can seek knowledge, peace, esthetic experiences, self-fulfillment, and so on. Fig. 5.1 presents Maslow's Hierarchy of Needs graphically.

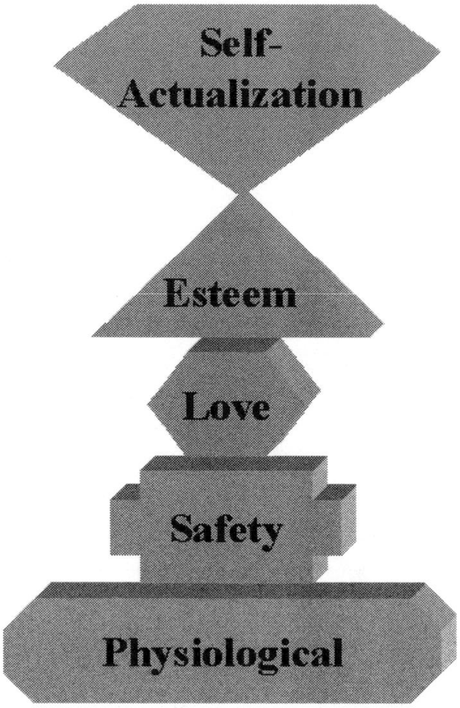

FIGURE 5.1. Maslow's Hierarchy of Needs.

I^3 *Does this hierarchy make sense to you? Why/why not? Can you see yourself or a friend in one of these stages? What might you do over the next four years to increase your changes of obtaining self-actualization at some point in your life?*

BTW

After all of those stages, do you need to WAKE UP? In early English times, lead cups were used to drink whiskey. The combination would sometimes knock them out for several days. When found lying on the side of the road they would be taken for dead and prepared for burial. They were laid out on the kitchen table for an eat and drink, and to wait and see if they would wake up, hence the custom of holding a "wake."

BTW

If that did not WAKE YOU UP, then "sleep tight." In the 1500s in Britain, beds consisted of a frames with ropes strung from side to side on which a "mattress" was supported. The ropes were twisted with a wooden key to tighten them to better support the big mattress, hence the term "sleep tight." "Mattresses" were often made of leaves and small brush, which could hold bugs, fleas, and ticks. Thus the term "good night and don't let the bed-bugs bite."

Special Education

Special education is typically defined as direct instructional activities or special learning experiences designed primarily for students identified as having exceptionalities in one or more aspects of the cognitive process or as being underachievers in relation to general level. Such services may be directed at students with physical, emotional, or cognitive learning disabilities.

Special education is a federal funding statute that provides financial aid to states to ensure a free, appropriate education to disabled children. Special education is defined as "specially designed instruction, at no cost to the parents, to meet the unique needs of a child with a disability" (34 CFR 300.26). "Specially designed instruction means . . . adapting, as appropriate to the needs of an eligible child . . . the content, methodology, or delivery of instruction."

There are many types of special education students. Some include those with attention deficit disorder (ADD) and attention deficit hyperactive disorder (ADHD); autism, behavioral disorders, such as anxiety, bipolar disorder, and obsessive-compulsive disorder, dyslexia, hearing and visual impairment, down syndrome, mental and physical retardation, speech impairment, and gifted students.

Each special education student will be provided the least restrictive environment as mandated by the Individuals with Disabilities in Education Act (IDEA) and Public Law 92-142. Extensive evaluations in language, reading, speech and auditory perception are typically completed for each child. From these evaluations, observations and parent input an Individualized Education Plan (IEP) is developed for each child.

I^3 *Let's try some activities that might help us understand how a special education student processes. Find a partner, a pen or pencil, a piece of paper, and a mirror. Use the attached sheet of a star. Have one person attempt to trace the star by looking into the mirror while the partner holds a piece of paper between the eyes of the person who is drawing and the star.*

What happened? How successful were you at this simple task? How did it make you feel?

I[3] *Please view the box below. What does it say? Is it difficult to read? Try again. Try something different, a different angle maybe. If all else fails try holding it lengthwise and read over it. Now what does it say? What does this exercise represent about special needs learners?*

____

____

VIEW FROM A
DIFFERENT ANGLE

I[3] *Please read the text in the box below. Is it difficult to read? Why? Try again and try to piece it together with what may make sense. What does this exercise represent about special needs learners?*

Special educa   s typically defined as direct structional activities or special l   ing experiences desig d primarily for students identified as having exce   nalities in one or more asp   f the   itive process or as b   nderachievers in relation to general level   ervices ma e directed at students wit physical, emotional, or co   e learning dis   ties.

Mainstreaming and Inclusion

Mainstreaming is an educational method that includes many different kinds of learners in the same classroom, instead of separating students according to their learning abilities. The term mainstreaming was first used in the 1970s and describes classrooms where students with disabilities and students who do not have disabilities are together. In a mainstreamed classroom, all students, including special education and gifted, learn together in the same classroom. Mainstreaming is now more commonly known as inclusion, and many school systems today are using inclusion in their districts. In any classroom setting, the teacher needs to be able to meet every student's needs. In a mainstreamed classroom, meeting every student's needs is more challenging because there are many different types of learners. Teachers who have mainstreamed classes are trained to provide different things for different students, making sure there is something for everyone.

Diverse Students

"If you treat an individual as he is, he will remain as he is. But if you treat him as if he were what he ought to be and could be, he will become what he ought to be and could be."

—GOETHE

FROM THE ISSUE DATED JANUARY 30, 2004

FRESHMAN SURVEY, 2003–4

THIS YEAR'S FRESHMEN AT 4-YEAR COLLEGES: A STATISTICAL PROFILE

TABLE 5.2. AGE, RACE, RELIGION

Age on Dec. 31, 2003	
17 or younger	1.8%
18	68.2%
19	28.7%
20	0.9%
21 to 24	0.4%
25 or older	0.1%
English is native language	
Yes	92.3%
No	7.7%
Racial and ethnic background	
White/Caucasian	75.7%
African-American/Black	9.6%
American Indian/Alaska Native	1.3%
Asian-American/Asian	7.7%
Native Hawaiian/Pacific Islander	0.8%
Mexican American/Chicano	3.7%
Puerto Rican	0.9%
Other Latino	2.2%
Other	3.0%
Religious preference	
Roman Catholic	29.7%
Baptist	11.1%
Methodist	5.8%
Lutheran	4.9%
Presbyterian	4.1%
Jewish	2.4%
Episcopal	1.8%
United Church of Christ	1.5%
Buddhist	1.2%
Islamic	0.8%
Islamic	0.8%
Hindu	0.7%
Eastern Orthodox	0.7%
Latter-day Saints (Mormon)	0.6%
Seventh-day Adventist	0.3%
Unitarian Universalist	0.3%
Quaker	0.2%
Other Christian	13.4%
Other religion	2.7%
None	17.6%

TABLE 5.3. HIGH-SCHOOL BACKGROUND, ACTIVITIES

Year of high-school graduation	
2003	98.3%
2002	1.0%
2001	0.2%
2000 or earlier	0.3%
Did not graduate but passed GED test	0.1%
Never graduated	0.1%

Average high-school grade	
A or A+	23.2%
A–	23.4%
B+	20.8%
B	20.4%
B–	7.1%
C+	3.4%
C	1.6%
D	0.1%

High school required community service for graduation	
No	68.7%
Yes	31.3%

TIME SPENT DURING LAST YEAR OF HIGH SCHOOL . . .

Hours per week	Studying or doing homework	Socializing with friends	Talking with teachers outside of class	Exercising or sports	Volunteer work	Working (for pay)	Student clubs/groups
None	2.7%	0.3%	9.7%	5.3%	29.4%	30.5%	27.5%
Less than 1	13.4%	1.3%	43.4%	9.8%	23.0%	2.6%	15.5%
1 to 2	21.6%	5.5%	30.7%	15.2%	23.6%	3.7%	25.2%
3 to 5	28.4%	17.1%	11.5%	18.9%	13.9%	7.0%	17.8%
6 to 10	18.7%	25.2%	3.0%	18.1%	5.5%	12.1%	7.5%
11 to 15	8.4%	18.8%	0.9%	13.9%	2.0%	13.8%	3.1%
16 to 20	4.1%	12.6%	0.4%	8.3%	1.0%	14.5%	1.5%
Over 20	2.8%	19.2%	0.4%	10.5%	1.7%	15.8%	1.9%

Hours per week	Watching TV	Partying	Household/childcare duties	Reading for pleasure	Playing video/ computer games	Prayer/ meditation
None	5.7%	22.8%	21.2%	25.3%	38.7%	36.2%
Less than 1	15.4%	14.9%	22.3%	26.7%	22.2%	33.8%
1 to 2	23.9%	17.9%	29.9%	23.8%	16.4%	19.1%
3 to 5	27.2%	20.3%	17.4%	14.6%	11.6%	6.9%
6 to 10	15.7%	13.0%	5.4%	5.8%	5.7%	2.2%
11 to 15	6.0%	5.6%	1.8%	2.1%	2.5%	0.7%
16 to 20	2.6%	2.7%	0.7%	0.8%	1.1%	0.4%
Over 20	3.4%	2.8%	1.2%	0.9%	1.7%	0.8%

TABLE 5.4. PARENTS

Parents' education (highest level)		
	Father	*Mother*
Grammar school or less	2.5%	2.3%
Some high school	4.1%	3.1%
High-school graduate	20.7%	21.0%
Postsecondary school other than college	4.0%	4.8%
Some college	15.2%	17.6%
College degree	28.2%	31.2%
Some graduate school	2.3%	2.9%
Graduate degree	23.0%	17.1%

Estimated parental income	
Less than $10,000	3.1%
$10,000 to $14,999	2.8%
$15,000 to $19,999	2.7%
$20,000 to $24,999	3.7%
$25,000 to $29,999	3.5%
$30,000 to $39,999	6.7%
$40,000 to $49,999	8.1%
$50,000 to $59,999	9.8%
$60,000 to $74,999	12.7%
$75,000 to $99,999	15.7%
$100,000 to $149,999	16.4%
$150,000 to $199,999	6.3%
$200,000 to $249,999	3.0%
$250,000 or more	5.5%

TABLE 5.5. MAKING THE CHOICE, SETTLING IN

Number of other colleges applied to for admission this year	
None	18.3%
1	12.2%
2	15.4%
3	16.7%
4	12.7%
5	8.8%
6	6.0%
7 to 10	8.1%
11 or more	1.8%
Miles from college to permanent home	
5 or less	4.8%
6 to 10	6.2%
11 to 50	25.6%
51 to 100	16.9%
101 to 500	34.1%
Over 500	12.4%
Student made first visit to college attended:	
Before applying	57.9%
After applying but before college acceptance	12.0%
After college acceptance but before making decision to attend	15.1%
After deciding to attend	15.0%
Housing plans during fall term:	
College dormitory	77.4%
With family or other relatives	16.4%
Other private home, apartment, or room	3.6%
Other campus student housing	1.9%
Fraternity or sorority house	0.4%
Other	0.3%

TABLE 5.6. FINANCES

Concern about financing college	
None (I am confident that I will have sufficient funds)	34.3%
Some (but I probably will have enough funds)	52.6%
Major (not sure I will have enough funds to complete college)	13.0%

NOTE: The statistics are based on survey responses of 276,449 first-year students entering 413 four-year colleges and universities in the fall of 2003. The figures were statistically adjusted to represent the total population of approximately 1.2 million first-time, full-time students at four-year institutions. Because of rounding or multiple responses, figures may add up to more than 100 percent.

"The American Freshman: National Norms for Fall 2003," published by the University of California at Los Angeles Higher Education Research Institute. Used with permission.

The Meaning of Culture

"Kids are the best . . . you can teach them to hate the things you hate, and they practically raise themselves what with the Internet and all."

—Homer Simpson

I^3 *Write down any ideas that come to you after reading this quote.*

____

____

A culture is all the things that make up a peoples entire way of life. Elements of culture include social organization, customs and traditions, language, art and literature, religion, forms of government and an economic system. Culture is a learned behavior. Each child goes through a process of enculturation as they grow up. Children learn by observing behaviors and symbols of their surroundings. Culture is an attribute of a group of people. Examples of cultural symbols might include Fig. 5.2 and Fig. 5.3.

FIGURE 5.2. The United States Flag

© Daimler-Chrysler AG

FIGURE 5.3. Mercedes Symbol

Cultural Identity

Cultural identity is a concept of identity in which the individual existence derives from his or her way of life. Your cultural identity is everything that makes you individual. Everyone has a cultural identity and as a teacher, this is one method which you can involve your students. Hopefully, you will be fortunate to teach a very diverse class of students and your cultural pool will be bountiful. In this case, there will be an increase in authentic, contextual moments from which students can learn about other environments first hand as well as learn from their peers, a very powerful teaching and learning technique.

Cultural identity is ever changing and at any point in history can be defined as the dominant culture of a society or group. Some people believe that cultural identity is a state of mind and heart. It's not about personal, habits, such as language, food, music, and attire. In William Shakespeare's play, *Hamlet,* the concept of cultural identity is explored through Hamlet's isolation, which is created by the conflict of his duty. Cultural identity is an important issue all over the world. In the United States there are more than 500 nations of American Indians. Many of them still have their own customs and traditions. The United States is also a land of immigrants from other countries. This makes the United States multicultural and multilingual. Teaching students with multiple first languages other than English can be challenging. These students are known as ESOL students. Helpful strategies to assist ESOL students include repeating and rephrasing your statements when it seems to be necessary, find lower grade level materials with more illustrations and less language, choose a proficient English-speaking student to serve as the ESOL student's partner, provide graphic organizers, use hand signals, and speak slowly and clearly.

Ethnicity and Race

Ethnicity is a term that is open to much debate and one that often causes great confusion. The word "ethnic" is derived from the Greek word ethnos, and simply means "nation" or "people." Many believe ethnicity as an ethnic group is a community of people who share cultural and/or physical characteristics including history, political system, religion, language, geographical origin, traditions, behaviors, foods, genetic similarities, and physical features. While others believe that it is strictly a cultural construct: there is simply no physical—no quantifiable—evidence that ethnic groups are much different from one another. Recently, ethnicity has taken on different connotations and tends to describe people who are often a minority in the country in which they live. We can see that there are some similarities between the term culture and ethnicity. As scholars and thinkers, we may realize and accept the similarities and differences and also appreciate diverse groups' beliefs on the concepts.

Whereas race is typically defined as people who are believed to belong to the same genetic stock or biologically, a taxonomic group that is a division of a species usually arises as a consequence of geographical isolation within a species. Race is a relatively modern idea. Ancient societies divided people amongst religion, class and language. Race has no genetic basis. Most variation is within, not between races. Ethnicity and race are often used in context with the concept of minorities. Minorities are groups of people who are smaller in number compared to other groups in a society, often because of racial, religious, ethnic, or political differences.

Stereotyping and Racism

Stereotyping is the process of assuming a person or group has one or more characteristics because most members of that group have (or are thought to have) the same characteristics. It is a simplification and generalization process that helps people categorize and understand their world, but at the same time it often leads to errors. When stereotypes are inaccurate and negative they lead to misunderstandings, which make resolving the conflict more difficult. The term "stereotype" was first used in the eighteenth century to describe a printing process designed to duplicate pages of type. A century later, psychiatrists started using the related term "stereotypy" to describe a behavior of "persistent repetitiveness and unchanging mode of expression" (Jones, 1977).

Racism is prejudice or discrimination based on the belief that race is the primary factor determining human traits and abilities. Racism includes the belief that genetic or inherited differences produce the inherent superiority or inferiority of one race over another. In the name of protecting their race from "contamination," some racists justify the domination and destruction of races they consider to be either superior or inferior. Racism takes many different forms, such as personal attacks, written or verbal threats, and damage to property. Unfortunately racism can exist in all races and cultures. Racists feel threatened by anyone who is from a different race or culture. We are not born racist. This approach is part of our culture and as such our views on this topic develop as we grow up and are enculturated by our surroundings.

Multicultural Education

Multicultural education relates to education and instruction designed for the cultures of several different races in an educational system. This approach to teaching and learning is based upon consensus building, respect, and fostering cultural pluralism within racial societies. Multicultural education acknowledges and incorporates positive racial idiosyncrasies into classroom atmospheres. As preservice teachers, we should prepare ourselves to teach a diverse, multicultural group of students. As noted above, there are many considerations for the teacher when in the classroom. There are many resources for lesson plans, demonstrations, and activities that will assist the teacher in addressing every student in their classroom. This text will not specifically include ideas or approaches to multicultural education for two main reasons. The first reason is that most education programs include a course on this topic and therefore our time will be more efficiently spent addressing our course objectives. Secondly, throughout the text and discussions, an intentional effort will be made by all to include broad examples, which are inclusive, not exclusive in the perception and working with students of all backgrounds.

I^3 *Consider all of the new diversity terms introduced in this section. Try to paraphrase and/or provide examples of these terms so that you can reflect on these and determine your own understanding of the challenges and potential misunderstandings.*

What Did You LEARN?

References

Jones, R. A. (1995). Perceiving Other People: Stereotyping as a Process of Social Cognition. In Miller, A. G. (Ed.), *In the Eye of the Beholder: Contemporary Issues In Stereotyping*. New York: Praeger Publishers.

Kohlberg, L. (1975). Accessed June 2004, from *http://www.haverford.edu/psych/ddavis/p109g/kohlberg.dilemmas.html*

34 CFR 300.26

Individuals with Disabilities in Education Act (IDEA)

Public Law 92-142

"The American Freshman: National Norms for Fall 2003," published by the American Council on Education and the University of California at Los Angeles Higher Education Research Institute. (2004). In

Accessed , from http://chronicle.com Section: Students
Volume 50, Issue 21, Page A30

2004 by The Chronicle of Higher Education

PowerPoint Outline to Assist In-Class Note-Taking

A. Learners' Individual Needs

a. Piaget's Model of Cognitive Development

b. Erikson's Psychosocial Development

c. Kolhberg's Model of Moral Development

d. Maslow's Model of a Hierarchy of Needs

B. Special Education

C. Diverse Students

D. The Meaning of Culture

a. Cultural identity

b. Ethnicity and Race

c. Stereotyping and Racism

E. Multicultural Education

6

Society and Teaching

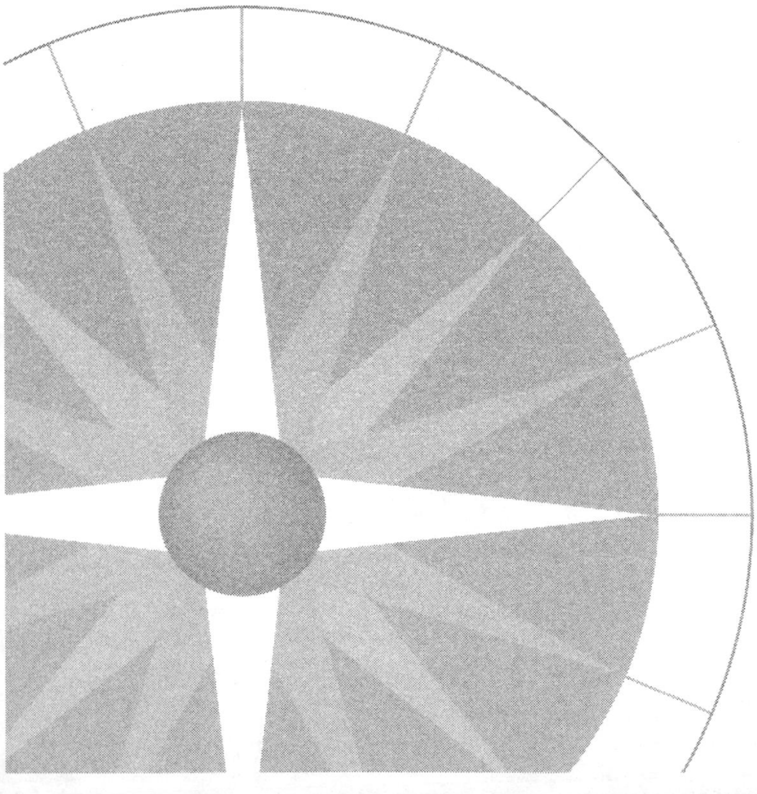

Guest Editorial: Michelle Wilcox, M.Ed., current Doctoral of Education Candidate, Director Adult Learning, St. Johns River Community College

So What If Kids Fail?

First, as John Lennon would have said, "Imagine." Let go of what you've learned to think that school should be, what legislators and administrators might think school should be . . . and IMAGINE!

WHAT IF . . .

. . . students could graduate from high school having failed a variety of things throughout the 13 years of formal education, without ever having to endure summer school to do more of what they didn't like anyway?

THINK ABOUT IT . . .

. . . when was the last time you used algebra in your everyday life or at work? If you're one of the 18% who actually does use it, just how well did you do in chorus when in high school? Oh . . . well, when was the last time you sang . . . driving in the car? In the shower?

. . . consider social studies classes. When was the last time you needed to know how many presidents there have been, or when Columbus discovered whatever landmass he's been credited with today? Could you be successful today in college, work, home, and family life if you had failed every social studies class you took? Are you sure you could survive if you couldn't name every state and capital, the date of the Louisiana Purchase, or recite the first paragraph of the Declaration of Independence?

. . . what if students fail English IV? After all, it is the critical language arts course with a focus on British literature. Is it possible to go to college and become successful if you've never read Shakespeare? Can you be a good nurse, computer programmer, commanding officer in the military, or pilot if you failed an English class in high school?

. . . and PE? How can anyone fail PE and ever become an author, sculptor, biochemist, or lawyer? It surely must not be possible, because children can fail high school and *not be allowed to graduate,* simply because they don't want to change clothes in front of a bunch of people they don't know, or because they just can't quite figure out how to hit a softball or spike volleyball. But there's no need to fail PE—you passed, didn't you? All you really have to do is "dress out" and sit on the bleachers, you don't actually have to be good at PE, or understand anything about physical health to pass it . . . so does it really matter if kids fail PE?

. . . and when is the last time you had to calculate the speed of light, or name all of the planets in order from the sun? How often do you have to identify the elements by their two-letter symbol? What if students can't do these things? What if they fail?

Now, think about this.

WHAT IF...

. . . instead of algebra, probability and statistics were part of the school curriculum? Isn't that what they need? Is it possible to create rigorous lessons the students can relate to, develop critical, logical thinkers, *and* interest students in research and discovery if you pose questions that require the use of probability, statistics and solid arithmetic skills to analyze a problem? Could you do that with third graders? Is there any grade level for which you couldn't do it?

Would we really consider someone successful in college, work, home, and family life if they weren't good citizens? Could you teach about history, and the development of economies around the world in such a way that demonstrates the *passion,* commitment, work ethic, and dedication to democracy and freedom of those who founded this country, fought for the rights we have today, and fought to help others around the world? Could you teach about those who fought against communism, totalitarianism, racism, slavery, and religious oppression, in such a way that students would be interested in knowing who those people were, in a way that might help develop their sense of responsibility, citizenship, and global concern for others? Could you put things in perspective so students can relate to a genuine sense of history, the people, times, and places, in a way that encourages students to become critical thinkers, to understand why things took place where they did because of who was there or because of the geography of the land, and encourage them to become actively involved? When was the last time you voted, paid a tax (did you buy gas, turn on a light, use a telephone—if so, you paid taxes other than sales tax on those things), or worried about someone listening or watching what you were doing in your home? Each of those has its roots in history and provides you with the privileges and freedoms you have today. Do you appreciate or expect those things? What if you had been born in Mexico, Afghanistan, India, or Columbia?

. . . instead of isolating the writing and critical analysis of literature from other areas of study, it was included in the study of history, mathematics, music, art, science, and careers? Isn't the only reason we have knowledge of history that people took the time to write about it? Can students grasp mathematical concepts and have the depth of understanding needed to use math if they don't understand the language (ask a high-school student, "What percent of the original purchase price did you save if you were given a 20-dollar discount on a 75-dollar item," and then decide if they need to understand the language.) Can you understand or appreciate music and art without understanding the politics and times in which they were created? Can you express that understanding or fully appreciate them without language? Can you understand DNA structure (a police detective may want to), or what it took to get two fully functional robots to land on Mars *and* have the ability to transmit data back and forth over *millions* of miles without reading, writing and critical analysis?

. . . PE classes were developed around lifelong activities designed to keep people in good physical condition? Do you think students might be more interested in PE classes if they revolved around things students could do as individuals and small teams or groups, such as walking, jogging, rock climbing, hiking, canoeing, surfing, and swimming? (How many people do you know who play medicine ball?) Could these things be taught, perhaps incorporated into other subjects (science, history, math, English), to promote good health, careers, and an in-depth understanding of those subjects? Can students really grasp a general understanding of "good physical health" without understanding the history of civilizations and the importance of health on survival? (How did they survive?) Isn't that related to science (diseases, vitamins, minerals, and so on) and math (calories, energy, volume, mass), and the ability to understand and critically analyze language, written or spoken?

. . . science was related to everyday life, and chemistry, physics, and biology were blended instead of taught independently, as if one has no connection to the other? Did you have breakfast today? Why? Did you have a biological need for food to provide energy? Did chemical reactions take place within your body? Did you use a microwave oven or electric range to help prepare your food? Where did the food come from? Is it natural or processed? What does that really *mean?* Have you ever been in a car accident? What happens when two masses collide? Do chemical, physical, and biological reactions occur; do police worry about things like explosions if gas and heat combust? What if one of the vehicles contains biological or chemical waste material from a hospital? Could you create rigorous and relevant science lessons that would require students to think critically, become engrossed in what they were learning and help them learn how they live science every day?

So, what if kids fail? Does it matter? Perhaps that depends on what they fail, what they were taught, and how that failure is measured (but that's another subject!). Think about the last time you failed at something—anything (a relationship, an academic test, meeting a deadline). Did you *learn* something from that? We learn best when things are relevant, when there is emotion attached, and expectations are high. What is it that students really need to know and be able to do? Do they need all of the details, or the ability to find the information, critically analyze it, and use it? I don't mean to suggest that students don't need to read, write, and apply basic math and science skills every day. They need much more if we expect to continue as a free, democratic, prosperous, and industrious nation. Should students fail and be denied access to higher education or careers because they "failed" in one area, even though they might be the next Jefferson, Edison, Chopin, Aristotle, or Picasso?

Maybe, just maybe, *we are the ones who have* really failed the students . . . and *they* haven't failed.

"The majority of public school students leave high school unprepared for more than low-paying work, unprepared for college and unprepared for the duties placed upon them by a democratic society. The schools have broken a covenant with students, and with society . . ."

—New York State Supreme Court Judge Leland DeGrasse

I³ *Write down any ideas that come to you after reading this quote.*

____

____

"To educate a man in mind, and not in morals, is to educate a menace to society."

—Theodore Roosevelt

I³ *Write down any ideas that come to you after reading this quote.*

____

____

I³ *How can you justify that both of these quotes may have merit?*

____

____

KWL

What Do You KNOW? **(prior knowledge)**

What Do You WANT to Know? **(objectives and goals)**

Are All Schools Alike?

> ***"Brainwashing is a system of befogging the brain so a person can be seduced into acceptance of what otherwise would be abhorrent to him. He loses touch with reality. Facts and fancy whirl round and change places. . . . However, in order to prevent people from recognizing the inherent evils in brainwashing, the Reds pretend that it is only another name for something already very familiar and of unquestioned respect, such as*** **education or reform."**
>
> —EDWARD HUNTER, 1956

I³ *Write down any ideas that come to you after reading this quote.*

"What's the difference between a bright, inquisitive five-year-old, and a dull, stupid nineteen-year-old? Fourteen years of the educational system."

—Bertrand Russell

I³ *Write down any ideas that come to you after reading this quote.*

I³ *How can you justify that both of these quotes may have merit?*

Since many of us have attended only a few schools, possibly only one elementary, one middle school and one secondary school, it may be difficult to answer this question. One might hypothesis that all schools are not exactly alike, but they most likely have common characteristics.

I³ *Before we begin, please list as many characteristics that you believe most schools have in common. Next, list a few aspects where you believe schools may differ.*

Is there a pattern? Do you see any common elements? Many countries develop a national template, which guides schools in their development and mission. Some believe that interpretation of these national goals or standards is highly regimented, while others observe a more random nature to the development.

I³ *What do you think of randomness? Things in nature often move in complicated ways. You have probably watched the way a butterfly moves. The molecules of the air that you are breathing move in a similar way. This type of motion we call random. You can also take a random walk. Go outside or to a large room and mark a spot on the ground. Take with you a coin. Stand on the spot and flip the coin. If the coin comes up heads, turn to the right and take a large step. If the coin comes up tails, turn to the left and take a large step. Keep doing this many times and see where you end up.*

How many times or how long did you flip the coin? Where did you end up? Why do you think this occurred?

If you flip the coin 25 times you will probably be about five steps away from where you started. This is because five times five equals 25. How far would you expect to be if you flipped the coin 100 times? When you try this, you will notice that sometimes you go much farther than you expect and sometimes you end up very close to where you started. But if you repeat it many times or get several of your friends to do it with you with coins of their own, the average distance should come out as expected. Often we can predict what will happen on the average even when the process is random.

Chances are there are many differences between your thoughts of schools and your colleagues. Some possible characteristics that you could have mentioned might include:

1. Floor space and classroom arrangement
2. Furniture and arrangement
3. Classroom organization that accommodates both didactic and constructivist instructional methods (I am sure many thought of this one)
4. Use of media such as television, computer projection devices, and computers
5. Temperature, air quality, and ventilation
6. Student access to hear and see each other and the teacher
7. Special needs of students who are physically challenged
8. Safety considerations
9. City, state, and federal building code and other legal considerations or requirements
10. Other learning considerations?

Metaphors for Schools

"Our schools have become vast factories for the manufacture of robots. We no longer send our young to them primarily to be taught and given the tools of thought, no longer primarily to be informed and acquire knowledge; but to be "socialized"—which in the current semantic means to be regimented and made to conform."

—Robert Lindner

I^3 *Write down any ideas that come to you after reading this quote.*

____

____

I^3 *Consider your high school environment for a moment. Can you provide your thoughts on what the type of metaphor school was like? (If you cannot think of any metaphors, please review the list and description below and select one, then describe how it fits your school.)*

____

____

____

____

____

____

Factories

"The strongest meshes of the school net are invisible. Unceasing competition for official favor in the dramatic fish bowl of a classroom delivers cowardly children, little people sunk in chronic boredom, little people with no apparent purpose for being alive."

—John Taylor Gatto

I^3 *Write down any ideas that come to you after reading this quote.*

____

____

A factory is typically thought of as a plant consisting of buildings with facilities for manufacturing. A factory is where you produce something efficiently. Schools may take an approach of their mission is to efficiently produce students who have the knowledge, skills, and dispositions to become literate, functioning citizens. Some believe this approach is directed more towards a vocational or skills-based philosophy of educating students in areas of securing skills necessary for securing a job. Obviously, relationships between students and faculty would be missing in this scenario. Students would feel like a number or a product being created or serviced until they were finished. This institutional approach may make student feel isolated and de-emphasize some of their avenues for learning.

Prisons

"Every time I pass a jailhouse or a school, I feel sorry for the people inside."

—Jimmy Breslin

I^3 *Write down any ideas that come to you after reading this quote.*

____

____

"Teachers who conform to the traditional institutional mode are out of place. They might find fulfillment as tap dance instructors or guards in maximum security prisons or proprietors of reducing salons or agents of the Federal Bureau of Investigation. But they damage teaching, children and themselves by staying in the classroom."

—National Education Association

I^3 *Write down any ideas that come to you after reading this quote.*

____

____

I^3 *How can you justify that both of these quotes may have merit?*

____

____

Prisons are a correctional institution where persons are confined while on trial or for punishment. There are a number of ways in which prisons are regulated, making sure that they are operated securely, just as there are a number of methods in which some schools may use to run their schools effectively. This metaphor correlates with a mandated education philosophy. Some students feel as though they are "nagged" and forced to go to school and sentenced to a minimum number of years to serve. Schools may validate this perspective by treating students like prisoners to be guarded and possibly punished. Physical attributes such as fences surrounding the school and possibly metal detectors at the entrance to schools as well as visitor check-in procedures may provide further evidence for this metaphor.

BTW

To nag is to annoy by constant urging or fault finding. European households of the early Middle Ages had a problem—rats infested every nook and corner, squirrels nested in the roofs, and the noise of gnawing was disturbing. The Germans developed the word *nagen*, from an old Scandinavian term meaning to gnaw. Eventually a person who gnawed at another was said to nag.

Homes

Some schools, especially in smaller districts may appear to have characteristics of a home, and be warm, friendly, nurturing, caring places. A student will feel like they belong, they are noticed (not guarded) and are accepted as a person. They may feel like teacher are similar to parents and caregivers. Physical characteristics such as furniture, lighting, temperature can play a major role in this environment. Typically absent are large fences and metal detectors such as in the Prison metaphor. These environments can assist some students in learning that operates on more of an affective domain.

Churches

A church is typically a place or building of public religious worship. The components of a church could be a main building or sanctuary for worship, a pulpit, seats or pews, and a balcony. Several direct analogies could be made between the physical characteristics of a church and a school. More importantly are the philosophical comparisons between what a church may offer and what typically a private, Christian school will provide.

Social Realities in Education

"Public education does not serve the public. It creates the public. And in creating the right kind of public . . ."

—Richard Riley

I³ *Write down any ideas that come to you after reading this quote.*

What is the role of education in socializing young people? There have been many debates on this topic as well as blame, credit, and otherwise. This is another component of a good pre-service candidate's philosophy to education. Understanding historical aspects of socialization in schools, the reform movements and ultimately synthesizing your beliefs and ideas on your obligations in this area. Students will spend a significant amount of their formative portion of their lives with teachers. To believe that teachers will not play a role in socializing may be naïve. Even if teachers agree not to play a role; that decision in itself will have an impact on how students behave in society.

Frequently, the direction of this conversation leans toward values and morals, which may or should be taught in schools in order to socialize and/or develop a person who will contribute a positive effect on society. The ideology of values and morals is obviously subjective and may put us on a slippery slope of well intentions.

"To suggest for a moment that morality and ethics are not being taught in government-controlled schools is ridiculous. . . . A definite point-of-view from a definite culture is being imposed. . . . It is outrageous that values taught in public schools are not the same ones held by Catholic parents, or by non-Catholic Christians and Jewish parents as well."

—Archbishop Edward Egan of New York

I^3 *Write down any ideas that come to you after reading this quote.*

____

____

I^3 *What are values? Provide some examples as well as some of your own values.*

____

____

____

____

I^3 *What are morals? Provide some examples as well as some of your own morals.*

____

____

____

____

It does not take long to see that these terms and what they mean are distinctly different for each of us. Consider how difficult it would be for a school district or even a school to create and impose a set of values and morals for everyone. Many schools have developed baseline values on conduct and behavior. However, just because these are difficult concepts, we should not avoid a discussion. It is only through dialogue and debate that we may arrive at a reasonable direction in which to pursue these issues.

Roles

"I doubt whether reams of propaganda pamphlets, endless reiteration that all is well with our schools, or even pressure tactics will again fool the American people into believing that education can safely be left to the 'professional' educators."

—Admiral Hyman G. Rickover

I³ *Write down any ideas that come to you after reading this quote.*

____

____

There are many people and entities involved in education; some include the federal and state governments, the districts, the schools, teachers, parents, and students. There are even more perspectives on the roles that each of these groups should play in the development and education of students. This is yet another area where pre-service teachers can consider their background, learn of historical approaches, and attempt to develop their own beliefs and philosophies on the best means to designate roles and responsibilities.

Schools

A school is a large group of fish. A school sometimes also means a public or nonprofit approved or accredited organizational entity devoted primarily to approved academic, vocational, or professional study and instruction, which operates primarily for educational purposes. It is also a place of learning with many varieties, including elementary, secondary, and high school; technical, professional, community college, and university; continuing education and graduate studies.

Traditional school roles are at times unclear as school members may be willing to do whatever is needed to ensure all students do well, physically, emotionally, socially, and academically. This approach may be framed in a mission statement, by a principal who requires or inspires it from their faculty and staff or by a community who endorses and rewards this type of an approach.

Teachers

"Schools will become clinics whose purpose is to provide individualized, psycho-social treatment for the student, and teachers must become psycho-social therapists."

—National Education Association

I³ *Write down any ideas that come to you after reading this quote.*

____

____

Teachers may take on a major role of socializing, caring, and being responsible for the outcomes of their students. This tends to be highly individualized, random and personalized. However, others believe that with the increase in accountability, testing, inclusion (mainstreaming), ESOL, special education, and decrease in resource teachers, such as in art, music, and physical education, teachers may become less able to individualize their care and attention to socializing students. Teachers who feel overwhelmed will exhibit stress and behave as most of us do, thereby becoming less effective, less personal and trying to find methods to lower their workload. As a new teacher, these demands will appear to be even more overwhelming as you become acclimated to a novel environment where everything is new to you. Many veteran teachers recommend trying to develop a routine as quickly as possible, create forms, organizational methods, plans, structures, and so on; anything that will assist the instruction in the future.

Parents

"We who are engaged in the sacred cause of education are entitled to look upon all parents as having given hostages to our cause."

—Horace Mann

I³ *Write down any ideas that come to you after reading this quote.*

____

____

The roles of parents differ dramatically from school to school and from greatly between social economic status. Some districts have policies against significant parental involvement and others have guidelines requiring some level of involvement. Parents are known to be from strong advocates to passive, apathetic participants. The full range of spectrum can be seen from parental perspectives as to their role and to the school and teachers role on raising their children. Some parents are intimately involved with student work, assignments, and completion of these works (possibly to the extent of managing their science fair project). At times, parents may feel as though they are the true client, as they are paying for education with their tax money and sending their children into the schools to receive services.

School Societal Issues

"Much more is to be gained by teaching disciplined historical thinking than by having students engage, while conceptually unprepared, the crucial issues that beset our society at the present."

—Dr. Kieran Egan

I³ *Write down any ideas that come to you after reading this quote.*

____

____

"Biographical history, as taught in our public schools, is still largely a history of boneheads: ridiculous kings and queens, paranoid political leaders, compulsive voyagers, ignorant generals—the flotsam and jetsam of historical currents."

—Martin Gardner

I³ *Write down any ideas that come to you after reading this quote.*

"*Teachers and administrators should come to see themselves as social engineers. They must equip themselves as change agents.*"

—Journal of Progressive Education, May 1949

I³ *Write down any ideas that come to you after reading this quote.*

I³ *How can you justify that these quotes may have merit?*

Students at Risk

Students at risk are at risk of dropping out of school. This brief, vague definition continues to be argued among the stake-holders of education. Some believe that adults place students at risk, including parents, teachers. and administrators. There are various reasons why a student might be classified as "as risk," including did not advance to another level, test scores were low, pregnant, or are a parent; substance abuse; placed in alternative education; expulsion; on probation; is an ESOL student; is homeless; and lives in a violent or abusive home, and/or in a low SES environment. Students who are living with one parent, a member of a minority group, have limited English proficiency, and so on are defined as at risk because, statistically, students in these categories are more likely to be among the lowest achievement groups or drop out of school. However, this approach rarely leads to any examination of fundamental aspects of the school (Natriello, et al., 1990). In addition, school attributes have been found to contribute to at-risk students. These characteristics include inflexible schedules; narrow curricula; a priority focus on basic/lower-order skills; inappropriate, limited, and rigid instructional strategies; inappropriate texts and other instructional materials; over-reliance on standardized tests to make instructional and curricular decisions; tracking; isolated pull-out programs; and teacher and administrators' beliefs and attitudes toward both students and their parents (Richardson & Colfer, 1990).

What are the systematic barriers to students at risk? The National Coalition of Advocates for Children (NCAC, 1988) provides the following possibilities:

1. Discrimination and Differential Treatment
2. Structural and Programmatic Barriers
3. The Societal Context: Declining Support for Schools, Children, and Families

Richardson & Colfer (1990) indicate that the responsibility for the at-risk status of a child, does not reside in one individual—be it the child, mother, or teacher—or in one institution—the school. Society creates schools in certain ways to meet its goals and expectations, thus creating environments in which certain children are at risk. The solution to the at-riskness of children and youth, then lies with us all.

Poverty

"Many students, especially those who are poor, intuitively know what the schools do for them. They school them to confuse process and substance. Once these become blurred, a new logic is assumed: the more treatment there is, the better are the results; or, escalation leads to success. The pupil is thereby "schooled" to confuse teaching with learning, grade advancement with education, a diploma with competence, and fluency with the ability to say something new. His imagination is "schooled" to accept service in place of value. Medical treatment is mistaken for health care, social work for the improvement of community life, police protection for safety, military poise for national security, the rat race for productive work. Health, learning, dignity, independence, and creative endeavor are defined as little more than the performance of the institutions which claim to serve these ends, and their improvement is made to depend on allocating more resources to the management of hospitals, schools, and other agencies in question."

—Ivan Illich

I³ *Write down any ideas that come to you after reading this quote.*

____

____

Poverty is the state of having little or no money and few or no material possessions. Poverty is synonymous with destitution. Destitution is a state without friends or money or prospects. The term poverty was first used in 1075. In recent years, research has recognized that poverty involves a wider set of deprivations, including vulnerability and exclusion from society, in addition to material destitution.

There are many effect of poverty on children in school, including nutritional, self-esteem, developmental, attitude, aptitude, connectedness, social norms, and so on.

An August 5, 1996 Department of Education (DOE) report found that even after accounting for poverty concentration in schools, the following was determined:

- Teacher absenteeism, an indicator of morale, was more of a problem in urban schools than in rural or suburban schools;
- Student behavior problems were more common in urban schools than in other schools, particularly in absenteeism, classroom discipline, weapons possession, and student pregnancy. However, the use of alcohol was less of a problem in urban schools that in rural schools;
- Students in high-poverty schools regardless of location were less likely to feel safe in school, or to spend much time on homework than those in low-poverty schools; eighth graders in urban and urban high-poverty schools scored lower on achievement tests, but their tenth-grade counterparts scored about the same as those in other locations;
- Students in urban and urban high-poverty schools were less likely to complete high school on time, but they completed post-secondary degrees at the same rate as others;
- Young adults who had attended urban and urban high-poverty schools had much higher poverty and unemployment rates later in life than those who had attended other schools.

I³ *What are some inferences and predictions you can make from this data?*

____

____

Violence

"Violence appears to be most commonly a result of threatened egotism—that is, highly favorable views of self that are disputed by some person or circumstance. . . . violence is perpetrated by a small subset of people with favorable views of themselves. . . . Viewed in this light, the societal pursuit of high self-esteem for everyone may literally end up doing considerable harm."

—Roy Baumeister, Joseph Boden, and Laura Smart, 2004

I³ *Write down any ideas that come to you after reading this quote.*

____

____

Violence is an act of aggression as one against a person who resists. It is physical and non-physical harm that causes damage and pain. It is a public health and safety condition that often results from individual, social, economic, political, and institutional disregard for basic human needs. Violence disrupts the school environment and results in a debilitation of personal development, which may lead to hopelessness and helplessness.

Several studies have indicated that over half of the students believe that an event such as the Columbine shooting could occur in their school. How accurate are these perceptions? Between 1993 and 2003, 270 violent deaths have occurred at schools across the nation, the majority being shooting deaths (The National School Safety Center's Report on School Associated Violent Deaths).

The following information comes from the U.S. Department of Education's National Center for Education Statistics (NCES, 2004).

- 57% of public elementary and secondary school principals stated that one or more incidents of crime or violence were reported to the police
- 10% of all public schools had one or more serious violent crimes (murder, rape, sexual battery, suicide, physical attack, or fight with a weapon, or robbery)
- The most reported crime was physical attacks or fights without a weapon
- Most of the serious violent crimes occurred in the middle and high schools
- A larger percentage of violent crimes occurred in city schools and in large schools

Violence in schools is also sensationalized by the news media. Many times there are news segments highlighting an arrest or an incident at a school. Students may bring weapons to school for a variety of reasons and when caught, the public quickly hears about the case.

- How much should you attempt to manage a violent situation?
- Where should the line be drawn in the classroom?
- Will the administration support you in your decision to discipline?

In 2004, in Duval County, Florida, there was an incident of violence on a middle-school bus returning students home that was on the national news. This event showed a video from the school bus of one student sitting in his seat while seven or eight other students stood above and beat him. There was no cause, reason, rationale, or justification. While observing the video, one can see the crowd behavior of joining in and when watched carefully, one particular young man who joins in the beating displays a gleeful smile while repeatedly striking the defenseless student.

I³ *Do you have any experiences with violence in the schools? If so, please share these below, if not, please share any examples, which you have seen or heard through the media. Finally, provide your thoughts on the current situation of violence in the schools and how you might handle a violent situation.*

____

____

____

____

Teen Pregnancy

In the United States, approximately 1 million teens get pregnant each year (Dehner, et al., 2002). Seventy percent of teens do not receive adequate care. Teen pregnancy is also associated with limiting the teen's chance for furthering her education and career aspirations (Aries, 2001). Something as important as pregnancy can certainly contribute to placing a student at risk of dropping out of school. Various districts have prevention programs and others have day care where the teen mother can bring their child to school, visit them at lunch, and continue to take classes to graduate. Schools routinely do not track the educational paths of pregnant and mothering students. As a result, quantitative research and subsequent theory and applications are minimal.

Substance Abuse

> ***"DARE relies on the old 'values clarification' approach wherein children are not told what is right or wrong, or permissible or impermissible, but rather they are helped to prize and act upon their own freely chosen values. Thus DARE does not tell children that they must not use drugs. Instead, DARE tells them that they have the 'right to say no,' implying that they have the 'right to say yes.'"***
>
> —Richard M. Evans, 1994

I³ *Write down any ideas that come to you after reading this quote.*

____

____

Substance abuse is the uncontrollable or excessive abuse of addictive substances, such as alcohol, drugs or other chemicals and the resultant physiological and/or psychological dependency, which develops with continued use. It is also defined as the taking of alcohol or other drugs at dosages that place a person's social, economic, psychological, and physical welfare in potential hazard, or endanger public health, morals, safety, or welfare. Substance abuse by the student or by persons at home can create a detrimental environment for the student and dramatically increase their level of risk. Many programs have been received with lukewarm attitudes.

> **BTW**
>
> Lukewarm means barely warm. Luke was a Middle English word, now obsolete meaning *warm,* which was based on *lew,* another word for warm. *Lew,* in turn was derived from the Old English word *hleow,* meaning *warm,* hence it all means "warm-warm."

Societal Perspectives—Examples to Consider

The following three scenarios present various perspectives on our society. Please read each of them and respond with your thoughts.

1. *Are We Rude?*
   People say you're rude. You walk around talking into that cell phone like you are the only person for miles. You curse like Madonna, your kids think the world is their personal playground, and you drive like a maniac.

   That's what respondents indicate on a national survey about America's manners. About 79% of over 2,000 adults surveyed by telephone said a lack of respect and courtesy in American society is a serious problem. Sixty-one percent believe things have gotten worse in recent years.

   Poor customer service has become so rampant that nearly half of those surveyed said that they have walked out of a store in the past year because of it. Half said they often see people talking on their cellular phones in a loud or annoying manner. And six drivers in ten said they regularly see other people driving aggressively or recklessly.

   Many people admitted to rude behavior themselves. More than one third said they use foul language in public. About the same percentage confessed to occasional bad driving.

   Do you see an epidemic of rudeness?
   What sorts of rude behavior bother you?
   Why are we becoming so rude?
   What do you think is contributing to this phenomenon?
   What is the best way to respond to rudeness?

2. *Vicious Dogs*
   This was a terrible tragedy. A woman was attacked and killed by two dogs belonging to a neighbor. One of the dogs, 110-pound Hera was held in isolation. A second dog, Bane, was put to death after the fatal attack in 2001. The owner of the dogs involved in the attack that killed a woman in the hallway outside her apartment said the dogs never showed any indications that they were violent. The couple could face manslaughter charges under a state law regarding dogs trained to fight, attack, or kill.

   In a news conference, the husband of the owner of the dogs said that his wife should not be held responsible.

   Do you have a dog (s)? If so, what type?
   So, do you think the owner of these dogs should be held responsible for manslaughter?

Do you think that certain breeds or types of dogs should be considered "dangerous" by virtue of their temperament and/or breeding patterns?
Should these animals be regarded as just "pets"?
What would you do if you were the judge in this case?
What would you do if you were the owners of the dogs?
What would you do if you were the spouse of the victim?

3. *Is Torture All Right?*

The United States has captured several known terrorists, who have recruited, trained, and assisted in terrorist activities. The capture of these people is very valuable, since they are suspected of planning further terrorist attacks and establishing al Qaeda cells around the world.

Intelligence believes that these prisoners can provide a treasure trove of information regarding the terrorist organization, possibly including plans for future attacks.

On the news, they were discussing the question of whether these people should be tortured—if necessary in order for the United States to gain valuable information about plans for future terrorists operatives.

Now torture is condoned by the international human rights groups, but that does not mean it is a method that is never used.

What do you think?
If torturing could lead to information which would prevent future terrorists attacks on the United States, would you believe it is an acceptable measure?
Is all fair in war?
What other options could you suggest?
If you were the head of the Intelligence Service, what would you do?
If you were a mother of a 911 victim, what would you do?
If you were the father of an admitted terrorist, what would you do?

KWL

What Did You LEARN?

References

Aries, Elizabeth. (2001). *Adolescent Behavior: Readings and Interpretations.* Columbus, OH: McGraw-Hill/Dushkin.

Baumeister, R., Boden, J., & Smart, L. (2004). Relation of Threatened Egotism to Violence and Aggression: The Dark Side of High Self-Esteem. *Psychological Review, 103(1),* 5.

Dehner, K., Leger, J., Burdrow, D. I., Herdia, S. (2002). Accessed February 12, 2002, from *http://www.bu.edu/cohis/teenpreg/teenpreg.htm*

Evans, R. M. (1994). *The Boston Globe,* September 21, 1994. Accessed June 2004, from *http://www.drcnet.org/DARE/excerpts.html#muddled*

Hunter, E. (1956). *Brainwashing.* New York: Pyramid Books.

Natriello, G., McDill, E. L., & Pallas, A. M. (1990). *Schooling disadvantaged children: Racing against catastrophe.* New York: Teachers College Press.

Richardson, V., & Colfer, P. (1990). Being at-risk in school. In J. Goodlad & P. Keating (Eds). *Access to knowledge: An agenda for our nation's schools.* New York: College Entrance Examination Board.

U.S. Department of Education's National Center for Education Statistics (NCES). Accessed June 8, 2004, from *http://712educators.about.com/gi/dynamic/offsite.htm?zi=1/XJ&sdn=712educators&zu=http%3A%2F%2Fnces.ed.gov%2Fpubs98%2Fviolence*

PowerPoint Outline to Assist In-Class Note-Taking

A. **Are All Schools Alike?**

  a. Metaphors for schools (factories, prisons, homes, churches)

B. **Social Realities in Education**

  a. Roles (Schools, Teachers, Parents)

  b. School Societal Issues

    i. Students at Risk

    ii. Poverty

    iii. Violence

    iv. Teen Pregnancy

    v. Substance Abuse

C. **Societal Perspectives—Examples to Consider**

7

School Governance

Guest Editorial: Gary Senn, PhD, Assistant Professor of Science Education and Director, Dupont Planetarium, University of South Carolina, Aiken

"I have a question regarding the education of my child. May I speak to the person in charge?" You might be surprised at the variety of answers to this question. One obvious answer might be, "Speak to your child's teacher." The classroom teacher has day-to-day contact with the student and provides direct oversight regarding the education of the student. The teacher plans the lessons and makes decisions on how to direct learning. However, is the teacher the one in charge of the education of the child? To whom is the teacher accountable?

Perhaps the department head or educational team leader provides oversight of the teacher. Perhaps this person determines when certain topics are covered or provides input into the structure of lessons. If the department head is not really responsible for the instruction that occurs with other teachers then perhaps an assistant principal is the person in charge. An assistant principal often has evaluation responsibility and it is quite likely that instruction will be influenced through the evaluation of teaching. A person in this position has authority over the educational process and a sense of being in charge might properly be assigned to this person.

If there is an assistant principal then there must be a principal. The principal might be a good answer to the question since that position has responsibility over the activities at the school. The principal has to make sure that the heating and air conditioning are in working order. The principal usually hires the teachers and determines where they will be teaching. The principal attends sporting activities to support the team and make sure the crowd does not get unruly. The principal makes sure that lunch is a smooth operation. The principal makes sure that the teachers have all of the supplies they need and might even provide teachers with a $75 budget to purchase all of the necessary instructional materials.

The person in charge of the education of a child would probably determine the content that is taught in the classroom. Who determines this? There are probably standards, goals, and objectives that direct what is taught in the classroom. These standards might be established by the school district. Who is in charge there? There is a superintendent and, perhaps, there are a number of assistant superintendents. These people supervise the principals and that provides further evidence that they might be the people in charge. What about state standards? The state department of education develops and adopts those. Maybe the state superintendent of schools or the commissioner for education is the one in charge.

The federal government has an influence on what is taught in the classroom. There are certain expectations on what is taught and on the qualifications of teachers that are directed at this level so perhaps one needs to identify a federal representative as the person in charge.

While standards and directives come from state and federal authorities, local school boards play an important role. School boards determine local policy and have authority over superintendents and principals. Perhaps it is someone on the school board who is in charge. How does one become a member of a school board and what qualifications are required? The public elects school board members and there typically is no set of required qualifications.

There was a student in a teacher preparation program, who became acquainted with a cashier at a grocery store. Over the course of time and many visits to the grocery store, the cashier and the student would talk about education and the impact it had on the cashier's children. This cashier had a very strong opinion on how schools should be governed and continued to insist that she could do a better job than those who were on the school board at the time. The student became a teacher and while he was in his second year of teaching, he was surprised to learn that this very same cashier was running for the school board. An even greater surprise that developed into concern was that this cashier was elected and then served on the school board.

Who is in charge of the education of children? It is difficult to say. One thing to consider, however, is that you should take care in how you treat your grocery cashier. She might be in charge of the education of your child some day.

> ***"Governance of many schools is such that you turn the steering wheel but the vehicle doesn't turn."***
>
> —U.S. Secretary of Education Rod Paige

I^3 *Write down any ideas that come to you after reading this quote.*

> ***"There is, on the whole, nothing on Earth intended for innocent people so horrible as a school."***
>
> —George Bernard Shaw

I^3 *Write down any ideas that come to you after reading this quote.*

I^3 *How can you justify that both of these quotes may have merit?*

KWL

What Do You KNOW? **(prior knowledge)**

What Do You WANT to Know? **(objectives and goals)**

Who Controls Schools?

"An education established and controlled by the State, should only exist, if it exist at all, as one among many competing experiments, carried on for the purpose of example and stimulus, to keep the others up to a certain standard of excellence."

—John Stuart Mill

I³ *Write down any ideas that come to you after reading this quote.*

"The major roadblock to the advance of school choice in the suburbs is not how to pursue a solution, but for families first to recognize there is a problem and that they have little choice or control over what their children are taught in public schools."

—George A. Clowes

I³ *Write down any ideas that come to you after reading this quote.*

I³ *How can you justify that both of these quotes may have merit?*

"That the National Education Association (NEA) advocated federal aid has surprised us at times but no longer. For control—real control—over the nation's children is being shifted rapidly to the National Education Association. That organization has about completed the job of cartelizing public school education under its own cartel. It is doing so under an organization known as the National Council for Accreditation of Teachers Education, an agency whose governing council is tightly NEA-controlled. The manner in which the NEA is usurping parental prerogatives by determining the type of education offered is very simple: control the education and hiring of teachers. NEA has no apprehension regarding federal control of public schools as a consequence of federal aid. It has control itself. . . . In the NEA scheme of things, it will be a simple matter to extend control over whatever Washington agency handles the funds."

—CHICAGO SUN-TIMES, OCTOBER 1962

I³ *Write down any ideas that come to you after reading this quote.*

___

___

"We are the biggest potential political fighting force in this country, and we are determined to control the direction of American education."

—CATHERINE BARON, PRESIDENT, NATIONAL EDUCATION ASSOCIATION, 1972

I³ *Write down any ideas that come to you after reading this quote.*

___

___

There many philosophies and possible entities in line aggressively pursuing control of the schools. Some of the parties include the National Educational Association, federal, state, and local authorities, local school districts and school boards, administrators, teachers, and teacher unions, parents and parent teacher organizations, students, taxpayers, minorities, and women, theorists, and researchers and corporations. Throughout this chapter, we will discuss the entities vying for control of the schools. The answer is typically a gray area, since control varies from state to state and district to district as well as from issue to issue. Many pre-service teachers are surprised by the intense interest in controlling the schools.

I³ *Why do you believe there is so much interest in controlling the schools? Why are there so many players in this game? Predict what a few of the players might gain if they were in control of the schools. Finally, which of the players do you believe should have a major control in the direction of the schools?*

___

___

___

___

Who Controls Me?

How Many Bosses Will I Have?

> ***"The person who says it can't be done should not interrupt the person doing it."***
>
> —CHINESE PROVERB

I³ *Write down any ideas that come to you after reading this quote.*

____

____

Of great concern to many pre-service and in-service teachers is autonomy. Many people ventured into the business of teaching because of the appeal of being in more control of their day-to-day activities. Strict oversight by a boss is typically an undesirable attribute of teaching and as so, an obvious question of pre-service teachers is how many bosses will I have? The response is not linear, however, ultimately, the news is not too bad. At times, simple luck plays a role in oversight structure.

BTW

The belief that four-leaf clovers are good luck come from the Druids, ancient residents of the British Isles. Several times a year, they gathered in oak groves to settle legal disputes and offer sacrifices . . . then they ended their rituals by hunting four-leaf clovers. Why? They believed a four-leaf clover enabled its owner to see evil spirits and witches and therefore avoid them.

National Education Association (NEA)

"Cardinal Principles of Education" (National Education Association (NEA) Commission on the Reorganization of Secondary Curriculum, 1918)

1. Health
2. Command of fundamental processes
3. Worthy home membership
4. Vocation
5. Civics
6. Worthy use of leisure
7. Ethical Character

"We are convinced that we stand today at the verge of a great culture. . . . but to achieve these things, many drastic changes must be made. A dying laissez-faire must be completely destroyed, and all of us, including the owners, must be subjected to a large degree of social control."

—NATIONAL EDUCATION ASSOCIATION, 1951

I^3 *Write down any ideas that come to you after reading this quote.*

____

____

The National Educational Association (NEA) is the largest education association and has over 2.7 million members that work across many disciplines and levels of education. The NEA is not necessarily your boss, however, it will be one of the many governing bodies, which will be guiding your profession, either directly or indirectly. NEA was founded in 1857 to elevate the character and advance the interests of the profession of teaching and to promote the cause of popular education in the United States. The NEA's current mission statement is to fulfill the promise of a democratic society, the NEA shall promote the cause of quality public education and advance the profession of education; expand the rights and further the interest of educational employees; and advocate human, civil, and economic rights for all.

Anyone who works for a public school system can join NEA and there are memberships for college students studying to become teachers. National dues are $13 per year. State and local dues are determined by individual state and local affiliates. There are some benefits in joining this organization as a pre-service teachers. Some of the benefits include discounts on professional and consumer products and services, including:

- mortgage plan with low down-payment options
- early-start investment plan for retirement
- health and life insurance
- dues rebate after graduation—during your first year of teaching and regular NEA membership, you will be eligible to receive a rebate of $20 for each year you were a student member.
- Scholarships
- Publications—NEA Today, Tomorrow's Teachers, and your state newsletter.

Federal Agency—U.S. Department of Education (USDOE)

In the United States, the federal role in education is limited. Because of the Tenth Amendment, most education policy is decided at the state and local levels. National standards are created broadly and forwarded to each state department of education, which interprets, typically increases their rigor, then provides and monitors district application of the standards. One of the most recent actions that the federal government has taken is enacting a law that governs education in the states. The No Child Left Behind (NCLB) law was enacted in 2001. Under *No Child Left Behind,* each state must measure every public school student's progress in reading and math. By school year 2007–2008, assessments in science will be underway. These assessments must be aligned with state academic content and achievement standards. They will provide parents with objective data on where their child stands academically. This law also proposes to supports learning in the early years, provide more information for parents about their child's progress, alert parents to important information on the performance of their child's school, give children and parents a lifeline, improve teaching and learning by providing better information to teachers and principals, ensure that teacher quality is a high priority, give more resources to schools, allow more flexibility, and focus on what works.

Congress also reauthorized the *Elementary and Secondary Education Act (ESEA),* the principal federal law affecting education from kindergarten through high school. In amending ESEA, the new law represents an overhaul of federal efforts to support elementary and secondary education in the United States. It is built on four common-sense pillars: accountability for results, an emphasis on doing what works based on scientific research, expanded parental options, and expanded local control and flexibility.

The U.S. DOE houses and supports organizations that provide research, evaluation, and statistics, including the Institute of Education Sciences, DOE's main agency for research, evaluation, and dissemination, statistics, and guidance to further evidence-based policy and practice; National Center for Education Statistics; National Assessment of Educational Progress, Policy and Program Studies Service and the National Research and Dissemination Centers for Career and Technical Education.

State Power

This text will use the state of Florida's Department of Education (FLDOE) as an example of state power in the educational arena. Each state has its own DOE with its own individual philosophies and governance.

The FLDOE has a governor, lieutenant governor, commissioner of education, a state board of education and a board of governors as well as the departments of accountability, research and measurement, administrative services, colleges and universities, community colleges, educational facilities, educational technology, educator certification, family and community outreach, general counsel, grants development, grants management, Just Read, Florida! office, K–12 public schools, leadership development and organizational improvement, personnel management, workforce education and blind services.

Governor

"If it is believed that these schools will be better managed by the governor and council, the commissioners of the literary fund, or any other general authority of the government, than by the parents within each ward, it is a belief against all experience. No my friend, the way to have good and safe government is not to trust it all to one but to divide it among the many, distributing to everyone exactly the functions he is competent to."

—Thomas Jefferson, February 2, 1816

"Governors must arm themselves with the power which knowledge gives."

—James Madison

I³ *Write down any ideas that come to you after reading this quote.*

____

____

The governor is the head of the state government. The governor is responsible for day-to-day operations of the state and is the chief law enforcement officer. The governor appoints not only the heads of departments under sole oversight of the governor, but also the heads of departments that are under both the governor and cabinet's oversight. The governor also appoints members of several regulatory boards and commissions, such as the commissioner of education.

Department of Education

1001.23 Specific powers and duties of the Department of Education. In addition to all other duties assigned to it by law or by rule of the State Board of Education, the department shall:

1. Adopt the school readiness uniform screening developed by the Florida Partnership for School Readiness, in accordance with the criteria itemized in chapter 1008.
2. Implement a training program to develop among state and district educators a cadre of facilitators of school improvement in accordance with the provisions of chapter 1008.
3. Identify the needs of the state system of public education as they relate to the development and production of materials used in instruction, in accordance with the requirements of chapter 1006.
4. After complying with the provisions of s. 257.37, the Department of Education may:
   a. Photograph, microphotograph, or reproduce on film or prints, documents, records, data, and information of a permanent character and destroy any of the documents after they have been photographed and after audit of the department has been completed for the period embracing the dates of the instruments. Photographs or microphotographs in the form of film or prints made in compliance with the provisions of this subsection shall have the same force and effect as the originals would have, and shall be treated as originals for the purpose of their admissibility in evidence. Duly certified or authenticated reproductions of such photographs or microphotographs shall be admitted in evidence equally with the original photographs or microphotographs.
   b. Destroy general correspondence that is over 3 years old; records of bills, accounts, vouchers, and requisitions that are over 5 years old and copies of which have been filed with the Chief Financial Officer; and other records, papers, and documents over 3 years old that do not serve as part of an agreement or understanding and do not have value as permanent records.

Commissioner of Education

The commissioner of education, who is sometimes referred to as the "education czar," will govern the state's educational arena along with three deputy commissioners—one for the state's 3,500 public schools, a second for its twenty-eight community colleges, and a third for the ten university campuses. The job of education commissioner or "czar" changes from an elected to an appointed position by the governor.

1001.10 Commissioner of Education; general powers and duties. The Commissioner of Education is the chief educational officer of the state, and is responsible for giving full assistance to the State Board of Education in enforcing compliance with the mission and goals of the seamless K–20 education system. To facilitate innovative practices and to allow local selection of educational methods, the State Board of Education may authorize the commissioner to waive, upon the request of a district school board, State Board of Education rules that relate to district school instruction and school operations, except those rules pertaining to civil rights, and student health, safety, and welfare. The Commissioner of Education is not authorized to grant waivers for any provisions in rule pertaining to the allocation and appropriation of state and local funds for public education; the election, compensation, and organization of school board members and superintendents; graduation and state accountability standards; financial reporting requirements; reporting of out-of-field teaching assignments under s. 1012.42; public meetings; public records; or due process hearings governed by chapter 120. No later than January 1 of each year, the commissioner shall report to the Legislature and the State Board of Education all approved waiver requests in the preceding year. Additionally, the commissioner has the following general powers and duties:

1. To appoint staff necessary to carry out his or her powers and duties.
2. To advise and counsel with the State Board of Education on all matters pertaining to education; to recommend to the State Board of Education actions and policies as, in the commissioner's opinion, should be acted upon or adopted; and to execute or provide for the execution of all acts and policies as are approved.
3. To keep such records as are necessary to set forth clearly all acts and proceedings of the State Board of Education.
4. To have a seal for his or her office with which, in connection with his or her own signature, the commissioner shall authenticate true copies of decisions, acts, or documents.
5. To recommend to the State Board of Education policies and steps designed to protect and preserve the principal of the State School Fund; to provide an assured and stable income from the fund; to execute such policies and actions as are approved; and to administer the State School Fund.
6. To take action on the release of mineral rights based upon the recommendations of the Board of Trustees of the Internal Improvement Trust Fund.
7. To submit to the State Board of Education, on or before August 1 of each year, recommendations for a coordinated K–20 education budget that estimates the expenditures for the State Board of Education, including the Department of Education, the Commissioner of Education, and all of the boards, institutions, agencies, and services under the general supervision of the State Board of Education for the ensuing fiscal year. Any program recommended to the State Board of Education that will require increases in state funding for more than 1 year must be presented in a multiyear budget plan.
8. To develop and implement a plan for cooperating with the Federal Government in carrying out any or all phases of the educational program and to recommend policies for administering funds that are appropriated by Congress and apportioned to the state for any or all educational purposes.
9. To develop and implement policies for cooperating with other public agencies in carrying out those phases of the program in which such cooperation is required by law or is deemed by the commissioner to be desirable and to cooperate with public and nonpublic agencies in planning and bringing about improvements in the educational program.
10. To prepare forms and procedures as are necessary to be used by district school boards and all other educational agencies to assure uniformity, accuracy, and efficiency in the keeping of records, the execution of contracts, the preparation of budgets, or the submission of reports; and to furnish at state expense, when deemed advisable by the commissioner, those forms that can more economically and efficiently be provided.
11. To implement a program of school improvement and education accountability designed to provide all students the opportunity to make adequate learning gains in each year of school as provided by statute and State Board of Education rule based upon the achievement of the state education goals, recognizing the following:
    a. The State Board of Education is the body corporate responsible for the supervision of the system of public education.

b. The district school board is responsible for school and student performance.
c. The individual school is the unit for education accountability.
d. The community college board of trustees is responsible for community college performance and student performance.
e. The university board of trustees is responsible for university performance and student performance.

12. To establish a Citizen Information Center responsible for the preparation, publication, and distribution of materials relating to the state system of seamless K–20 public education.
13. To prepare and publish annually reports giving statistics and other useful information pertaining to the Opportunity Scholarship Program.
14. To have printed or electronic copies of school laws, forms, instruments, instructions, and rules of the State Board of Education and provide for their distribution.
15. To develop criteria for use by state instructional materials committees in evaluating materials submitted for adoption consideration. The criteria shall, as appropriate, be based on instructional expectations reflected in curriculum frameworks and student performance standards. The criteria for each subject or course shall be made available to publishers of instructional materials pursuant to the requirements of chapter 1006.
16. To prescribe procedures for evaluating instructional materials submitted by publishers and manufacturers in each adoption.

The commissioner's office shall operate all statewide functions necessary to support the State Board of Education and the K–20 education system, including strategic planning and budget development, general administration, and assessment and accountability.

State Board of Education (SBE)

Florida Statutes 1001.01 State Board of Education indicates that the state board shall be a citizen board consisting of seven members who are residents of the state appointed by the Governor to staggered 4-year terms, subject to confirmation by the Senate. Members of the state board shall serve without compensation but shall be entitled to reimbursement of travel and per diem expenses. The SBE is the chief implementing and coordinating body of public education in Florida, and it shall focus on high-level policy decisions. It has authority to adopt rules pursuant to implement the provisions of law conferring duties upon it for the improvement of the state system of K–20 public education. It may delegate its general powers to the Commissioner of Education.

The State Board of Education has the following duties:

a. To adopt comprehensive educational objectives for public education.
b. To adopt comprehensive long-range plans and short-range programs for the development of the state system of public education.
c. To exercise general supervision over the divisions of the Department of Education as necessary to ensure coordination of educational plans and programs and resolve controversies and to minimize problems of articulation and student transfers, to ensure that students moving from one level of education to the next have acquired competencies necessary for satisfactory performance at that level, and to ensure maximum utilization of facilities.
d. To adopt for state universities and community colleges, and from time to time modify, minimum and uniform standards of college-level communication and computation skills generally associated with successful performance and progression through the baccalaureate level and to identify college-preparatory high school coursework and postsecondary-level coursework that prepares students with the academic skills necessary to succeed in postsecondary education.

e. To adopt and submit to the Governor and Legislature, on or before September 1 of each year, a coordinated K-20 education budget that estimates the expenditure requirements for the State Board of Education, including the Department of Education, the Commissioner of Education, and all of the boards, institutions, agencies, and services under the general supervision of the State Board of Education for the ensuing fiscal year. Any program recommended by the State Board of Education, which will require increases in state funding for more than 1 year, must be presented in a multiyear budget plan.
f. To hold meetings, transact business, keep records, adopt a seal, and perform such other duties as may be necessary for the enforcement of all laws and rules relating to the state system of public education.
g. To approve plans for cooperating with the Federal Government.
h. To approve plans for cooperating with other public agencies in the development of rules and in the enforcement of laws for which the state board and such agencies are jointly responsible.
i. To review plans for cooperating with appropriate nonpublic agencies for the improvement of conditions relating to the welfare of schools.
j. To create such subordinate advisory bodies as are required by law or as it finds necessary for the improvement of education.
k. To constitute any education bodies or other structures as required by federal law.
l. To assist in the economic development of the state by developing a state-level planning process to identify future training needs for industry, especially high-technology industry.
m. To assist in the planning and economic development of the state by establishing a clearinghouse for information on educational programs of value to economic development.
n. To adopt cohesive rules for education system-wide issues.
o. To authorize the allocation of resources in accordance with law and rule.
p. To contract with independent institutions accredited by an agency whose standards are comparable to the minimum standards required to operate a postsecondary educational institution at that level in the state. The purpose of the contract is to provide those educational programs and facilities, which will meet needs unfulfilled by the state system of public postsecondary education.
q. To recommend that a district school board take action consistent with the state board's decision relating to an appeal of a charter school application.
r. To enforce system-wide education goals and policies.
s. To establish a detailed procedure for the implementation and operation of a system-wide K-20 technology plan that is based on a common set of data definitions.
t. To establish accountability standards for existing legislative performance goals, standards, and measures, and order the development of mechanisms to implement new legislative goals, standards, and measures.
u. To adopt criteria and implementation plans for future growth issues, such as new colleges and universities and campus mergers, and to provide for cooperative agreements between and within public and private education sectors.
v. To develop, and periodically review for adjustment, a coordinated 5-year plan for postsecondary enrollment and annually submit the plan to the Legislature.
w. To approve a new program at the professional level or doctoral level
x. To review, and approve or disapprove, degree programs identified as unique pursuant to s. 1007.25.
y. To recommend to the Legislature a plan for implementing block tuition programs and providing other incentives to encourage students to graduate within 4 years.

The State Board of Education adopted the Sunshine State Standards (SSS) as the basis for education in public schools. Florida educators developed the SSS, and all school districts reviewed the Standards before their adoption.

1001.03 Specific powers of State Board of Education.

1. **PUBLIC K-12 STUDENT PERFORMANCE STANDARDS**—The State Board of Education shall approve the student performance standards known as the Sunshine State Standards in key academic subject areas and grade levels.
2. **DIRECT-SUPPORT ORGANIZATION OF THE DEPARTMENT OF EDUCATION**—The State Board of Education shall govern issues relating to use of property, facilities, and personal services between the Department of Education and its direct-support organization and shall certify that the organization operates at all times in a manner consistent with the goals and best interest of the department.
3. **PROFESSIONAL CERTIFICATES**—The State Board of Education shall classify school services, designate the certification subject areas, establish competencies, including the use of technology to enhance student learning, and certification requirements for all school-based personnel, and prescribe rules in accordance with which the professional, temporary, and part-time certificates shall be issued by the Department of Education to applicants who meet the standards prescribed by such rules for their class of service.
4. **PROFESSIONAL TEACHER ASSOCIATIONS**—The State Board of Education shall ensure that not-for-profit, professional teacher associations that offer membership to all teachers, non-instructional personnel, and administrators, and that offer teacher training and staff development at no fee to the district, shall be given equal access to voluntary teacher meetings, be provided access to teacher mailboxes for distribution of professional literature, and be authorized to collect voluntary membership fees through payroll deduction.
5. **IDENTIFICATION OF CRITICAL TEACHER SHORTAGE AREAS**—The State Board of Education shall identify critical teacher shortage areas.
6. **CAPITAL OUTLAY BOND AND MOTOR VEHICLE TAX ANTICIPATION CERTIFICATE RESOLUTIONS**—The State Board of Education shall issue bonds and approve resolutions regarding the expenditure of funds for capital projects and purposes pursuant to the State Constitution and other applicable law.
7. **ARTICULATION ACCOUNTABILITY**—The State Board of Education shall develop articulation accountability measures that assess the status of system-wide articulation processes, and shall establish an articulation accountability process.
8. **SYSTEMWIDE ENFORCEMENT**—The State Board of Education shall enforce compliance with law and state board rule by all school districts and public postsecondary educational institutions.
9. **MANAGEMENT INFORMATION DATABASES**—The State Board of Education shall continue to collect and maintain, at a minimum, the management information databases for state universities, and all other components of the public K-20 education system.
10. **COMMON PLACEMENT TESTING FOR PUBLIC POSTSECONDARY EDUCATION**—The State Board of Education shall develop and implement a common placement test to assess the basic computation and communication skills of students who intend to enter a degree program at any community college or state university.
11. **MINIMUM STANDARDS FOR NONPUBLIC POSTSECONDARY EDUCATION**—The State Board of Education shall adopt minimum standards relating to nonpublic postsecondary education and institutions.
12. **COMMON POSTSECONDARY DEFINITIONS**—The State Board of Education shall adopt, by rule, common definitions for associate in science degrees and for certificates.

13. **CYCLIC REVIEW OF POSTSECONDARY ACADEMIC PROGRAMS**—The State Board of Education shall provide for the cyclic review of all academic programs in community colleges and state universities at least every 7 years. Program reviews shall document how individual academic programs are achieving stated student learning and program objectives within the context of the institution's mission. The results of the program reviews shall inform strategic planning, program development, and budgeting decisions at the institutional level.
14. **UNIFORM CLASSIFICATION SYSTEM FOR SCHOOL DISTRICT ADMINISTRATIVE AND MANAGEMENT PERSONNEL**—The State Board of Education shall recommend to the Legislature, a uniform classification system for school district administrative and management personnel that will facilitate the uniform coding of administrative and management personnel to total district employees.

Board of Governors

The Florida Board of Governors consists of 17 members, 14 of who are appointed by the Governor. In addition to the 14 members appointed by the Governor, the Board of Governors automatically includes the Commissioner of Education, the Chair of the Advisory Council of Faculty Senates and the President of the Florida Student Association. The statewide Board of Governors coordinates the State University System. It also supports the role of the 11 individual University Boards of Trustees that were originally established with the implementation of the new K–20 education system and are reauthorized under this amendment.

Local Power

School Districts are the local governing agency for education.

School District

Public school districts have various legal and educational responsibilities. Some of these include selection of curriculum materials, staff assignments, employee hires and dismissals, labor negotiations and contracts, monitoring revenues and expenditures, compliance with state and federal laws, management of facilities, staff development, purchasing, technology planning, strategic planning, public information, student transportation, student performance standards, and student assessments.

School Board

"The [school district system] seems impervious to reform from within. In my experience, those who join district boards, even those who start out reform-minded, eerily become co-opted and wind up defending the system tooth and nail. It's just like watching Invasion of the Body Snatchers."

—Lisa Graham Keegan, former Superintendent of Public Instruction, State of Arizona

I³ *Write down any ideas that come to you after reading this quote.*

____

____

> ***"In the first place, God made idiots. That was for practice. Then he made school boards."***
>
> —Mark Twain

I³ *Write down any ideas that come to you after reading this quote.*

____

____

I³ *How can you justify that both of these quotes may have merit?*

____

____

What Does the School Board Actually Do?

Theoretically school boards may perform a variety of duties such as creating and approving an annual budget, developing and confirming a school calendar, negotiating contracts, approving curriculum materials, and closing or constructing schools. In addition, a school board can create a mission and vision for the school district. These guidelines can include an educational philosophy, student outcomes, assessment techniques, cultural diversity, and future considerations. In addition, the school board, searches, interviews, hires, evaluates, and terminates the district superintendent.

School District Budget

Funds for operating a school district are developed, modified, and proposed by the school board of that county. Typical revenues include federal sources, state, and local sources, with state sources being the most significant contributor and the federal sources being very low. Expenditures may include instruction, personnel services, instructional media services, instruction and curriculum services, instructional staff training, administration, facilities maintenance and construction, food services, transportation services, and community services. Clearly, the instruction is the highest expenditure, typically seen as ten times that of any other one service and well over half of the total expenditures of the district budget. For example, a 125,000 student district budget can be in the area of $1.5 billion.

How Do I Become a School Board Member?

1001.34 Membership of district school board. Each district school board shall be composed of not less than five members. Each member of the district school board shall be a qualified elector of the district in which she or he serves, shall be a resident of the district school board member residence area from which she or he is elected, and shall maintain said residency throughout her or his term of office.

1001.35 Term of office. District school board members shall be elected at the general election in November for terms of 4 years.

1001.361 Election of board by district wide vote. Notwithstanding any provision of local law or any county charter, the election of members of the district school board shall be by vote of the qualified electors of the entire district in a nonpartisan election as provided in chapter 105. Each candidate for district school board member shall, at the time she or he qualifies, be a resident of the district school board member residence area from which the candidate seeks election. Each candidate who qualifies to have her or his name placed on the ballot shall be listed according to the district school board member residence area in which she or he resides. Each qualified elector of the district shall be entitled to vote for one candidate from each district school board member residence area. The candidate from each district school board member residence area who receives the highest number of votes in the general election shall be elected to the district school board.

1001.395 District school board members; compensation.

1. Each district school board shall annually determine the salary of its members at the first regular meeting following the organizational meeting held pursuant to s. 1001.371. The proposed salary to be adopted shall be noticed at the time of the meeting notice and shall not be increased during the meeting. The salary adopted by the district school board shall be in effect during the succeeding 12 months.
2. This section shall apply to any district school board member elected or reelected at the November 2002 general election or any subsequent general election and to any person appointed to fill a vacancy in the office of any such member.

1001.41 General powers of district school board. The district school board, after considering recommendations submitted by the district school superintendent, shall exercise the following general powers:

1. Determine policies and programs consistent with state law and rule deemed necessary by it for the efficient operation and general improvement of the district school system.
2. Adopt rules to implement the provisions of law conferring duties upon it to supplement those prescribed by the State Board of Education and the Commissioner of Education.
3. Prescribe and adopt standards as are considered desirable by it for improving the district school system.
4. Contract, sue, and be sued. The district school board shall constitute the contracting agent for the district school system.
5. Perform duties and exercise those responsibilities that are assigned to it by law or by rules of the State Board of Education or the Commissioner of Education and, in addition thereto, those that it may find to be necessary for the improvement of the district school system in carrying out the purposes and objectives of the education code.
6. Assign students to schools.
7. Enter into agreements for accepting credit card, charge card, and debit card payments as compensation for goods, services, tuition, and fees, as authorized by law.

1001.42 Powers and duties of district school board. The district school board, acting as a board, shall exercise all powers and perform all duties listed below:

1. **REQUIRE MINUTES AND RECORDS TO BE KEPT**—Require the district school superintendent, as secretary, to keep such minutes and records as are necessary to set forth clearly all actions and proceedings of the school board.
2. **CONTROL PROPERTY**—Subject to rules of the State Board of Education, control property and convey the title to real and personal property.
3. **ADOPT SCHOOL PROGRAM**—Adopt a school program for the entire school district.
4. **ESTABLISHMENT, ORGANIZATION, AND OPERATION OF SCHOOLS**—Adopt and provide for the execution of plans for the establishment, organization, and operation of the schools of the district.
5. **PERSONNEL**

6. **STUDENT WELFARE**
7. **COURSES OF STUDY AND OTHER INSTRUCTIONAL MATERIALS**—Provide adequate instructional materials for all students.
8. **TRANSPORTATION OF STUDENTS**—After considering recommendations of the district school superintendent, make provision for the transportation of students to the public schools or school activities they are required or expected to attend; authorize transportation routes arranged efficiently and economically; provide the necessary transportation facilities.
9. **SCHOOL PLANT**—Approve plans for locating, planning, constructing, sanitating, insuring, maintaining, protecting, and condemning school property.
10. **FINANCE**—Take steps to assure students adequate educational facilities through the financial procedure authorized.
11. **RECORDS AND REPORTS**—Provide for the keeping of all necessary records and the making of all needed or required reports.
12. **COOPERATION WITH OTHER DISTRICT SCHOOL BOARDS**—May establish and participate in educational consortia that are designed to provide joint programs and services to cooperating school districts. The State Board of Education shall adopt rules providing for the establishment, funding, administration, and operation of such consortia.
13. **ENFORCEMENT OF LAW AND RULES**—Require that all laws and rules of the State Board of Education or of the district school board are properly enforced.
14. **SCHOOL LUNCH PROGRAM**—Assume such responsibilities and exercise such powers and perform such duties as may be assigned to it by law or as may be required by rules of the State Board of Education or, as in the opinion of the district school board, are necessary to ensure school lunch services, consistent with needs of students; effective and efficient operation of the program; and the proper articulation of the school lunch program with other phases of education in the district.
15. **PUBLIC INFORMATION AND PARENTAL INVOLVEMENT PROGRAM**
16. **IMPLEMENT SCHOOL IMPROVEMENT AND ACCOUNTABILITY**—Maintain a system of school improvement and education accountability as provided by statute and State Board of Education rule. This system of school improvement and education accountability shall be consistent with, and implemented through, the district's continuing system of planning and budgeting required. This system of school improvement and education accountability shall include, but is not limited to, the following:
17. **LOCAL-LEVEL DECISIONMAKING**
18. **OPPORTUNITY SCHOLARSHIPS**—Adopt policies allowing students attending schools that have been designated as performance grade category "F," failing to make adequate progress, for 2 school years in a 4-year period to attend a higher performing school in the district or an adjoining district or be granted a state opportunity scholarship to a private school.
19. **AUTHORITY TO DECLARE AN EMERGENCY**—May declare an emergency in cases in which one or more schools in the district are failing or are in danger of failing and negotiate special provisions of its contract with the appropriate bargaining units to free these schools from contract restrictions that limit the school's ability to implement programs and strategies needed to improve student performance.
20. **SCHOOL-WITHIN-A-SCHOOL**—In order to reduce the anonymity of students in large schools, adopt policies to encourage any large school to subdivide into schools-within-a-school that shall operate within existing resources.
21. **FLORIDA VIRTUAL SCHOOL**—Provide students with access to enroll in courses available through the Florida Virtual School and award credit for successful completion of such courses. Access shall be available to students during or after the normal school day and through summer school enrollment.
22. **ADOPT RULES**

I³ ***School Board Activity:*** *Each student will be assigned a group and each group will research a local school board member. The group will develop a plan to gather information on the school board member, so that in class, the group can answer AT LEAST the following questions as if they were a board member. (Note—you may wish to decide amongst group members who will contact the member by phone or email, who will research them on the Internet, who will research in the library, etc.)*

1. Background (born, worked, traveled, and so on).
2. Education (high school, undergraduate degree, graduate, continuing education, and so on).
3. Educational philosophy.
4. Political affiliation.
5. Favorite projects.
6. Strengths and weaknesses.
7. Typically in favor or opposed to superintendents ideas—can you provide an example?
8. Typically in favor or opposed to mayors ideas—can you provide an example?
9. How would you vote for this person?
10. Something unusual about this person.

Superintendent

1001.46 District school superintendent; election and term of office. The district school superintendent shall be elected for a term of 4 years or until the election or appointment and qualification of his or her successor.

1001.461 District school superintendent; procedures for making office appointive.

1. Pursuant to the provisions of s. 5, Art. IX of the State Constitution, the district school superintendent shall be appointed by the district school board in a school district wherein the proposition is affirmed by a majority of the qualified electors voting in the same election making the office of district school superintendent appointive.

1001.47 District school superintendent; salary.

1. Each district school superintendent shall receive as salary the amount indicated pursuant to this section. However, a district school board, by majority vote, may approve a salary in excess of the amount specified in this section.
2. Notwithstanding the provisions of chapter 145 to the contrary, the annual salaries of elected district school superintendents for 1993 and each year thereafter shall be established at the same amounts as the district school superintendents were paid for fiscal year 1991–1992.
3. This section does not apply to a district school superintendent appointed pursuant to the terms of s. 1001.50.
4. a. There shall be an additional $2,000 per year special qualification salary for each district school superintendent who has met the certification requirements established by the Department of Education. Any district school superintendent who is certified during a calendar year shall receive in that year a pro rata share of the special qualification salary based on the remaining period of the year.
   b. In order to qualify for the special qualification salary provided by paragraph (a), the district school superintendent must complete the requirements established by the Department of Education within 6 years after first taking office.

   c. After a district school superintendent meets the requirements of paragraph (a), in order to remain certified the district school superintendent shall thereafter be required to complete each year a course of continuing education as prescribed by the Department of Education.
5. a. The Department of Education shall provide a leadership development and performance compensation program for district school superintendents, comparable to chief executive officer development programs for corporate executive officers.
   b. Upon the successful completion of both phases and demonstrated successful performance, as determined by the department, a district school superintendent shall be issued a Chief Executive Officer Leadership Development Certificate and shall be given an annual performance salary incentive of not less than $3,000 nor more than $7,500 based upon his or her performance evaluation.
   c. A district school superintendent's eligibility to continue receiving the annual performance salary incentive is contingent upon his or her continued performance assessment and follow-up training prescribed by the department.

1001.49 General powers of district school superintendent. The district school superintendent shall have the authority, and when necessary for the more efficient and adequate operation of the district school system, the district school superintendent shall exercise the following powers:

1. GENERAL OVERSIGHT—Exercise general oversight over the district school system in order to determine problems and needs, and recommend improvements.
2. ADVISE, COUNSEL, AND RECOMMEND TO DISTRICT SCHOOL BOARD—Advise and counsel with the district school board on all educational matters and recommend to the district school board for action such matters as should be acted upon.
3. RECOMMEND POLICIES—Recommend to the district school board for adoption such policies pertaining to the district school system as the district school superintendent may consider necessary for its more efficient operation.
4. RECOMMEND AND EXECUTE RULES—Prepare and organize by subjects and submit to the district school board for adoption such rules to supplement those adopted by the State Board of Education as, in the district school superintendent's opinion, will contribute to the efficient operation of any aspect of education in the district. When rules have been adopted, the district school superintendent shall see that they are executed.
5. RECOMMEND AND EXECUTE MINIMUM STANDARDS—From time to time prepare, organize by subject, and submit to the district school board for adoption such minimum standards relating to the operation of any phase of the district school system as are needed to supplement those adopted by the State Board of Education and as will contribute to the efficient operation of any aspect of education in the district and ensure that minimum standards adopted by the district school board and the state board are observed.
6. PERFORM DUTIES AND EXERCISE RESPONSIBILITIES—Perform such duties and exercise such responsibilities as are assigned to the district school superintendent by law and by rules of the State Board of Education.

1001.51 Duties and responsibilities of district school superintendent. The district school superintendent shall exercise all powers and perform all duties listed below and elsewhere in the law, provided that, in so doing, he or she shall advise and counsel with the district school board. The district school superintendent shall perform all tasks necessary to make sound recommendations, nominations, proposals, and reports required by law to be acted upon by the district school board. All such recommendations, nominations, proposals, and reports by the district school superintendent shall be either recorded in the minutes or shall be made in writing, noted in the minutes, and filed in the public records of the district school board. It shall be presumed that, in the absence of the record required in this section, the recommendations, nominations, and proposals required of the district school superintendent were not contrary to the action taken by the district school board in such matters.

1. **ASSIST IN ORGANIZATION OF DISTRICT SCHOOL BOARD**—Preside at the organization meeting of the district school board and transmit to the Department of Education, within 2 weeks following such meeting, a certified copy of the proceedings of organization, including the schedule of regular meetings, and the names and addresses of district school officials.
2. **REGULAR AND SPECIAL MEETINGS OF THE DISTRICT SCHOOL BOARD**—Attend all regular meetings of the district school board, call special meetings when emergencies arise, and advise, but not vote, on questions under consideration.
3. **RECORDS FOR THE DISTRICT SCHOOL BOARD**—Keep minutes of all official actions and proceedings of the district school board and keep such other records, including records of property held or disposed of by the district school board, as may be necessary to provide complete information regarding the district school system.
4. **SCHOOL PROPERTY**—Act for the district school board as custodian of school property.
5. **SCHOOL PROGRAM; PREPARE PLANS**—Supervise the assembling of data and sponsor studies and surveys essential to the development of a planned school program for the entire district and prepare and recommend such a program to the district school board as the basis for operating the district school system.
6. **ESTABLISHMENT, ORGANIZATION, AND OPERATION OF SCHOOLS, CLASSES, AND SERVICES**—Recommend the establishment, organization, and operation of such schools, classes, and services as are needed to provide adequate educational opportunities for all children in the district.
7. **PERSONNEL**—Be responsible, as required herein, for directing the work of the personnel.
8. **COURSES OF STUDY AND OTHER INSTRUCTIONAL AIDS**—Recommend such plans for improving, providing, distributing, accounting for, and caring for textbooks and other instructional aids as will result in general improvement of the district school system.
9. **TRANSPORTATION OF STUDENTS**—Provide for student transportation.
10. **SCHOOL PLANT**—Recommend plans, and execute such plans as are approved, regarding all phases of the school plant program.
11. **FINANCE**—Recommend measures to the district school board to assure adequate educational facilities throughout the district, in accordance with the financial procedure.
12. **RECORDS AND REPORTS**—Recommend such records as should be kept in addition to those prescribed by rules of the State Board of Education; prepare forms for keeping such records as are approved by the district school board; ensure that such records are properly kept; and make all reports that are needed.
13. **COOPERATION WITH OTHER AGENCIES**
14. **ENFORCEMENT OF LAWS AND RULES**—Require that all laws and rules of the State Board of Education, as well as supplementary rules of the district school board, are properly observed and report to the district school board any violation that the district school superintendent does not succeed in having corrected.
15. **COOPERATE WITH DISTRICT SCHOOL BOARD**—Cooperate with the district school board in every manner practicable to the end that the district school system may continuously be improved.
16. **VISITATION OF SCHOOLS**—Visit the schools; observe the management and instruction; give suggestions for improvement; and advise supervisors, principals, teachers, patrons, and other citizens with the view of promoting interest in education and improving the school conditions of the district.
17. **CONFERENCES, INSTITUTES, AND STUDY COURSES**—Call and conduct institutes and conferences with employees of the district school board, school patrons, and other interested

citizens; organize and direct study and extension courses for employees, advising them as to their professional studies; and assist patrons and people generally in acquiring knowledge of the aims, services, and needs of the schools.

18. **PROFESSIONAL AND GENERAL IMPROVEMENT**—Attend such conferences for district school superintendents as may be called or scheduled by the Department of Education and avail himself or herself of means of professional and general improvement so that he or she may function most efficiently.
19. **RECOMMEND REVOKING CERTIFICATES**—Recommend in writing to the Department of Education the revoking of any certificate for good cause, including a full statement of the reason for the district school superintendent's recommendation.
20. **MAKE RECORDS AVAILABLE TO SUCCESSOR**—Leave with the district school board and make available to his or her successor, upon retiring from office, a complete inventory of school equipment and other property, together with all official records and such other records as may be needed in supervising instruction and in administering the district school system.
21. **RECOMMEND PROCEDURES FOR INFORMING GENERAL PUBLIC**—Recommend to the district school board procedures whereby the general public can be adequately informed of the educational programs, needs, and objectives of public education within the district.
22. **SCHOOL IMPROVEMENT AND ACCOUNTABILITY**—Recommend procedures for implementing and maintaining a system of school improvement and education accountability as provided by statute and State Board of Education rule.
23. **PARENTAL INVOLVEMENT**—Fully support and cooperate.
24. **QUALITY TEACHERS**—Fully support and cooperate in the application of the guiding principles of Better Educated Students and Teachers (BEST) Florida Teaching.
25. **ORDERLY CLASSROOMS AND SCHOOL BUSES**—Fully support the authority of each teacher and school bus driver to remove disobedient, disrespectful, violent, abusive, uncontrollable, or disruptive students from the classroom and the school bus and the authority of the school principal to place such students in an alternative educational setting, when appropriate and available.
26. **OTHER DUTIES AND RESPONSIBILITIES**—Perform such other duties as are assigned to the district school superintendent by law or by rules of the State Board of Education.

1001.32 Management, control, operation, administration, and supervision. The district school system must be managed, controlled, operated, administered, and supervised as follows:

1. **DISTRICT SYSTEM**—The district school system shall be considered as a part of the state system of public education. All actions of district school officials shall be consistent and in harmony with state laws and with rules and minimum standards of the state board and the commissioner. District school officials, however, shall have the authority to provide additional educational opportunities, as desired, which are authorized, but not required, by law or by the district school board.
2. **DISTRICT SCHOOL BOARD**—District school boards shall operate, control, and supervise all free public schools in their respective districts and may exercise any power except as expressly prohibited by the State Constitution or general law.
3. **DISTRICT SCHOOL SUPERINTENDENT**—Responsibility for the administration and management of the schools and for the supervision of instruction in the district shall be vested in the district school superintendent as the secretary and executive officer of the district school board, as provided by law.
4. **SCHOOL PRINCIPAL OR HEAD OF SCHOOL**—Responsibility for the administration of any school or schools at a given school center, for the supervision of instruction therein, and for

providing leadership in the development or revision and implementation of a school improvement plan required shall be delegated to the school principal or head of the school or schools in accordance with rules established by the district school board.

1001.33 Schools under control of district school board and district school superintendent.

1. Except as otherwise provided by law, all public schools conducted within the district shall be under the direction and control of the district school board with the district school superintendent as executive officer.
2. Each district school board, each district school superintendent, and each district and school-based administrator shall cooperate to apply the following guiding principles of Better Educated Students and Teachers (BEST) Florida Teaching:
   a. Teachers lead, students learn.
   b. Teachers maintain orderly, disciplined classrooms conducive to student learning.
   c. Teachers are trained, recruited, well compensated, and retained for quality.
   d. Teachers are well rewarded for their students' high performance.
   e. Teachers are most effective when served by exemplary school administrators.

The superintendent interviews, hires, evaluates and terminates the principals.

Principal

1001.54 Duties of school principals.

1. a. A district school board shall employ, through written contract, public school principals.
   b. The school principal has authority over school district personnel.
   c. The school principal shall encourage school personnel to implement the guiding principles for Better Educated Students and Teachers (BEST) Florida Teaching.
   d. The school principal shall fully support the authority of each teacher and school bus driver to remove disobedient, disrespectful, violent, abusive, uncontrollable, or disruptive students from the classroom and the school bus and, when appropriate and available, place such students in an alternative educational setting.
2. Each school principal shall provide leadership in the development or revision and implementation of a school improvement plan.
3. Each school principal must make the necessary provisions to ensure that all school reports are accurate and timely, and must provide the necessary training opportunities for staff to accurately report attendance, FTE program participation, student performance, teacher appraisal, and school safety and discipline data.
4. Each school principal is responsible for the management and care of instructional materials.
5. Each school principal shall fully support and cooperate in the implementation of s. 1002.23.

The principal interviews, hires, evaluates, and terminates the teachers.

Teacher

"Too many teachers are not qualified in the subject they're teaching. Too many states do not test to make sure teachers know what they're teaching. Too many states that do test set the bar for passing way too low."

—ROD PAIGE, U.S. SECRETARY OF EDUCATION, JUNE 2002

I^3 *Write down any ideas that come to you after reading this quote.*

Teacher's duties include:

Everything.

1012.32 Qualifications of personnel.

1. To be eligible for appointment in any position in any district school system, a person shall be of good moral character; shall have attained the age of 18 years, if he or she is to be employed in an instructional capacity; and shall, when required by law, hold a certificate or license issued under rules of the State Board of Education or the Department of Children and Family Services. Previous residence in this state shall not be required in any school of the state as a prerequisite for any person holding a valid Florida certificate or license to serve in an instructional capacity.
2. a. Instructional and noninstructional personnel who are hired to fill positions requiring direct contact with students in any district school system or university lab school shall, upon employment, file a complete set of fingerprints taken by an authorized law enforcement officer or an employee of the school or district who is trained to take fingerprints. These fingerprints shall be submitted to the Department of Law Enforcement for state processing and to the Federal Bureau of Investigation for federal processing. The new employees shall be on probationary status pending fingerprint processing and determination of compliance with standards of good moral character. Employees found through fingerprint processing to have been convicted of a crime involving moral turpitude shall not be employed in any position requiring direct contact with students. Probationary employees terminated because of their criminal record shall have the right to appeal such decisions. The cost of the fingerprint processing may be borne by the district school board or the employee.
   b. Personnel who have been fingerprinted or screened pursuant to this subsection and who have not been unemployed for more than 90 days shall not be required to be re-fingerprinted.

1012.33 Contracts with instructional staff, supervisors, and school principals.

1. a. Each person employed as a member of the instructional staff in any district school system shall be properly certified pursuant to s. 1012.56 or s. 1012.57 or employed pursuant to s. 1012.39 and shall be entitled to and shall receive a written contract as specified in this section. All such contracts, except continuing contracts as specified in subsection (4), shall contain provisions for dismissal during the term of the contract only for just cause. Just cause includes, but is not limited to, the following instances, as defined by rule of the State Board of Education: misconduct in office, incompetency, gross insubordination, willful neglect of duty, or conviction of a crime involving moral turpitude.
   b. A supervisor or school principal shall be properly certified and shall receive a written contract as specified in this section. Such contract may be for an initial period not to exceed 3 years, subject to annual review and renewal. The first 97 days of an initial contract is a probationary period. During the probationary period, the employee may be dismissed without cause or may resign from the contractual position without breach of contract.

After the first 3 years, the contract may be renewed for a period not to exceed 3 years and shall contain provisions for dismissal during the term of the contract only for just cause, in addition to such other provisions as are prescribed by the district school board.

2. Any person so employed on the basis of a written offer of a specific position by a duly authorized agent of the district school board for a stated term of service at a specified salary, and who accepted such offer by telegram or letter or by signing the regular contract form, who violates the terms of such contract or agreement by leaving his or her position without first being released from his or her contract or agreement by the district school board of the district in which the person is employed shall be subject to the jurisdiction of the Education Practices Commission. The district school board shall take official action on such violation and shall furnish a copy of its official minutes to the Commissioner of Education.
3. Each district school board shall provide a professional service contract as prescribed herein. Each member of the instructional staff who completed the following requirements prior to July 1, 1984, shall be entitled to and shall be issued a continuing contract in the form prescribed by rules of the state board pursuant to s. 231.36, Florida Statutes (1981). Each member of the instructional staff who completes the following requirements on or after July 1, 1984, shall be entitled to and shall be issued a professional service contract in the form prescribed by rules of the state board.

The teacher does NOT interview, hires, evaluate and terminate the parents. They do welcome, assist, guide and provide various opportunities to communicate with the parents concerning their children.

Parents

"The only real measure of a teacher's competence, over time, is whether parents want the services of that teacher."

—Unknown

I³ *Write down any ideas that come to you after reading this quote.*

____

____

"Education will always do whatever makes the parents most uncomfortable, that's their forte."

—Jesse Ventura

I³ *Write down any ideas that come to you after reading this quote.*

____

____

"Parents give up their rights when they drop their kids off at public school."

—Federal District Judge Melinda Harmon ruling against parents suing a Texas School district

I³ *Write down any ideas that come to you after reading this quote.*

____

____

I³ *How can you justify that both of these quotes may have merit?*

____

____

Parents are an integral part of a student's education. One of the most critical components is parental involvement as cited by principals.

The parents do NOT interview, hire, evaluate, and terminate the teachers.

Students

Students are more than recipients of this incredible system of education. They can be a full participatory member and significantly contribute when their ideas and beliefs are solicited, heard and intelligently addressed.

Funding and Salary

1011.01 Budget system established. The State Board of Education shall prepare and submit a coordinated K–20 education annual legislative budget request to the Governor and the Legislature on or before the date provided by the Governor and the Legislature. The board's legislative budget request must clearly define the needs of school districts, community colleges, universities, other institutions, organizations, programs, and activities under the supervision of the board and law or the General Appropriations Act assigns that to the Department of Education.

1011.04 Levying of taxes.

1. Upon receipt of the certificate of the property appraiser giving the assessed valuation of the county and of each of the special tax school districts pursuant to s. 200.065, the district school board shall determine by resolution the amounts necessary to be raised for current operating purposes and for each district bond interest and sinking fund and the millage necessary to be levied for each such fund, including the voted millage. A certified copy of the resolution shall thereupon be filed with the county property appraiser, and the district school board shall also order the property appraiser to assess the several millages certified by the school board against the appropriate taxable property in the school district.
2. The property appraiser shall then assess the taxes as ordered by the district school board. Tax millages so assessed shall be clearly designated and separately identified as to source on the tax bill for other county taxes.
3. The collector shall collect said taxes and pay over the same promptly as collected to the district school depository or depositories to be used as provided by law; provided, that all taxes authorized herein shall be assessed and collected on railroad, street railroad, sleeping car, parlor car, and telegraph company property in the manner now provided by law.

1011.19 Sources of district school fund. The district school fund shall consist of funds derived from the district school tax levy; state appropriations; appropriations by county commissioners; local, state, and federal school food service funds; any and all other sources for school purposes; national forest trust funds and other federal sources; and gifts and other sources.

1011.62 Funds for operation of schools. If the annual allocation from the Florida Education Finance Program to each district for operation of schools is not determined in the annual appropriations act or the substantive bill implementing the annual appropriations act, it shall be determined as follows:

1. COMPUTATION OF THE BASIC AMOUNT TO BE INCLUDED FOR OPERATION—The following procedure shall be followed in determining the annual allocation to each district for operation:
   a. *Determination of full-time equivalent membership.* During each of several school weeks, including scheduled intercessions of a year-round school program during the fiscal year, a program membership survey of each school shall be made by each district by aggregating the full-time equivalent student membership of each program by school and by district. The department shall establish the number and interval of membership calculations, except that for basic and special programs such calculations shall not exceed nine for any fiscal year. The district's full-time equivalent membership shall be computed and currently maintained in accordance with regulations of the commissioner.
   b. *Determination of base student allocation.* The base student allocation for the Florida Education Finance Program for kindergarten through grade 12 shall be determined annually by the Legislature and shall be that amount prescribed in the current year's General Appropriations Act.
   c. *Determination of programs.* Cost factors based on desired relative cost differences between the following programs shall be established in the annual General Appropriations Act. The Commissioner of Education shall specify a matrix of services and intensity levels to be used by districts in the determination of the two weighted cost factors for exceptional students with the highest levels of need. For these students, the funding support level shall fund the exceptional students' education program, with the exception of extended school year services for students with disabilities.

BTW

Throwing pennies into a well. Ancient people believe spirits living in springs and fountains demanded tribute—usually flesh. Young Mayan girls, for example, were sometimes tossed into the Well of Sacrifice, where they would marry the spirits. Today, we just toss spirits a penny or two for luck.

1012.05 Teacher recruitment and retention.

1. The Department of Education, in cooperation with teacher organizations, district personnel offices, and schools, colleges, and departments of all public and nonpublic postsecondary educational institutions, shall concentrate on the recruitment of qualified teachers.
2. The Department of Education shall:
   a. Develop and implement a system for posting teaching vacancies and establish a database of teacher applicants that is accessible within and outside the state.
   b. Advertise in major newspapers, national professional publications, and other professional publications and in public and nonpublic postsecondary educational institutions.

c. Utilize state and nationwide toll-free numbers.
d. Conduct periodic communications with district personnel directors regarding applicants.
e. Provide district access to the applicant database by computer or telephone.
f. Develop and distribute promotional materials related to teaching as a career.
g. Publish and distribute information pertaining to employment opportunities, application procedures, and all routes toward teacher certification in Florida, and teacher salaries.
h. Provide information related to certification procedures.
i. Develop and sponsor the Florida Future Educator of America Program throughout the state.
j. Develop, in consultation with school district staff including, but not limited to, district school superintendents, district school board members, and district human resources personnel, a long-range plan for educator recruitment and retention.
k. Identify best practices for retaining high-quality teachers.
l. Develop, in consultation with Workforce Florida, Inc., and the Agency for Workforce Innovation, respectively, a plan for accessing and identifying available resources in the state's workforce system for the purpose of enhancing teacher recruitment and retention.
m. Develop and implement a First Response Center to provide educator candidates one-stop shopping for information on teaching careers in Florida and establish the Teacher Lifeline Network to provide online support to beginning teachers and those needing assistance.

1012.07 Identification of critical teacher shortage areas.

1. The term "critical teacher shortage area" applies to mathematics, science, career education, and high priority location areas. The State Board of Education may identify career education programs having critical teacher shortages. The State Board of Education shall adopt rules necessary to annually identify other critical teacher shortage areas and high priority location areas. The state board shall also consider teacher characteristics such as ethnic background, race, and sex in determining critical teacher shortage areas. School grade levels may also be designated critical teacher shortage areas. Individual district school boards may identify other critical teacher shortage areas. Such shortages must be certified to and approved by the State Board of Education. High priority location areas shall be in high-density, low-economic urban schools and low-density, low-economic rural schools and shall include schools which meet criteria which include, but are not limited to, the percentage of free lunches.

1012.231 BEST Florida Teaching salary career ladder program; assignment of teachers.

1. SALARY CAREER LADDER FOR CLASSROOM TEACHERS—Beginning with the 2004–2005 academic year, each district school board shall implement a salary career ladder for classroom teachers as defined in s. 1012.01(2)(a). Performance shall be defined as designated in s. 1012.34(3)(a)1.-7. District school boards shall designate categories of classroom teachers reflecting these salary career ladder levels as follows:
   a. *Associate teacher.* Classroom teachers in the school district who have not yet received a professional certificate or those with a professional certificate who are evaluated as low-performing teachers.
   b. *Professional teacher.* Classroom teachers in the school district who have received a professional certificate.
   c. *Lead teacher.* Classroom teachers in the school district who are responsible for leading others in the school as department chair, lead teacher, grade-level leader, intern coordinator, or professional development coordinator. Lead teachers must participate on a regular basis in the direct instruction of students and serve as faculty for professional development

activities as determined by the State Board of Education. To be eligible for designation as a lead teacher, a teacher must demonstrate outstanding performance pursuant to s. 1012.34(3)(a)1.–7. and must have been a "professional teacher" pursuant to paragraph (b) for at least 1 year.

d. *Mentor teacher.* Classroom teachers in the school district who serve as regular mentors to other teachers who are either not performing satisfactorily or who strive to become more proficient. Mentor teachers must serve as faculty-based professional development coordinators and regularly demonstrate and share their expertise with other teachers in order to remain mentor teachers. Mentor teachers must also participate on a regular basis in the direct instruction of low-performing students. To be eligible for designation as a mentor teacher, a teacher must demonstrate outstanding performance and must have been a "lead teacher" pursuant to paragraph (c) for at least two years.

Promotion of a teacher to a higher level on the salary career ladder shall be based upon prescribed performance criteria and not based upon length of service.

2. **TEACHER ASSIGNMENT**—School districts may not assign a higher percentage than the school district average of first-time teachers, temporarily certified teachers, teachers in need of improvement, or out-of-field teachers to schools with above the school district average of minority and economically disadvantaged students or schools that are graded "D" or "F." District school boards are authorized to provide salary incentives to meet this requirement. No district school board shall sign a collective bargaining agreement that fails to provide sufficient incentives to meet this requirement.
3. **STATE BOARD AND SCHOOL DISTRICT PLANS**—The State Board of Education shall develop a long-range plan to implement a differentiated pay model for teachers beginning in the 2004–2005 academic year, based upon the differentiated classroom teacher categories in subsection (1). No later than December 1, 2003, the State Board of Education shall approve guidelines and criteria for the district plans. District school boards shall develop plans to implement the salary career ladder prescribed in this section and submit these plans to the State Board of Education by March 1, 2004.

The average statewide teacher pay in Florida is $50,000. The beginning salary of a degreed certified teacher with no experience in Duval County, Florida is $30,000/academic year (less than a full year).

I³ *Do you believe this is sufficient compensation? Why/why not? If you could, how would you develop a plan to pay teachers more? Remember, where funds come from to pay teachers, so if you are going to increase teacher pay, you will need to consider several factors which will be affected.*

____

____

____

____

____

____

____

KWL

What Did You LEARN?

References

State of Florida. Description of Florida government roles. State of Florida Web site. Accessed November 15, 2004, from *http://www.flsenate.gov/Statues/index.cfm?App_mode=Display_Statue&URL=Ch1001/ch1001.htm*

State of Florida. Description of Commissioner of Education duties. State of Florida Web site. Accessed November 15, 2004, from *http://www.flsenate.gov/Statutes/index.cfm?App_mode=Display_Index&Title_Request=XLVIII#TitleXLVIII*

CHAPTER 7—SCHOOL GOVERNANCE

PowerPoint Outline to Assist In-Class Note-Taking

A. **Who Controls Schools**

B. **Who Controls Me?**

   a. How Many Bosses Will I Have?

C. **National Education Association (NEA)**

D. **Federal Agency—U.S. Department of Education (USDOE)**

E. **State Power**

   a. Governor

   b. Department of Education

   c. Commissioner of Education

   d. Board of Education

   e. Board of Governors

F. **Local Power**

   a. School Districts

b. School Board

c. Superintendent

d. Principal

e. Teacher

f. Parents

g. Students

G. Funding and Salary

8

Legal and Ethical Concerns for Educators

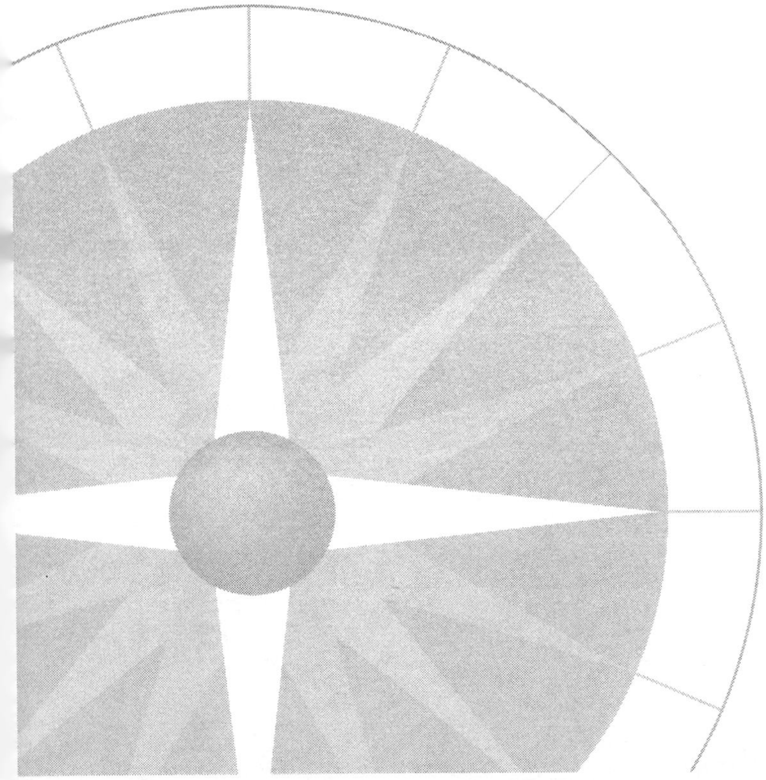

Guest Editorial: Professor Tim Richardson, Seneca College/University of Toronto, Ontario, Canada

The circumstances, which affect legal and ethical considerations in the new millennium, are circumstances caused by drastic changes in the

- political environment (regional, national, and international), and the consequent rules and regulations effecting educators locally and regionally
- social-cultural environment (along with linguistic and religious influences)
- technological environment (which effects communication regionally and globally)
- economic environment (which influences corporate objectives and consumer priorities)

There has always be pressure on educators—even Socrates, Plato and Aristotle had limiting considerations imposed by the conflicts the Greeks were involved in at various times. However the intensity of the technological environment of the new millennium, (most infamous in the form of the WWW) facilitates a global audience for local issues, and together with a highly competitive economic environment, challenges decision makers to respond in ways that can intensify the impact of the four environments listed at the outset.

Legal concerns affecting the pedagogical and administrative activities of educators are now concerns that are influenced by

- the political environment in the immediate jurisdiction, (city, county, state)
- the political dynamic at the national level, and
- politics at the global level.

These political environments, at various levels, are in turn effected by economic forces, which are no longer local and regional, but also national and international. The political environments are also effected by a worldwide shift in the social-cultural environment such that many groups of *identified cultures* use technology and economic power to exert pressure on national governments and international organizations where previously such pressure would have been squashed.

The competitive nature of the global broadcast networks, and their technological wizardry allow them to bring stories to the forefront at a startling speed, and consequently regional issues can gain international exposure in a short period of time. To serve up an example, just as this guest editorial was being written (second week of July 2004) a small story out of New Brunswick (a small Maritime province in eastern Canada) came to prominence at such a speed that within a matter of forty-eight hours, millions and millions of people worldwide had heard about this blind French-speaking student who was barred from speaking French with his seeing-eye dog. UNB student Yvan Tessier, who wanted to be in the English Language immersion program at the University of New Brunswick, wanted to have his seeing eye dog accompany him to his English classes but was told he could not speak French to the dog while in English class (due to the principles of language immersion). Tessier responded by saying "the dog is not bilingual!" and the university then threatened to restrict Tessier from the ESL classes. Tessier spoke to the Canadian press, who in turn ran the story on the international wire, and due to the sensational nature of the piece, it was picked up as a human interest story by media outlets worldwide who love stories about such things: "good guy gets limited by red tape."

The British based BBC ran the story and informed millions of Europeans; several American and Canadian print and broadcast media ran the story, which reaches over 300 million people in North America. As a result of the story being circulated on TV, and the Internet worldwide, UNB felt embarrassed and publically announced they would change their regulations. UNB's policy reversal might not have happened if it were not for the technological environment that made it possible for this story to spread so fast and so far.

How will this story of Tessier and similar cases affect educators deliberating on pedagogical and administrative issues? The answer is that rules and regulations you enact will not only be judged by the students, parents, and community in your immediate jurisdiction, but may also be exposed to the world if a sensational topic is deemed worthy of being fed into the global media pipeline for instant consumption worldwide.

Ethical concerns affecting the pedagogical and administrative activities of educators are no longer simple issues (as if they ever were before). The underlying social-cultural environment, upon which the ethical/religious opinions are based, is now multicultural in most urban areas of the major countries. While educators in the 1970s through the 1990s might have dealt with social integration challenges among children of somewhat proximate groups, now there are challenges raised by integration among cultural groups from very different parts of the world. It is one thing to have the challenges of dealing with children whose heritage comes from three or four different European countries, but it is very different when you mix in children from regions in the Middle East, Asia, and Latin America because people who are integrating are people with no knowledge of even the most basic understandings of the other culture. While the enthusiasms and curiosities of youth may mean that multicultural integrations usually end up harmonious, this is sadly not the case with their adult parents, whose votes affect the politics of the school board and other elected officials.

In early 2004, the French educational system was reeling from worldwide media coverage of a controversial law that deals with restrictions on what students may wear to school, in relation to obvious religious symbols such as head coverings and crucifixes. This situation (as yet unresolved at the time this chapter went to print) reveals how the ethical concerns of educators can be hijacked by different religious and cultural groups all striving to substantiate their concerns.

Legal and ethical concerns for educators, as we move further into the millennium, will continue to be challenged more and more by national and international forces, which will increase effect and affect the local and regional rules and regulations, and the officials caught up in scripting those regulations.

> ***"To suggest for a moment that morality and ethics are not being taught in government-controlled schools is ridiculous. . . . A definite point-of-view from a definite culture is being imposed. . . . It is outrageous that values taught in public schools are not the same ones held by Catholic parents, or by non-Catholic Christians and Jewish parents as well."***
>
> —Archbishop Edward Egan of New York

I³ *Write down any ideas that come to you after reading this quote.*

____

____

"Opportunity may knock only once, but temptation leans on the doorbell."

—UNKNOWN

I^3 *Write down any ideas that come to you after reading this quote.*

I^3 *How can you justify that both of these quotes may have merit?*

KWL

What Do You KNOW? (prior knowledge)

What Do You WANT to Know? (objectives and goals)

Am I Fit to Be a Teacher?

"Courage is being scared to death . . . but saddling up anyway."

—John Wayne

I^3 *Write down any ideas that come to you after reading this quote.*

____

____

Legal Concerns

Some of the many possible legal issues for teachers include student rights, disabled students, student supervision, special education students, negligence, confidentiality, students with ADD, avoiding lawsuits and liability, dealing with parents, reporting requirements, and disciplining students.

When speaking of legal concerns that teachers have, there have been many headlines that highlight how teachers did not adhere to legal guidelines. Some teachers believe that even if there are no ill intentions, a student could make false accusations on the teacher's behavior toward them. When accusations are made, the school district is legally bound to investigate. Once the legal process begins, intrusion into the life of the victim teacher can be intense. Even if the charges are found to be false, typically the teacher will find it difficult to teach even if they can secure another position. How do teachers deal with the possibility of legal issues and still provide the best, caring services to the students? Do they refuse to be alone with students? A good rule of thumb is to interact with several students at one time and if a sensitive issue arises, or if there is a troubled student, it is best if the teacher gathers support and other professionals as quickly as possible to resolve student's needs safely.

I^3 *What do you believe is lost in the student-teacher relationship, when teachers feel the need to be conservative in their approach?*

____

____

____

____

Tenure

Tenure is a form of job security for teachers who have successfully completed a probationary period of employment. Its initial and primary purpose is to protect competent teachers from arbitrary nonrenewal of contract for reasons unrelated to the educational process, such as personal beliefs, academic freedom, and personality conflicts with administrators or school board members.

Tenure is a right of holding or occupying land or a position for a certain amount of time. The term was first used in the English feudal land system, whereby all land belonged to the king but was lent out to lords for a certain period of time; the lord never owning, but having tenure in the land. Used in modern law mostly to refer to a position a person occupies. In an academic setting, tenure is the employment status of a person who holds an academic appointment that is continuous until terminated by retirement or dismissal. The termination of a continuous tenure appointment shall be only pursuant to university policy. Tenure means guaranteed job security, usually granted by law after a specified number of years of satisfactory service, which cannot be rescinded except for specified reasons. Although contrary to popular believe, it is possible to terminate a tenured teacher for poor performance. Many school districts have developed tenure programs, whereby after three years a faculty member is tenured and will receive a continuing contract, unless there are special circumstances that would prevent rehiring. Recently, because some teachers had significantly decreased their level of effort after securing tenure, some districts have modified their tenure policies. In some cases, after obtaining tenure, a tenure teacher will maintain tenure only if they receive "satisfactory" or "exceeds satisfactory" annual evaluations. If the teacher falls below this level, they lose tenure and must begin the tenure process again. Knock on wood, securing tenure will not a problem for those of you who complete a teacher education program.

BTW

Knocking on wood. The English touch wood for luck; Americans prefer the more sounding knock. These actions reflect the early Christian worship for the cross. Making contact with wood is a way of connecting symbolically with this holy article of Christianity. Others see the custom as a survivor of the medieval tradition of sanctuary. In the days when any fugitive could find protection behind the doors of a church, touching the wood of these doors would be a signal that he was safe.

Professional Code of Ethics

"The early bird gets the worm, but the early worm gets eaten."

—Anonymous

I^3 *Write down any ideas that come to you after reading this quote.*

____

____

"Only when we have something to value, will we have something to evaluate . . . and we cannot value something that we cannot share, exchange and examine."

—Lee Shulman

I^3 *Write down any ideas that come to you after reading this quote.*

____

____

I³ *How can you justify that both of these quotes may have merit?*

Ethics are motivation based on ideas of right and wrong. They are a system of moral principles, rules, or standards that govern the conduct of members of a group. Ethical codes of conduct approach human behavior from a philosophical standpoint by stressing objectively defined, but essentially idealistic, standards (or laws) of right and wrong, good/evil, and virtue/vice.

What are morals?

Some aspects of various definitions indicate that morals are a code of good conduct laid down out of the experience of the race to serve as a uniform yardstick for the conduct of individuals and groups. Morals are actually laws. Also, they could be personal standards or rules of conduct that guide an individual toward making judgments about permissible behavior with regard to basic human values (e.g., human equity, individual freedoms, respect for others.).

What are values?

Values are the ideas we have about what is good and what is bad, and how things should be. We have values about family relationships (regarding, for instance, the role of the husband with respect to the wife), about work relationships (regarding, for instance, how employers should treat employees) and about other personal and relationships issues (regarding, for example, how children should behave towards adults, or how people should follow particular religious beliefs).

I³ *Please list some of the ethical ideas you would include if you were to develop a professional code of ethics for teachers.*

NEA'S PROFESSIONAL CODE OF ETHICS FOR TEACHERS

CODE OF ETHICS OF THE EDUCATION PROFESSION

PREAMBLE

The educator, believing in the worth and dignity of each human being, recognizes the supreme importance of the pursuit of truth, devotion to excellence, and the nurture of the democratic principles. Essential to these goals is the protection of freedom to learn and to teach and the guarantee of equal educational opportunity for all. The educator accepts the responsibility to adhere to the highest ethical standards.

The educator recognizes the magnitude of the responsibility inherent in the teaching process. The desire for the respect and confidence of one's colleagues, of students, of parents, and of the members of the community provides the incentive to attain and maintain the highest possible degree of ethical conduct. The Code of Ethics of the Education Profession indicates the aspiration of all educators and provides standards by which to judge conduct.

The remedies specified by the NEA and/or its affiliates for the violation of any provision of this Code shall be exclusive and no such provision shall be enforceable in any form other than the one specifically designated by the NEA or its affiliates.

PRINCIPLE I

Commitment to the Student

The educator strives to help each student realize his or her potential as a worthy and effective member of society. The educator therefore works to stimulate the spirit of inquiry, the acquisition of knowledge and understanding, and the thoughtful formulation of worthy goals.
In fulfillment of the obligation to the student, the educator—

1. Shall not unreasonably restrain the student from independent action in the pursuit of learning.
2. Shall not unreasonably deny the student's access to varying points of view.
3. Shall not deliberately suppress or distort subject matter relevant to the student's progress.
4. Shall make reasonable effort to protect the student from conditions harmful to learning or to health and safety.
5. Shall not intentionally expose the student to embarrassment or disparagement.
6. Shall not on the basis of race, color, creed, sex, national origin, marital status, political or religious beliefs, family, social or cultural background, or sexual orientation, unfairly—
   a. Exclude any student from participation in any program
   b. Deny benefits to any student
   c. Grant any advantage to any student
7. Shall not use professional relationships with students for private advantage.
8. Shall not disclose information about students obtained in the course of professional service unless disclosure serves a compelling professional purpose or is required by law.

PRINCIPLE II

Commitment to the Profession

The education profession is vested by the public with a trust and responsibility requiring the highest ideals of professional service.
In the belief that the quality of the services of the education profession directly influences the nation and its citizens, the educator shall exert every effort to raise professional standards, to promote a climate that encourages the exercise of professional judgment, to achieve conditions that attract persons worthy of the trust to careers in education, and to assist in preventing the practice of the profession by unqualified persons.

NEA'S PROFESSIONAL CODE OF ETHICS FOR TEACHERS *(CONT.)*

In fulfillment of the obligation to the profession, the educator—

1. Shall not in an application for a professional position deliberately make a false statement or fail to disclose a material fact related to competency and qualifications.
2. Shall not misrepresent his/her professional qualifications.
3. Shall not assist any entry into the profession of a person known to be unqualified in respect to character, education, or other relevant attribute.
4. Shall not knowingly make a false statement concerning the qualifications of a candidate for a professional position.
5. Shall not assist a noneducator in the unauthorized practice of teaching.
6. Shall not disclose information about colleagues obtained in the course of professional service unless disclosure serves a compelling professional purpose or is required by law.
7. Shall not knowingly make false or malicious statements about a colleague.
8. Shall not accept any gratuity, gift, or favor that might impair or appear to influence professional decisions or action.

—Adopted by the NEA 1975 Representative Assembly (NEA, 1975)

Ethical Teaching Attitudes

Case Studies

"What would you do in these situations?"

Case Study #1

Your grandmother, Yolanda is seventy-five years old and has been in poor health for many years. She has verbally indicated that she wants to die naturally when the time comes. Her daughter does not agree and has indicated she will ask the doctors to resuscitate if necessary to keep her mother alive. Yolanda has a stroke and is not on a life support system.

1. How would you feel in this situation?

____

____

2. What ethical principles would guide you in this case?

____

____

3. What alternatives are there for resolving this dilemma?

____

____

4. What are the possible consequences for each of the alternatives?

5. How would you prioritize the alternatives?

6. What is your plan of action?

Case Study #2

You are the judge in a divorce settlement. The wife indicates that she wants the couples frozen embryos so that she could have children and ask her husband for child support. The husband wants the embryo's to be destroyed.

1. How would you feel in this situation?

2. What ethical principles would guide you in this case?

3. What alternatives are there for resolving this dilemma?

4. What are the possible consequences for each of the alternatives?

5. How would you prioritize the alternatives?

6. What is your plan of action?

Case Study #3

You discover that your best friend's spouse is having an extramarital affair.

1. How would you feel in this situation?

2. What ethical principles would guide you in this case?

3. What alternatives are there for resolving this dilemma?

4. What are the possible consequences for each of the alternatives?

5. How would you prioritize the alternatives?

6. What is your plan of action?

I^3 *Write your own ethical case study.*

Legal Responsibilities as a Teacher

Tort Liability

A tort is any wrongful act, not involving a breach of contract, for which a civil action may be taken. Only torts involving negligence constitute legal grounds for damage suits. It is not criminal because the act was not intentional.

You may be held liable for an accident as a teacher if you are negligent in performing your duty. Negligent acts may include teaching a course that you are not trained or certified to teach, failing to warn students about hazards, being absent or inattentive from your room when an accident occurs, and making students perform a hazardous activity.

There are three main duties that are required of you as a teacher to avoid liability for an accident. You must provide appropriate, pertinent and safe instruction; attentive and active supervision; and you must provide maintenance on instructional materials and equipment. If you fail in any of these areas, you can be in neglect. Negligence includes careless conduct, failure to use appropriate care, conduct in spite of hazard, and unreasonable risk.

Cases of negligence are classified as torts. A teacher-student relationship is such that the teacher has the ability to prevent injury to the student. This may occur in a traditional classroom setting where a teacher ignores safety issues with the classroom itself, or material in the classroom; or it could occur on a field trip. The best method to avoid tort liability is to maintain common sense and awareness of your student's behavior. Do not hope for luck to keep you or your students safe, take action and be proactive.

BTW

Horseshoe over a Door. History has shown horseshoes displayed with the heels both up and down. They can be found on silver coins from 300 B.C., displayed on banners, and most recently above the door of many homes. More often than not, horseshoes placed above the door have the heels up and the ground surface of the shoe facing out. It is said that a horseshoe placed in this position over the door is good luck for all who are in this home. However, there are also horseshoes displayed with the heels down. The reasoning here is that from this shoe (with the heels down) good luck will flow down upon all who come and go through this doorway. The tradition of putting a horseshoe over the door to bring good luck and keep the devil away has long been tradition. The story behind this tradition has many variations.

Once upon a time, a wise old blacksmith was hard at work making horseshoes. The sound of the anvil attracted the attention of the devil. He saw that the smith was making horseshoes, and he thought it would be a good idea to get his own hoofs shod. So the devil made a deal with the smith and stood to be shod. The wise blacksmith saw whom he was dealing, and so he nailed on a red-hot shoe, driving the nails square into the center of the devil's hoof. The devil then paid him and left; but the honest blacksmith threw the money into the forge fire, knowing it would bring him bad luck. Meanwhile, the devil walked some distance and began to suffer the greatest torture from the new shoes. The more he danced and pranced and kicked and swore, the more they hurt him. Finally, after he had gone through the most fearful agony, he tore them off and threw them away. From that time to this, whenever the devil sees a horseshoe he turns and runs—anxious to keep out of the way of those torturous devices.

Child Abuse Reporting

All fifty states have passed some form of a mandatory child abuse and neglect reporting law in order to qualify for funding under the Child Abuse Prevention and Treatment Act (CAPTA). Eighteen states have broad statutes requiring "any person" to report child abuse. CAPTA mandates child abuse is any act or failure to act resulting in imminent risk of serious harm, death, serious physical or emotional harm, sexual abuse, or exploitation of a child by a parent or caretaker who is responsible for the child's welfare. Failure to report suspected child abuse can result in criminal or civil liability. Remember, when you report child abuse, you are reporting suspected child abuse—you are not making a determination about whether the child is abused or neglected as defined by the law.

Teachers working with children should be aware of their students and able to detect some signs of child abuse such as physical signs including bruising, burns, bone fractures, or poor hygiene. In addition, the teacher may notice behavioral signs of abuse such as little emotion when physically hurt, withdrawn, mood swings, and erratically and dramatically changed behavior.

There are many ways to respond to a potential child abuse scenario, although each situation is uniquely different. The initial step is to share the information with other professionals as soon as possible. Continue to gather data on student behavior and then discuss with colleagues as well as compare notes and brainstorm possible strategies. Ask the school professionals as to your role in assisting the student and if they believe you should talk to the student and/or be involved in their discussions.

Corporal Punishment

"I believe that there is no longer any use for corporal punishment in schools and much to be gained by suppressing it."

—B. F. Skinner

I³ *Write down any ideas that come to you after reading this quote.*

____

____

I³ *What are your thoughts on or prior experiences with corporal punishment in schools?*

____

____

____

____

According to a consumer research poll commissioned by the Family Research Council, 76% of the more than 1,000 Americans surveyed said that spanking was an effective form of discipline in their home when they were children (Family Research Council, 1994). Americans perceive lack of discipline to be the biggest problem in public education today and studies show strong public support for corporal punishment (Flynn, 1994). However, many psychologists believe that spanking is an improper form of discipline and a systematic review of the research literature on corporal punishment found that 83% of the 132 identified articles in psychosocial journals were opinion-driven editorials and devoid of empirical data (Lyons, Anderson, & Larson, 1993).

I³ *What are your thoughts on this data? What questions do you have about the research?*

There are currently 27 U.S. states that ban corporal punishment in schools. In Florida, more than half of the districts in the state do not allow corporal punishment. The trend appears to be that the northern and western states typically ban this approach. In 2,000, 342,038 students were subjected to corporal punishment out of a total public school enrollment of 46,306,355, which is less than 1% of the student population. Tennessee (4.2%), Alabama (5.4%), Arkansas (9.1%), and Mississippi (9.8%) lead the country with corporal punishment incidents.

Hymen and Wise (1979) indicate that there is no evidence that discipline is better when corporal punishment is used, and in many places the schools and homes with the most corporal punishment have had the worst discipline. Parents and teachers who participate in corporal punishment in an attempt to control children may be setting an example the children try to follow (Bandura, 1977). Some view this as the hypocrisy of "Do what I say, not what I do."

I³ *What are your thoughts on this data? What questions do you have about the research?*

I³ *How can you justify the polarization of views and research on this topic?*

Copyright Laws

Copyright is a form of protection provided by the laws of the United States to the authors of "original works of authorship," including literary, dramatic, musical, artistic, and certain other intellectual works. This protection is available to both published and unpublished works. It is illegal for anyone to violate any of the rights provided by the copyright law to the owner of copyright. These rights, however, are not unlimited in scope. One major limitation is the doctrine of "fair use," of the 1976 Copyright Act.

Fair Use

Under the Copyright Act of 1976, the "fair use" exemption places a limit on exclusive rights to promote free speech, learning, scholarly research, and open discussion. Educators may use portions of copyrighted material if the purpose and character of the use is educational in nature, previously published, not a substantial part of the entire work and if the marketability of the work is not impaired by the use. These standards do not provide specific guidance for educators, scholars, and students and may be subjective in their interpretation. Copying by teachers should be limited and infrequent and should include a notice of the author's copyright. Four major factors to consider for fair use are character of use, nature of the work to be used, amount of work, and market effect.

Several categories of material are generally not eligible for federal copyright protection. Works that have *not* been fixed in a tangible form of expression; titles, names, short phrases, and slogans; familiar symbols or designs; mere variations of typographic ornamentation, lettering, or coloring; mere listings of ingredients or contents; ideas, procedures, methods, systems, processes, concepts, principles, discoveries, or devices, as distinguished from a description, explanation, or illustration; and works consisting *entirely* of information that is common property and containing no original authorship (e.g., standard calendars, height and weight charts, tape measures and rulers, etc.)

Technology, Education, and Copyright Harmonization Act of 2002 (TEACH)

"Anyone who tells you computers are more effective than anything else is either dumb or lying."

—Larry Cuban, Stanford University

I^3 *Write down any ideas that come to you after reading this quote.*

____

____

"It is appallingly obvious our technology has exceeded our humanity."

—Albert Einstein

I^3 *Write down any ideas that come to you after reading this quote.*

____

____

I^3 *How can you justify that both of these quotes may have merit?*

____

____

The same copyright exist regardless if the work is electronic or in a traditional format. A recent addition to the copyright law is the Technology, Education, and Copyright Harmonization Act of 2002 or TEACH Act. This describes technological protection systems that have been implemented to protect digitized copyrighted works and prevent infringement, including upgradeable and self-repairing systems. Since the rapid influx and development of technology affect the educational arena, there is special consideration for the interaction of how these two will exist appropriately. The TEACH Act expands the scope of educators' rights to display works and make copies integral for using technology in education. This act attempts to parallel the rights and limitations that are given for traditional teaching.

Legal Rights

Freedom of Expression

There are currently seven states that have adopted a student expression law. Some believe that the First Amendment ensuring freedom of speech is no different in schools than in the greater society outside of the school grounds. Some districts have developed guidelines to set forth rules and regulations in order to preserve the educational process and create an environment conducive to learning, balanced against the individual student's right to freedom of expression under the First Amendment. The First Amendment declares that "Congress shall make no law . . . abridging the freedom of speech." It seems as though this law would be clear and enable anyone to say anything, anywhere. However, other considerations deemed more important may trump this law, such as safety and providing all students with a safe, secure, nurturing environment to learn.

I³ *What are your thoughts on freedom of expression?*

____

____

____

____

____

____

Freedom of Speech and Press: What Is Your Opinion?

Please read these statements and provide your opinion whether you agree or disagree and why.

1. There should be limits on our freedom of speech and press.
2. People should be able to say or print any opinion about the president of the United States.
3. School principals should have complete control over what is printed in the school newspaper.
4. People who strongly oppose a government policy should be able to legally burn an American flag.
5. Students should be able to wear protest symbols in schools.
6. The government should be able to ban violent Web sites on the Internet to protect children.
7. There should be laws to ban people from making insulting statements about someone's gender, racial background, or religion.
8. During a war, the government should be allowed to place more restrictions on freedom of speech and press.
9. The government should ban art, music, or TV shows that encourage illegal behavior such as drug use or violence against police.
10. The government should make it illegal to take photographs of famous people without their permission.

Dress Codes

> ***"Now they're talking about making kids wear uniforms in school . . . this is pretty stupid. Don't these schools do enough damage making these kids think alike, now they want them to look alike too?"***
>
> —George Carlin

I³ *Write down any ideas that come to you after reading this quote.*

____

____

Many districts are concerned with school dress codes and have taken action to address the concerns. Some districts have developed policies or regulations, while others have determined school uniforms are the best resolution. Some districts have indicated their belief that the development of attitudes and behavior patterns in dress and grooming should be a part of each student's total educational experience. Some schools recommend that teachers be aware of particular attire such as oversized pants and shirts, garments that are cut-off or torn, wearing of all one color on a consistent and frequent basis, heavy overcoats, or belts with large, heavy metal buckles. Others have restrictions against wearing items containing offensive words or those with dual meaning; garments that expose midriffs, cleavage, buttocks or undergarments; sexually suggestive; and indoor hats or sunglasses cannot be worn. In addition, tattoos that depict anything prohibited in these rules must be covered at all times and at no time will bandannas or hairnets be allowed.

Though many people agree with mandatory school uniforms, there are still just as many people opposed to them. One of the arguments opposing uniforms are that they deliberately violate a student's First Amendment rights such as blatantly ignoring a student's fundamental right to freedom of expression. Another argument is that in the long run, uniforms stunt a child's personal development. A child's personal development is inhibited by forcing them into conformity and by suppressing peaceful means of expressing emotions (Cohn, 1996).

I³ *What do you think of dress codes? Did you have dress codes at your secondary school? Which of the prior rules do you believe are unnecessary?*

____

____

____

____

____

____

____

____

____

____

Due Process

Due process is a term of U.S. law that refers to fundamental procedural legal safeguards of which every citizen has an absolute right when a state or court purports to take a decision that could affect any right of that citizen. The most basic right protected under the due process doctrine is the right to be given notice, and an opportunity to be heard. The procedure or process required for a given judgment to be fair. Fairness here is specified in terms of the process rather than the outcome.

Schools create their own process or procedure for student misconduct. When a student has broken a school rule, the administration then follows this procedure to determine the outcome of the student's actions.

Reasonable Search and Seizure

Many states have common reasonable search and seizure laws for identifying potential problems on school grounds. The searches must be complete in accordance with the legal, state, district, and school regulations. Typically the principal, assistant principal, or security assistant may search a student on the school premises or on a school-sponsored activity if he/she has a reasonable belief that you possess something that is illegal. The search will be typically be held in front of a third-party adult and anything taken will be returned within a reasonable time, unless it is illegal to have the item or the item. They may search any part of the school, which includes your locker. If your locker is searched, the school official should make reasonable effort to obtain your consent before he/she searches it. Students are protected from unreasonable search and seizure by the fourth amendment. Some problems arise in a lack of clarity of the application of the Fourth Amendment in school settings. The Fourth Amendment protects individuals from unreasonable searches by law enforcement.

"The right of people to be secure in their persons, houses, papers, and effects, against unreasonable searches and seizures, shall not be violated, and no Warrants shall issue, but upon probable cause, supported by Oath or affirmation, and particularly describing the place to be searched, and the persons or things to be seized."

—FOURTH AMENDMENT

I³ *What do you think about search and seizure rules?*

____

____

____

____

____

____

____

____

____

____

____

KWL

What Did You LEARN?

____

____

____

____

____

____

____

____

____

____

____

References

Bandura, A. (1977). *Social learning theory.* Englewood Cliffs, NJ: Prentice Hall.

Cohn, C. (1996). Mandatory school uniforms. *The School Administrator,* Vol. 5, 22–25.

Flynn, C. P. (1994). Regional differences in attitudes toward corporal punishment. *Journal of Marriage and the Family,* 56, 314–324.

Hymen, I., & Wise, J. (1979). *Corporal punishment in American education: readings in history, practice, and alternatives.* Philadelphia: Temple University Press.

Lyons, J. S., Anderson, R. L., & Larson, D. B. (1993). The use and effects of physical punishment in the home: a systematic review. Presentation to the Section on Bio-Ethics of the American Academy of Pediatrics, Annual Meeting, Washington, DC, November 2, 1993.

Trumbull, M.D., Dean A. and Ravenel, M.D., S. Dubose. *Spare the Rod? New Research Challenges Spanking Critics.* Downloaded from http://www.fotf.ca/familyfacts/analysis/100196.html

Voter/Consumer Research Poll, *National Values.* Commissioned by the Family Research Council, 1994.

PowerPoint Outline to Assist In-Class Note-Taking

A. Am I Fit to Be a Teacher?

B. Legal Concerns

C. Tenure

D. Professional Code of Ethics

a. NEA's Professional Code of Ethics for Teachers

E. Ethical Teaching Attitudes

a. Case Studies

F. Legal Responsibilities as a Teacher

a. Tort Liability

b. Child Abuse Reporting

c. Corporal Punishment

d. Copyright Laws

G. **Legal Rights**

a. Freedom of Expression

b. Dress Codes

c. Due Process

9

Historical Aspects of Education in America

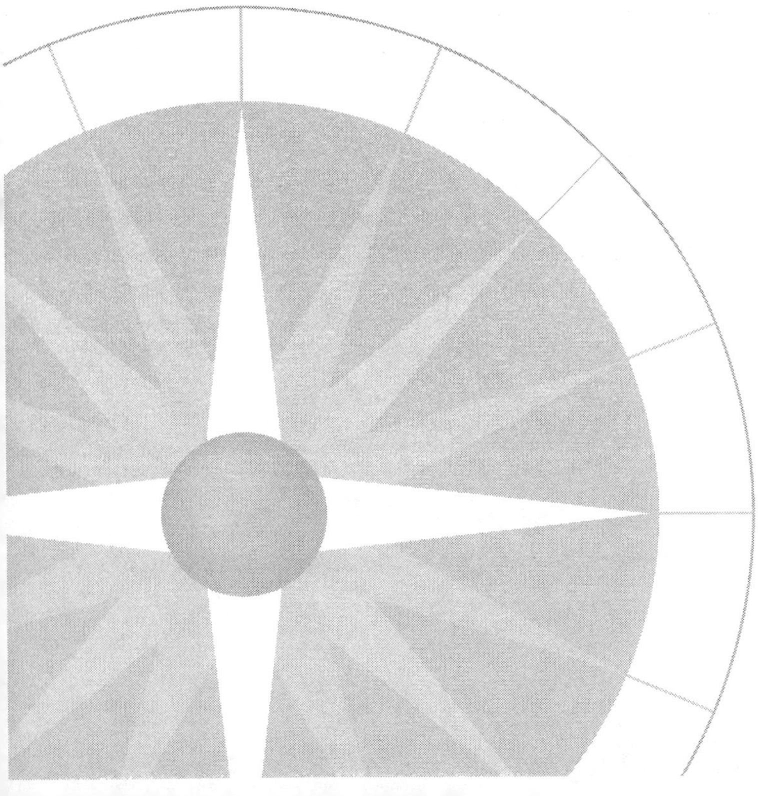

Guest Editorial: William Russell, Doctoral Candidate,
Florida State University

The Educational Times They Are A-Changin'!

Through out the history of education, education has been manipulated to the needs and wants of society. Education is like pop music, the diva of the educational world is whatever idea or concept is the most popular, not necessarily what is most effective. In recent years there are three major educational issues.

1. Integrating Technology into the Classroom
2. Standardized Tests
3. Reading

These concepts have been written about in educational journals/books and discussed among the academia long before the diva insurgence came.

These concepts/ideas, among many others, have been in education for years, but do not become important until some one with authority recognizes the importance. Social and economical trends help decide what is most important in education. During the race for the moon, educators thought science and math were the most important, so what happened, students were smothered with science and math content. In the early days of our nation, religion was extremely important, so what happened, students were educated by reading the Bible. Educational trends have happened throughout history and will continue to happen in education.

The educational times they are a-changin', and will continue to do so as the social and economic values of society change. The best thing educators can do to prepare for the inevitable change is to be flexible.

"To know nothing of what happened before you were born is to remain ever a child."

—Cicero

I^3 *Write down any ideas that come to you after reading this quote.*

"Many public-school children seem to know only two dates—1492 and 4th of July; and as a rule they don't know what happened on either occasion."

—Mark Twain

I^3 *Write down any ideas that come to you after reading this quote.*

I^3 *How can you justify that both of these quotes may have merit?*

KWL

What Do You KNOW? **(prior knowledge)**

What Do You WANT to Know? **(objectives and goals)**

History of Education

> ***"The purpose of Compulsory Education is to deprive the common people of their commonsense."***
>
> —G. K. Chesterton, 1929

I^3 *Write down any ideas that come to you after reading this quote.*

"For most Americans, all history is ancient history and the best thing about the past is that it's over."

—Raymond Seitz, former U.S. Ambassador to Britain

I³ *Write down any ideas that come to you after reading this quote.*

____

____

I³ *How can you justify that both of these quotes may have merit?*

____

____

As a rule of thumb, most pre-service candidates have not observed many classrooms. Let us take a moment to determine our class's background on history in general. Please access the form at the back of this chapter entitled "Historic Figures." Form a small group and discuss these individuals and their accomplishments. Finally, determine a short list of five people from the list or others whom are not on that list, if you are aware of them, who have had the greatest impact of our global society over the past millennium.

BTW

Rumor is that old English law declared that it was okay for a man to beat his wife but had to use a stick no larger in diameter than his thumb.

What would you LIKE to know about the history of education?

1. ____
2. ____
3. ____
4. ____
5. ____

If you said "nothing," then you might want to reconsider being a teacher. Now this does not mean that unless you memorize the dates of the first schools, amendments, NEA presidents, and so on, that you do not wish to be a teacher or cannot be an effective teacher. However, if you are not interested in the history of your chosen vocation, regardless of what it is, then you might wish to rethink how intrinsically motivated you are about the discipline. When people actively and intentionally pursue a goal, they typically are excited about it, involved in it, and are interested in what occurred concerning the background of the goal before they begin. So, in order for you to validate pursuing a teaching career, somewhat of an interest in the history of education should be natural. So, mind your Ps and Qs and read on.

BTW

This one is interesting because there are many different interpretations on what it means.

1. Ale was served at local taverns out of a "tankard"—you were charged by the angle of your elbow: half-way up—you drank a pint; all the way up—you drank a quart. Since the quart cost so much more than the pint, you were warned to "mind your Ps and Qs"
2. "Minding one's Ps and Qs" is a typesetter's admonition. When you handle individual character type slugs, you need to be careful of how you store and retrieve the "Ps and Qs", because they look so much alike
3. It stands for "mind your pints and quarts," a saying that came into existence long before any typesetters could be concerned about mistaking "Ps and Qs" on a typewriter! The expression was intended for people to mind how many pints and quarts they drank, or in other words, to behave!
5. It's just a shorthand way of saying "mind your pleases and thank yous"—something you tell your kids when they go off to spend the night at a friend's house so that they will be polite. Maybe this is a colloquial definition, because the pints and quarts thing sounds more like a general "take care" kind of warning.

When, where, and by whom was the first school established?

Questions such as when, where, who, and how are good points to begin when tracing how we arrived at our current educational system. This text will present a few highlights, but you are encouraged to research various aspects, which you believe to be relevant or particularly interesting to you and your career pursuits.

In 1635, the first grammar school was established in Boston. The next year, Harvard University was founded. At this time, a school's main function was to teach people to read so that they are able to read the Bible. Schools were typically associated with a church in that region and the main purpose of an institute for higher learning was for young men who wished to pursue a career in religion. In the late 1700s, each region of the United States took different approaches to education. The northeast focused on primary school for boys, whereas the midwest engaged in elementary education and the south decidedly abstained from educational responsibility. In 1821, the first high school was opened in Boston for the sons of the mechanics. From 1836–1850, while serving on the Massachusetts Board of Education, Horace Mann took the first step toward teacher professional development. In the 1920s, John Dewey called for a progressive form of education. Dewey would serve as a foundational pioneer in the field of education, his work and ideology in curriculum development is still cited today.

BTW

The citrus soda 7-UP was created in 1929; "7" was selected because the original containers were 7 ounces. "UP" indicated the direction of the bubbles.

Timing is everything and just as a education was developing a progressive approach, society seem to desire a return to traditional education during the postwar era of the 1950s. In 1954, the historic case of *Brown vs. Board of Education* in Topeka, Kansas indicated that separate but equal schools are unconstitutional. The court declared in 1955 that schools must be desegregated "with all deliberate speed." The Brown decision gave tremendous forward motion to the 1964 Civil Rights Act (Title IV).

Remember, other worldly events help shape the direction and philosophy of education in the United States. In 1949, the Soviet Union exploded its first nuclear bomb. America's monopoly on nuclear weapons is over. In 1952, the United States developed the H-Bomb. In 1955, the Soviet Union dropped the world's first airborne H-bomb. Also, the Soviets displayed long-range missiles, capable of delivering a nuclear bomb to America. Eisenhower doubled the rate of B-52 bomber production. In 1957, the Soviet Union tested the world's first Intercontinental Ballistic Missile (ICBM). On October 4, 1957, the Soviet Union launched the world's first manmade satellite, Sputnik. America pushed its own satellite project forward; the satellite Vanguard failed to launch and is a national humiliation for America. The United States successfully tests its first Atlas ICBM. In 1958, the first U.S. satellite, Explorer 1, is launched into orbit and NASA is formally established. Congress passes the National Defense Education Act to encourage young people to pursue the fields of math, science, and engineering. In 1959, exactly 2 years after the first Sputnik launch, the Soviets sent the first spacecraft around the moon. Luna 3 took pictures of the moon's far side and sent them to Earth. Between 1958 and 1961, six more Sputniks were launched into orbit, all larger than the first. They improved re-entry and recovery efforts in preparation for manned flight. In 1961, Soviet cosmonaut Yuri Gagarin became the first person to orbit the Earth. One month later on May 5th, the first astronaut was sent briefly into space aboard Freedom 7. Alan Shepard spent 15 minutes in suborbital space but did not orbit the Earth. This flight demonstrated that a man could control a craft during weightlessness and high G-force stress.

"I believe that this nation should commit itself to achieving the goal, before this decade is out, of landing a man on the moon and returning him safely to the Earth."

—John F. Kennedy, May 25, 1961

"We would get under our desks and stay there until we were told to come out or in some cases, in some of the classrooms we had coat-rooms off the side of each classroom and we'd walk through and we'd get our coat and we'd go out into the hallways and we would literally duck down facing against the wall. In that way we thought we were protecting ourselves from the bombs and from any damage that would be done to us."

—Jean Asam, American

"In the 1950s it didn't even cross our minds that the Americans were frightened of a Soviet invasion. We thought they believed we only had peaceful aims; that all we wanted was to live in peace. . . . We thought that we had something to be frightened of, because they were capitalists and that was something terrible for us. We believed that they sucked the blood of the workers. It didn't even cross our minds that the Americans were scared of us."

—Galina Mishnia, Russian

I³ *Compare and contrast ideas that you may infer from these quotes.*

____

____

____

____

I³ *How can you justify that both of these quotes may have merit?*

____

____

Think about these questions in the context of education and how the outcomes of these affected how we educate today.

1. What was the arms race and why did it escalate?
2. How did the arms race affect domestic and educational concerns?
3. How did the arms race and science contribute to the continuation of the Cold War?

The Elementary and Secondary Education Act (ESEA) was enacted in 1965 to provide guidance and funds to K–12 schools. On January 8, 2002, President George Bush signed the *No Child Left Behind (NCLB) Act.* This act reauthorizes and amends federal education programs established under the Elementary and Secondary Education Act (ESEA) of 1965. The major focus of NCLB, i.e., ESEA, is to provide all children with a fair, equal, and significant opportunity to obtain a high-quality education. The U.S. Department of Education is emphasizing four pillars within the bill: accountability, flexibility, research-based education, and parent options. In essence, it is a national extension of the standards-based education reform efforts.

I³ *Why would a president re-enact an act which was almost 40 years old? What are some potential problems of this act? What are some advantages?*

____

____

____

____

____

Organization of Schools

In the United States there are free public schools and private schools, which parents must pay tuition. The money to pay for the public schools comes from local property taxes. Public schools are divided into districts, which is governed by a school board (refer to Chapter 6 for more information). The school board selects a superintendent, who is the director of the school district. There are several types of schools in the United States, including pre-school, kindergarten, elementary, and secondary (which includes middle, junior, and high school). There are also post-secondary schools, which include vocational, technical colleges, community colleges, and universities.

Developing and Implementing the Curriculum

There are several definitions of curriculum. For this text, curriculum will be the subject matter that teachers and students cover in their studies. It describes and specifies the methods, structure, organization, balance, and presentation of the content. It is a plan of instruction that details what students are to know, how they are to learn it, what the teacher's role is, and the context in which learning and teaching will take place. It is a comprehensive overview, including activities planned for delivery to the students, the scope of content, the sequence of materials, interpretation, and balance of subject matter, and motivational, instructional, and assessment techniques to be used. Basically, it is everything seen and unseen, intentional and unintentional, and perceived and unperceived that occurs in school.

Types of Curriculum

Curriculum can be categorized into multiple types, in order to understand and address it more clearly. Many believe that the four major curriculum types are explicit (public), hidden (affective), null (missing), and extracurricular. The explicit curriculum is generally thought of as the public curriculum. This is what is written down, approved by school boards, facilitated by superintendents and principals, and taught by teachers. The hidden curriculum deals with the affective domain, such as attitudes and perspectives. How a student feels about the content or their self-efficacy is important and will greatly affect how efficiently and effectively they will learn. The null curriculum is material or concepts that should be included, but is missing. For instance, some schools may not offer life skills, or how to gain acceptance to college, or information on careers. It is up to all involved parties to consider whether null curriculum should be created and transferred into explicit curriculum. Finally, there is extracurricular, which is any activity outside of the formalized explicit curriculum. Examples such as music, athletics, clubs, and other organizations are extracurricular.

How Is the Curriculum Developed?

Remember, everything taught in the public schools must align with the national and/or state standards. Therefore, curriculum will be developed by administrators and teachers in the discipline area by interpreting and determining the best practice for teaching the standards.

Do I Have to Teach the Curriculum?

Yes. As a student, it may have appeared at times, that your teacher was teaching anything they desired (hopefully that was actually the case). Actually, they were teaching the standards specifically designed for that particular discipline.

How Do I Teach the Curriculum?

As a teacher, the state will instruct you WHAT to teach and you will determine the best way HOW to teach it. Your academic methods courses will assist you in developing the ideal ways to teach a particular concept. Typically, pre-service teachers will take methods courses in science, math, literacy, music, art, and physical education.

Will I Have to Teach a Class That I Am Unqualified to Teach?

Maybe. Currently, as much as 30% of teachers nationwide are teaching out of their field. If you are asked to teach a class that does not align itself well with your background, then you will either make a choice to ask not to teach it. In that case, the principal may have to terminate your contract, or select to teach out of field. If you teach out of field, you should have a mentor and assistance. You may wish to continue teaching out of field for a while and wait until a course opens that aligns itself closer to your experience or you may wish to transfer to a school that has openings in your area. Also, as implementation of the *No Child Left Behind Act* continues, schools will be required to ensure that all teachers are highly qualified in each academic subject they teach, further increasing the staffing pressures created by out-of-field teaching and teacher turnover. In Florida, employment of out-of-field teachers is regulated. The employment or assignment of out-of-field teachers may occur when a qualified and appropriately certificated teacher is unavailable. Any teacher who is employed or assigned out-of-field shall be required to satisfy the course credit requirement in state board of education. A teacher may receive in-field designation if they pass a Florida subject area test, demonstrate subject area competencies via several established venues, pass successful experiences in the field, and pass systematic observations and favorable evaluations of classroom instruction by their supervisor.

Reform Efforts

Shanker (1990) argued that contemporary school reform proposals do not imagine different kinds of schools, but emphasize improving traditional schools—primarily at the secondary school level, traditional governance systems, and administrative bureaucracies. Typical reform recommendations are wide-ranging. Sizer (1992) indicated that school reform efforts can be divided into three general types. They include the oblique strategy, in which the government promotes reform at long-range increased regulations, testing, or teacher salaries. The second type is the direct approach, which is the re-engineering of individual schools. The final type is called systemic and the change mechanism are the parents.

Reform efforts over the years include open classrooms, closed classrooms, collaboration, testing, and certification of new teachers, teaching using technology, performance standards, high stakes testing, more science and mathematics, and more homework.

In all actuality, we have not deviated significantly from 5 decades ago, where students were all sitting in desks arranged in straight rows positioned toward the front of the classroom, where a teacher lectured orally, then provided a written assessment.

In earlier sections of this text, we spoke of progressivism, constructivism, and active learning—methodologies that COULD be viewed as a reforming traditional education. However, these approaches have not been widely accepted and integrated into the curriculum.

I^3 *Why do you believe this is the case? If we have developed a better "mouse trap," as an educational culture, why are we not using it?*

____

____

____

____

____

BTW

Have you read "Who Moved My Cheese?" by Spencer Johnson?

Cheese represents what makes us happy and fulfilled, including financial, spiritual, physical, or mental well-being.

- The more important your cheese is, the more you want to hold on to it.
- To keep your cheese, you may need to change.
- The possibility of losing our cheese makes us afraid.
- We should smell our cheese often to know when it's getting old.
- Movement in a new direction helps you to find cheese.
- The quicker you let go of old cheese, the sooner you will find new cheese.
- Old beliefs do not lead you to new cheese.
- So move with the cheese and enjoy it!

The point of the story is that we have to be alert to changes in the cheese, and be prepared to go running off in search of new sources of cheese when the cheese we have runs out or goes bad.

I^3 *Have you checked your cheese recently? How does it look? What would be the first thing that you would do if you noticed it smelling poorly?*

___

___

___

___

Chapter 68 National Education Reform

The United States Code is the official, subject matter order, compilation of the Federal laws of a general, and permanent nature that are currently in force. The U.S. Code is compiled by the Office of the Law Revision Counsel of the United States House of Representatives. Title 20 of the Code includes Education and Chapter 68 is the National Education Reform. The purpose of this chapter is to provide a framework for meeting the National Education Goals established by

1. promoting coherent, nationwide, systemic education reform;
2. improving the quality of learning and teaching in the classroom;
3. defining appropriate and coherent federal, state, and local roles and responsibilities for education reform and lifelong learning;
4. establishing valid and reliable mechanisms;
5. supporting new initiatives at the federal, state, local, and school levels to provide equal educational opportunity for all students to meet high academic and occupational skill standards and to succeed in the world of employment and civic participation;
6. providing a framework for the reauthorization of all federal education programs
7. stimulating the development and adoption of a voluntary national system of skill standards and certification to serve as a cornerstone of the national strategy to enhance workforce skills; and
8. assisting every elementary and secondary school that receives funds under this chapter to actively involve parents in supporting the academic work of their children.

National Education Goals

Eight National Education Goals were created by the governors and the Congress to improve learning and teaching in the nation's education system. These goals help provide a national framework for education reform and promote certain specific changes needed to ensure equitable educational opportunities and high levels of educational achievement for all students.

The goals include:

Goal 1—Ready to Learn
Goal 2—School Completion
Goal 3—Student Achievement and Citizenship
Goal 4—Teacher Education and Professional Development
Goal 5—Mathematics and Science
Goal 6—Adult Literacy and Lifelong Learning
Goal 7—Safe, Disciplined, and Alcohol- and Drug-Free Schools
Goal 8—Parental Participation

I^3 *What do you think of these goals? Are there some that you would not include? Are there some that you believe are missing?*

____

____

____

____

Standards-Based Education

"'Less is more' we keep telling ourselves. Students learn more when we teach less—but teach it well."

—(Dempster, 1993).

What is a standard? A standard is a basis for comparison, a reference point against which other things can be evaluated. In addition, standards indicate the level of performance on the criterion being assessed that is considered satisfactory in terms of the purpose of the evaluation.

I^3 *Please create at least four standards for toilet paper.*

1. ______________________________
2. ______________________________
3. ______________________________
4. ______________________________
5. ______________________________

An educational standard must be specific enough so that everyone interprets it in the same manner in order to understand what students need to learn. The standards must permit a fair and accurate judgment of whether the standards have been met. Ideally, they should be able to be achieved in a variety of ways.

An extensive international study called the Third International Mathematics and Science Study (TIMSS) gathered significant amounts of data on how other countries teach and how the achievement levels of their students compare to those in the United States. One very interesting result is that although U.S. science textbooks attempt to cover 930% more topics than do German textbooks and 433% more topics than do Japanese textbooks, both German and Japanese students significantly outperform U.S. students in science achievement as well (Schmidt, McKnight, & Raizen, 1996).

I³ *What does this mean? Please take a moment and seriously consider these statements and critically evaluate some of the possibilities as a student and a pre-service teacher.*

Assessment differs greatly in standard-based education. In this case, assessment is closely aligned with what is taught or the curriculum. This approach also compares students with the criterion or standard and not with their peers. Standards-based assessment also incorporates new forms of assessment. Authentic and alternative assessment is ideal for this standards-based education. Standards-based assessment ideally should

- involve activities that are valued and engaging, such as found in the real world;
- model curriculum reform;
- focus on objectives;
- lead to improved learning by engaging students in meaningful activities;
- lead to more appropriate accountability.

Assessment will be discussed in detail in a later chapter.

Education Action Research

Action research in an education setting is research conducted by classroom teachers and possibly educational researchers, typically concurrent with their teaching. This approach offers a powerful combination of theory and application. If a teacher would like to know how a particular method of teaching will affect their students' achievement, intrinsic motivation, behavior, or other characteristic, they can develop a plan to implement and test their methodology in the context of their classroom. Many times these studies are more authentic, and therefore more generalizable to other similar settings. For instance, if a fourth-grade public school teacher collects action research data on how effective concept mapping was as an alternative formative assessment and found the result positive, then another fourth-grade public school class across the country could expect to receive similar results.

Action research is another way to engage your students in addition to increase their participation and achievement. When students know that they are a part of a research program, a phenomenon called the Hawthorn Effect occurs. The Hawthorn Effect is where the participants in research projects try to please the researcher by trying harder than they would normally.

BTW

Did you know that apples, not caffeine, are more efficient at waking you up in the morning or that diddly-squat actually comes from early American carnival lingo as workers referred to nickels and dimes, the going rate for games of chances as "diddle-e-squat." Also, no piece of paper can be folded more than seven times and most dust particles in your house are made from dead skin or Tonto's nickname for the Lone Ranger, "Kemo Sabe," actually means "soggy shrub" in Navaho. These could be trivial tidbits of useless knowledge or they could be the item that may catch your student's attention.

Instructional Technology

A final aspect of educational reform is the use of instructional technology to enhance teaching and learning. There is significant data which offers insight to using technology in the classroom. Extensive information on how teachers can use technology to supplement their teaching will be provided in a later chapter of this text.

I^3 *What are your thoughts on using technology in teaching? What specific types of lessons and concepts can you consider when using this tool?*

____

____

KWL

What Did You LEARN?

____

____

____

____

____

References

Dempster, F. N. (1993). Exposing our students to less should help them learn. *Phi Delta Kappan, 74(6),* 432–437.

Shanker, A. (1990). The end of the traditional model of schooling—and a proposal for using incentives to restructure our public schools. *Phi Delta Kappan, 71,* 345–357.

Sizer, T. R. (1992). School reform—what's missing? *World Monitor, 5(11),* 20–28.

Schmidt, W. H., McKnight, C. C., & Raizen, S. A. (1996). *Splintered vision: An investigation of U.S. science and mathematics education: Executive summary.* Lansing, MI: U.S. National Research Center for the Third International Mathematics and Science Study, Michigan State University.

HISTORIC FIGURES FORM

Activity to Learn and Evaluate People Who Impacted the Past Millennium

Sridhara 1000	Indian mathematician who discovered the importance of zero.
William the Conqueror 1027–1087	Led the Norman conquest of England and usurped the English throne.
Pope Urban II 1042–1099	Inaugurated the Crusades.
Bhaskara 1114–1185	Indian mathematician who developed a decimal number system.
Saladin 1138–1193	Muslim leader who recaptured Jerusalem from the Crusaders.
Genghis Khan 1162–1227	Mongol conqueror.
Aquinas, St. Thomas 1225–1274	Produced *Summa Theologica*—a statement of Catholic theological doctrines.
Edward I 1239–1307	King of England who helped end feudalism.
Polo, Marco 1254–1324	Gave Europeans the first view of life in the far east.
Osman 1258–1324	Turkish leader who is considered the founder of the Ottoman dynasty.
Alighieri, Dante 1265–1321	Italian poet, composed "The Divine Comedy."
Tamerlane 1336–1405	Turkish Mongol conqueror.
Petrarch 1304–1374	Italian poet and humanist.
Chaucer, Geoffrey 1343–1400	English poet, composed "The Canterbury Tales."
Cheng Ho 1371–1435	Chinese diplomat and explorer who opened China's trade.
Gutenberg, Johann 1400–1468	Developed movable type and the printing press for mass printing.
Yung Lo 1403–1424	Chinese emperor of Ming dynasty who opened up China's trade.
Joan of Arc 1412–1431	Patron saint of France who turned the Hundred Years' War in France's favor.
Medici, Lorenzo de' 1449–1492	Italian banker, statesman, and Renaissance patron of art and scholarship.
Queen Isabella I 1451–1504	Created a united kingdom of Spain and financed Columbus's voyage.
Columbus, Christopher 1451–1506	Explored the Americas.
Da Vinci, Leonardo 1452–1519	Painter, sculptor, architect, engineer, and scientist of the high Renaissance.

HISTORIC FIGURES FORM (*continued*)

Gama, Vasco da 1460–1524	Discovered direct route from Europe to India around Africa.
Machiavelli, Niccolo 1469–1527	Political philosopher who advised rulers to employ ruthless use of force.
Copernicus, Nicolaus 1473–1543	Discovered the moon and planets revolve around the sun.
Michelangelo 1475–1564	Renaissance painter, sculptor, and architect.
Pizarro, Francisco 1475–1541	Spanish adventurer who conquered Inca Empire in Peru.
Magellan, Ferdinand 1480–1521	Leader of the first expedition to circumnavigate the earth.
Luther, Martin 1483–1546	Inaugurated the Protestant Reformation.
Cortes, Hernando 1485–1547	Spanish conqueror of Mexico.
Loyola, St. Ignatius of 1491–1556	Founder of the Order of the Jesuits.
Henry VIII 1491–1547	King of England and founder of the Church of England.
Suleiman 1494–1566	Sultan of Turkey when the Ottoman Empire reached its zenith.
Calvin, John 1509–1564	Protestant theologian and moralist.
Queen Elizabeth I 1533–1603	English monarch.
Tokugawa, Ieyasu 1542–1616	Founder of Japan's Tokugawa dynasty who opened trade with China.
Cervantes, Miguel de 1547–1616	Spanish writer, best known for "Don Quixote."
Shakespeare, William 1550–1604	Playwright and poet.
Bacon, Francis 1561–1626	Philosopher who realized science and technology could transform the world.
Galilei, Galileo 1564–1642	Discovered uniform rate of acceleration and law of inertia.
Harvey, William 1578–1657	Discovered the circulation of blood and the function of the heart.
Hobbes, Thomas 1588–1679	Philosopher who provided a secular justification for the political state.
Shah Jahan 1592–1666	Indian emperor who built the Taj Mahal and the Pearl Mosque.
Descartes, Rene 1596–1650	French mathematician and philosopher.

HISTORIC FIGURES FORM (*continued*)

Cromwell, Oliver 1599–1658	English Civil War leader who led the parliamentary forces to victory.
Milton, John 1606–1674	English poet, composed "Paradise Lost."
Rembrandt 1606–1669	Dutch Baroque artist who is one of the greatest painters of western art.
Locke, John 1632–1704	English philosopher who presented ideas of constitutional democracy.
Louis XIV 1638–1715	King of France whose reign is the longest in European history.
Newton, Sir Isaac 1642–1727	English mathematician and scientist, formulated the four laws of mechanics.
Peter the Great 1672–1725	Russian czar who instituted a policy of westernization.
Bach, Johann Sebastian 1685–1750	Composer.
Montesquieu 1689–1775	French political philosopher.
Voltaire 1694–1778	Writer, historian, philosopher, and leading figure of the French Enlightenment.
Franklin, Ben 1706–1790	Businessman, scientist, writer, and politician.
Rousseau, Jean-Jacques 1712–1778	Philosopher whose writings paved the way for the French Revolution.
Mozart, Wolfgang Amadeus 1719–1787	Composer.
Smith, Adam 1723–1790	Presented the first comprehensive and systematic theory of economics.
Kant, Immanuel 1724–1804	Philosopher who sought to find the nature and limits of human knowledge.
Washington, George 1732–1799	First U.S. president.
Watt, James 1736–1819	Inventor of the first practical steam engine, key industrial revolution figure.
Jefferson, Thomas 1743–1826	Third U.S. president, author of the Declaration of Independence.
Jenner, Edward 1749–1823	Developed smallpox vaccination.
Madison, James 1751–1836	Fourth U.S. president who made the Bill of Rights part of the Constitution.
Wollstonecraft, Mary 1759–1797	English feminist who advocated equality of education between sexes.
Dalton, John 1766–1844	Introduced the atomic hypothesis into the mainstream of science.

HISTORIC FIGURES FORM (*continued*)

Bonaparte, Napoleon 1769–1821	French general and emperor.
Beethoven, Ludwig Van 1770–1827	Composer.
Hegel, George 1770–1831	German idealist philosopher.
Austen, Jane 1775–1817	English novelist, wrote "Pride and Prejudice."
Chaka d. 1898	Zulu warrior chief.
Clausewitz, Karl von 1780–1831	Prussian soldier and military theorist who published "On War."
Bolivar, Simon 1783–1830	Played a dominant role in the liberation of five South American countries.
Daguerre, Louis 1787–1851	Developed the first practical method of photography.
Faraday, Michael 1791–1867	Discovered the law of electromagnetic induction.
Morse, Samuel 1791–1872	Invented the telegraph and Morse code.
Babbage, Charles 1792–1871	Designed and built computing machines anticipating the modern computer.
Darwin, Charles 1809–1882	Originator of the theory of organic evolution by means of natural selection.
McCormick, Cyrus 1809–1884	Inventor of the first reaping machine.
Lincoln, Abraham 1809–1865	Sixteenth U.S. president who led the Union in the Civil War.
Poe, Edgar Allen 1809–1849	American writer.
Barnum, P. T. 1812–1870	American showman and circus innovator. 1810–1891 Dickens, Charles English novelist.
Stanton, Elizabeth Cady 1815–1902	Chief political strategist and theorist of the U.S. women's rights movement.
Thoreau, Henry David 1817–1862	American writer, philosopher, and naturalist, composed "Walden."
Gandhi, Mohandas K. 1869–1948	Leader of Indian independence and prophet of non-violent revolution.
Lenin, Vladimir Ilich 1870–1924	Political leader primarily responsible for establishing Communism in Russia.
Rutherford, Ernest 1871–1937	Central figure in the discovery of radioactivity and nuclear physics.
Caruso, Enrico 1871–1937	Central figure in the discovery of radioactivity and nuclear physics.

HISTORIC FIGURES FORM (*continued*)

Frost, Robert 1874–1963	American poet, composed "The Road Not Taken."
Marconi, Guglielmo 1874–1937	Inventor of the radio.
Churchill, Winston 1874–1965	British prime minister during W.W.II.
Griffith, D. W. 1875–1948	Pioneering American often called the Father of the Motion Picture.
Reza Shah Pahlavi 1878–1944	Shah of Iran who modernized country and emancipated women.
Abdul-Aziz d. 1953	First king of Saudi Arabia and father of 79 children.
Stalin, Joseph 1879–1953	Brutal general secretary of Communist party in USSR.
Einstein, Albert 1879–1955	Formulated the theory of relativity.
Sanger, Margaret 1879–1966	Pioneer birth control advocate and founder of Planned Parenthood.
Keller, Helen 1880–1968	Blind and deaf author, lecturer, and pacifist.
Fleming, Alexander 1881–1955	Discoverer of penicillin.
Picasso, Pablo 1881–1973	Painter and sculptor, generally considered greatest artist of the twentieth century.
Roosevelt, Franklin D. 1882–1945	Thirty-second U.S. president who established the New Deal.
Woolf, Virginia 1882–1941	English author and feminist.
Joyce, James 1882–1941	Irish novelist and poet, wrote "Ulysses."
Gibran, Khalil 1883–1931	Lebanese-American writer, author of "The Prophet."
Keynes, John Maynard 1883–1946	British economist that said recovery from a recession is through employment.
Roosevelt, Eleanor 1884–1962	Human rights and civil rights, first U.S. delegate to the U.N.
Ben-Gurion, David 1886–1973	First prime minister of Israel, regarded as the father of his country.
O'Keefe, Georgia 1887–1986	American artist and one of the founders of Modernism.
Hitler, Adolf 1889–1945	Leader of the Nazi party.
Zworykin, Vladimir 1889–1982	Primary developer of the television.

HISTORIC FORM (*continued*)

Chaplin, Charlie 1889–1977	English motion-picture actor, director, producer, and composer.
Ho Chi Minh 1890–1969	Vietnamese Communist leader.
Haile Selassie I 1892–1975	Emperor who brought Ethiopia to independence and modernity.
Graham, Martha 1893–1997	Choreographer and dancer.
Mao Zedong 1893–1976	Chinese head of state, led Communist Party to power in China.
Fitzgerald, F. Scott 1896–1940	American writer of novels and short stories.
Earhart, Amelia 1898–1937	American aviator.
Anderson, Marian 1897–1993	First black opera singer to perform at the Met.
Meir, Golda 1898–1978	Israeli premier and one of the founders of the state of Israel.
Hemingway, Ernest 1899–1961	American novelist and short story writer.
Hitchcock, Alfred 1899 –1980	Film director.
Ellington, Duke 1899–1974	American jazz composer, bandleader and pianist.
Pol Pot 1928–1998	Leader of the Khmer Rouge guerrilla movement of Cambodia.
King Jr., Martin Luther 1929–1968	Martyred leader of the American civil rights movement.
Frank, Anne 1929–1945	German diarist, symbol of the Holocaust.
Armstrong, Neil 1930–	The first man on the moon.
O'Connor, Sandra Day 1930–	First woman U.S. Supreme Court justice.
Achebe, Chinua 1930–	Nigerian novelist and first African author to be read globally.
Ailey, Alvin 1931–1989	Dancer and choreographer.
Morrison, Toni 1931–	Nobel Prize-winning novelist, composed "Song of Solomon."
Gorbachev, Mikhail 1931–	Soviet premier and pivotal figure in the decline and fall of the Soviet empire
Tutu, Desmond 1931–	South African clergyman, civil rights activist and Nobel laureate.

HISTORIC FORM (*continued*)

Aquino, Corazon 1933–	First woman president of the Philippines.
Steinem, Gloria 1934–	American feminist, activist, author, and founder of "Ms." magazine.
Pavarotti, Luciano 1935–	Italian tenor.
Presley, Elvis 1935–1977	Singer, actor, and early pioneer of rock-and-roll music.
Mehta, Zubin 1936–	Indian-American conductor.
Cosby, Bill 1937–	American entertainer.
Hussein, Saddam 1937–	President of Iraq.
Pele 1940–	Brazilian soccer player.
Dylan, Bob 1941–	American musician and songwriter.
Hawking, Steven 1942–	Theoretical physicist related general relativity to quantum mechanics.
Walker, Alice 1944–	Pulitzer prize winning author, composed "The Color Purple."
Spielberg, Steven 1947–	American filmmaker.
Ride, Sally 1951–	First American woman in space.
Tenzin Gyatso 1935–	Fourteenth Dalai Lama and Nobel laureate.
Bhutto, Benazir 1953–	Pakistani prime minister.
Winfrey, Oprah 1954–	American TV talk show host and actress.
The Beatles 1960–1970	Band that revolutionized pop music.
Gates, Bill 1955–	Chairman and CEO of Microsoft.
Kahn, Robert E. 1948–	TCP/IP protocol, computer language that gave birth to the Internet.
Wilmut, Ian 1944–	Embryologist, cloned "Dolly."

List five people in order of who have had the greatest impact of our global society over the past millennium and a brief rationale as to why you have chosen these folks.

1. ______________________________

Rationale ______________________________

____

____

____

2. ______________________________

Rationale ______________________________

____

____

____

3. ______________________________

Rationale ______________________________

____

____

____

4. ______________________________

Rationale ______________________________

____

____

____

5. ______________________________

Rationale ______________________________

____

____

____

PowerPoint Outline to Assist In-Class Note-Taking

A. History of Education

B. Organization of Schools

C. Developing and Implementing the Curriculum

D. Types of Curriculum

Explicit (public)

Hidden (affective)

Null (missing)

Extracurricular

a. How Is the Curriculum Developed?

b. Do I Have to Teach the Curriculum?

c. How Do I Teach the Curriculum?

d. Will I Have to Teach a Class That I Am Unqualified to Teach?

E. Reform Efforts

a. Chapter 68 National Education Reform

i. National Education Goals

ii. Standards-Based Education

iii. Education Action Research

F. Instructional Technology

10

Instructional Technology

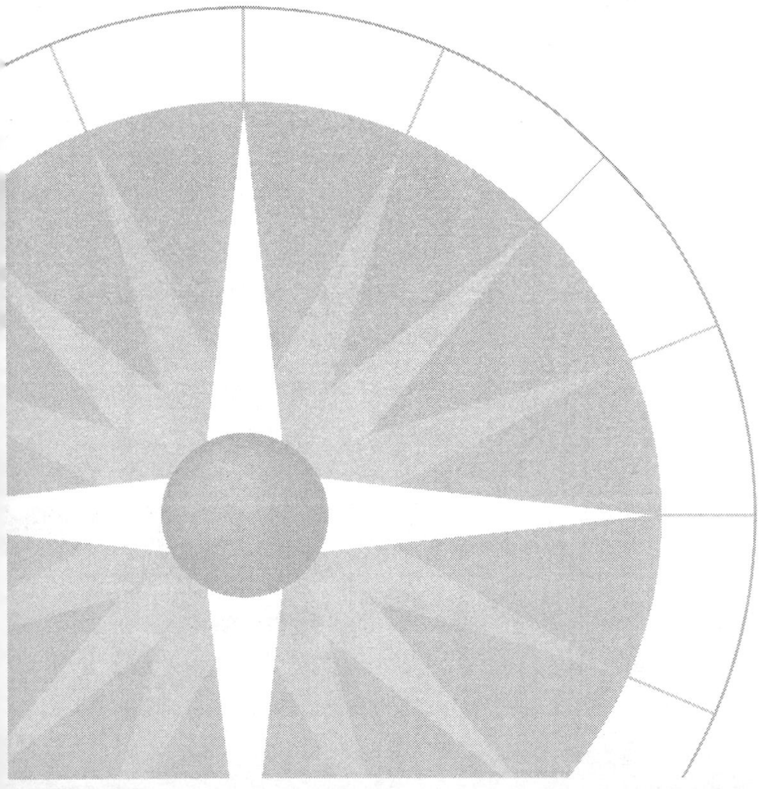

Guest Editorial: David Jaffee, PhD—Sociologist Professor, Associate Dean, College of Arts and Sciences, UNF

I AM NOT A TV: Confessions of a Professor

"I am not a TV"!

That is what I repeatedly tell my students. But I'm not sure they get it, because when I tell them this they continue to stare at me with expressionless faces. Again, they have failed to see the profound insight, or even the humor, of my observation. Again, they confirm my thesis.

How did I come to the revelation that, in the eyes of my students, I am a television set? As a sociologist I should probably say that I arrived at this proposition after many years of careful data collection and observation in undergraduates courses with disengaged students. But that would be untrue. In fact, for many years I never really noticed student expressions and demeanor. Fresh out of graduate school, with an abundance of self-important intellectual energy coupled with some nervousness about public speaking, the strategy was to lecture endlessly. I would just focus on a spot above the students' heads at the back of the class and pontificate on things sociological. However, over time, as I became more self-confident and also more concerned with classroom dynamics, I thought it might be worth taking a peek at their faces. This was a big mistake.

Most of the students either stared at me with no expression whatsoever—even when I attempted a joke, or asked a question, or launched into an animated diatribe—or they were looking elsewhere (like out the window, or at their notebooks, or at one another). Occasionally, some would just get up and walk out of the classroom and then return a few moments later. Either no eye contact, glazed eye contact, or total disregard for my human existence. And then it hit me—they think I'm a TV.

How else can you explain this behavior? When we watch TV—let's say a standup comic —we can wear any expression we want, we can fail to laugh at the jokes, we can fall asleep, we can go to the fridge for a beer. None of this has any impact on the comic. "It" continues to perform because it cannot see us. Students treat professors the same way. They assume we can't see them. So, it makes no difference what *they* do. Under these circumstances, why should students bother wasting valuable energy on social niceties like a nod of the head, a smile, or any other social cue acknowledging the humanity of the instructor?

I once had a student who "sat" in the front row sleeping through the entire class period. At the end of class I told him he would be more comfortable sleeping in a bed. He was incredibly embarrassed, horrified, and shocked that I had "caught him" engaging in this deviant academic behavior, even though he committed the crime directly beneath my nose. Did he think I was blind? Did he think I was totally insensitive to his behavior? No, he thought I was a talking head who could not see the television audience.

Another form of antisocial classroom behavior that further cements the case for my thesis, is represented by the student who strolls (some actually strut), into class 10 minutes late, right in front of the lecturing instructor. It is often the same student who, 15 minutes later, gets up to leave the class, only to schlep (they are now getting tired) back in 5 minutes later, with absolutely no self-conscious awareness of the social impact of these actions. I should report that this behavior is clearly on the rise. There are a number of possible explanations. Maybe there is an evolutionary process underway involving a shrinking bladder capacity. Maybe students are much more active today in the stock market and must constantly contact their broker. Or, what I really suspect, students don't believe a TV set will mind one way or the other.

There is a well-known concept in sociology called "the looking-glass self." It says that our sense of self is shaped by the reactions of others. Now, if my sense of self hinged on the reaction of my students, I would be selling advertising time to commercial sponsors or maybe trying to figure out a way to convert myself into a full screen model (it's a good thing I don't come with a remote).

I am now in the habit of confronting students about their classroom demeanor and making comments to students when they walk into class late. Students really hate this. They long for the good old days when I stared at the back of the room and lectured to the collective unconscious. But those days are past and my student evaluations reflect it. After all, who wants a TV that not only observes the viewer but evaluates their behavior? How would you like it if your TV could comment on your posture ("don't slouch") or your eating habits ("do you really *need* that second piece of cheesecake?").

So, I am not sure what strategy to pursue. However, I have been entertaining the idea of taping myself lecturing and then having media services televise the lectures to my students. This would make student behavior perfectly congruous with the educational delivery mode. I would also be integrating technology and teaching (some people think this is important). Yes, a true "televersity"! Don't worry, I would still hold office hours and attend department meetings. And if students missed a lecture they could always catch a rerun.

KWL

***What Do You KNOW?* (prior knowledge)**

***What Do You WANT to Know?* (objectives and goals)**

"I would trade all of my technology for an afternoon with Socrates."

—Steve Jobs

"Life Is Not Fair"

1. Life is not fair; get used to it.
2. The world won't care about your self-esteem. The world will expect you to do something BEFORE you feel good about yourself.
3. You will NOT make $40K out of high school. You won't be vice president with a car phone until you earn both.
4. If you think your teacher is tough, wait till you get a boss, he doesn't have tenure.
5. Flipping burgers is not beneath your dignity. Your grandparents had a different word for this, they called it opportunity.
6. If you mess up, it's not your parents' fault, so don't whine about your mistakes, learn from them.
7. Before you were born, your parents weren't as boring as they are now. They got that way from paying your bills, cleaning your clothes, and listening to you talk about how cool you are. So before you save the rain forest from the parasites of your parents' generation, try delousing the closet in your own room.
8. Your school may have done away with winners and losers, but life has not. In some schools they have abolished failing grades; they will give you as many times as you want to get the right answer. This doesn't bear the slightest resemblance to anything in real life.
9. Life is not divided into semesters. You don't get summers off and very few employers are interested in helping you find yourself. Do that on your own time.
10. Television is NOT real life. In real life, people actually have to leave the coffee shop and go to their jobs.

"And remember, be nice to nerds, chances are you'll end up working for one."

—Bill Gates

I^3 *Compare and contrast these ideas integrating your experiences, ideas, and beliefs about technology and technology in education.*

Introduction

"It is appallingly obvious our technology has exceeded our humanity."

—ALBERT EINSTEIN

I³ *Write down any ideas that come to you after reading this quote.*

____

____

"If I had a dollar for every time somebody in high school made fun of me, I—oh, wait, I do."

—BILL GATES

I³ *Write down any ideas that come to you after reading this quote.*

____

____

I³ *How can you justify that both of these quotes may have merit?*

____

____

Please keep in mind that as this section is being written, dozens of changes are occurring in the realm of technology and it is practically impossible to keep current on the fluid arena of technology.

In 1990, a normal, consumer-oriented computer cost about $4,000 and could hold almost two megabytes (Mb) of hard drive information, which equals about $2,000/Mb. Remember, that one byte equals one character and 1,024 bytes is a kilobyte (Kb). Similarly 1,024 Kb is one Mb. One thousand Mb equals one Gb (gigabyte). In the year 2000, the price dropped significantly to $1,000 for a similar household-use computer, although the storage spaced increased to 128 Mb, which is about $10/Mb. Although in 1949, *Popular Mechanics* believed that "computers in the future may weigh no more than 1.5 tons," it seems that the trend is much different than predicted. Extrapolating this data to the year 2010, computers should cost about $300 and provide 100,000 Mb (or 100 Gbs), which will result in a cost per Mb of 0.003. Regardless how close this approximation is, a clear significant trend can be observed that the cost per memory unit has decreased dramatically. Even though in 1942, Thomas Watson, chairman of IBM said, "I think there is a world market for maybe five computers." And even as recent as 1977, Ken Olson, president of Digital Equipment Corporation believed that "There is no reason anyone would want a computer in their home."

What is the point of this data? History demonstrates that as we can develop higher capability items at a less cost, the ability to universally apply these items increases, especially in the consumer arena. Once the item is mainstreamed, the possibility of using the item in the classroom becomes feasible.

We currently have more computers and peripherals (printers, scanners, cameras, etc.) in the schools than ever before. This chapter will attempt to share some of the trends, applications, uses, insights, and future ideas for using technology to enhance teaching and learning.

Current trends and issues in technology include capacity, bandwidth, compression, wireless, security, and accessibility. A few short years ago, Palm developed a unique technology device called a Personal Digital Assistant (PDA). The intent was to help organize schedules, contacts, addresses, and so on. However, this quickly evolved into other functions, which included email, web browsing, and telephony. The PDA morphed into what is known now as wireless handheld computers and can do many of the same functions as a normal computer.

To help you put the wireless handheld phenomenon into perspective, let me share a few stories, which may demonstrate the current mainstream-ability of these devices. One maker of the handheld device has partnered with a refrigerator producing company. At first, one might wonder what the two firms have to collaborate on to make a profit. It seems that refrigerators are, as many consumer devices constantly looking for ways to improve and upgrade the abilities of their product. So, they are pilot testing the addition of a wireless handheld computer inside of the unit. The handheld will scan the bar codes on the food placed in the unit and then inform the consumer when there is a need for additional product or even something useful as the milk or mayonnaise has past its expiration date. In addition, the wireless handheld device also has communication capabilities, so they already have these units in automobiles. Ideally, one could be traveling in their car and wish to stop by the grocery store. They can call their home and since they are not at home, their answering service answers. The person can ask the answering machine to connect them to the refrigerator. The refrigerator will download a list of items needed to the wireless handheld computer screen and the person will have the information with them when they shop.

Another scenario has developed where a handheld device maker has partnered with a golf club producer. A chip is inserted into the driver and after the swing, the golfer can view their swing and the handheld device provides suggestions on how their swing can be modified. In addition, another chip is inserted into their golf ball and if they cannot find it in the rough, the handheld computer has a tracking system that will enable them to find the ball.

An example that will demonstrate the abilities of making cheaper, smaller chips or storage units has occurred in several fields, especially in biotech. This micro-azation or computer hardware is typically called *nanotechnology.* For comparison, 10 nanometers is 1,000 times smaller than the diameter of a human hair. Nanotechnology is the branch of engineering that deals with things smaller than 100 nanometers (especially with the manipulation of individual molecules). So, the limitations of functioning in the physical environment of chips has been overcome by chemically coating devices with material and then engineering their function at a molecular level. Although research in this field dates back to Richard P. Feynman's classic talk in 1959, the term nanotechnology was first coined by K. Eric Drexler in 1986 in the book, *Engines of Creation.* Recall that Feynman worked with Oppenheimer and Einstein on the atomic bomb.

One very useful medical application of nanotechnology is currently being used and a company has already provided an initial public offering (IPO) to sell its stocks. In this case, a very small nanotechnology robot is placed inside of a gel tablet for the patient with upper gastrointestinal (GI) problems to swallow. The robot continues through the upper GI tract collecting 20 photos every second and ultimately being painlessly egested and disposed of. The data is analyzed and if any polyps are observed, then another nanotechnology gel pill is swallowed, which contains another type of technology that attacks only the detrimental polyp in question in a "Pac man" like fashion. All of this is accomplished avoiding intrusive, costly, painful surgery. A similar process is currently being explored to address open-heart surgery and the plaque that causes cardiovascular problems.

Other more pedestrian uses for nanotechnology are for rapid and more accurate pregnancy determination and more controversial for consumer DNA testing, which can provide a genetic predisposition to disease. And there is even now nanotechnology paint. This paint works under the same theory used in the air bag industry. On a micro scale, the paint appears similar to a raisin, with rough ridges. If a wall or car door is hit, the "raisin" behaves like an air bag and propels paint outward to fill in the gash.

Amazing? Yes, and some people believe that we are nearing the end of advancement. However, as rapidly and productive as we have been in recent years, I am certain that the end is nowhere in sight. In the 1950s, a U.S. patent officer resigned, indicating that he believed that in a few years, his job would be boring, since there would be nothing new to patent. Until a teacher can stand at the front of the room, hold their arm out and switch on their wristwatch to project a hologram of Abraham Lincoln reciting the Gettysburg Address, I will say that we have quite far to go.

Why Use Technology?

"Much computer use in schools these days involves computer 'enhanced' instruction—things like simulations. . . . There's no evidence that this helps to the degree that promoters promise. . . . I remain a skeptic because so many claims have been made without questioning."

—Larry Cuban, Stanford University

I³ *Write down any ideas that come to you after reading this quote.*

____

____

There is a cultural shift from the importance of possessing knowledge in one's own memory to be able to effectively search for and use the information needed for particular purposes. Therefore, it becomes increasingly important for the individual to possess some knowledge of computer technology. Undoubtedly, the individual would be greatly advantaged if they could gain this knowledge at an early age, perhaps as a student. There can be little doubt about the advantages the computer possesses over any textbook as a tool for learning. Firstly, the student is able to access a vastly more superior range of information from the computer, as too is the teacher. Available computer programs, such as the Internet, provide an excellent opportunity to access an astronomical quantity of information. In fact, the Internet provides greater access to a larger bank of knowledge for teachers and it enhances the quality and quantity of information that teachers provide for their students. The teacher as the primary source of knowledge no longer suffices in a world where knowledge doubles every 7 years and 10,000 scientific articles are published every year (Forman, 1987). Technology can be a mechanism to supplement traditional instruction, focusing on use of the web as a teaching tool that establishes an extension in the regular classroom. Forman (1987) also indicates that technology can add the ability for students to choose how, when, and where they participate in the learning experience and to bring together a vast wealth of previously unavailable learning resources. If this approach works, one might say, "don't look a gift horse in the mouth."

BTW

Never look a gift horse in the mouth comes from the way to tell if a horse is happy or not—by peering into its mouth. Thus, if you are given a horse as a gift, it would be insulting to check what condition it's in—sort of like looking at a price tag on a gift. Also, the way you tell a horse's age is by looking at his teeth. The saying simply means that if someone presents you with a gift horse you shouldn't immediately open its mouth to see if it is an old nag or a young horse.

Technology Literacy

> ***"The key to helping the next generation of American children be bright, literate, intellectually self-sufficient, steeped in the most important areas of knowledge? It all comes down to computers in the classrooms. Get rid of them."***
>
> —BOB GREENE, CHICAGO TRIBUNE

I³ *Write down any ideas that come to you after reading this quote.*

Technology literacy includes basic computers skills, use of technology, and application of computers skills, information, acquisition, presentation, communication, and problem-solving. Throughout time, humans have utilized different technological tools to enhance both basic communication and learning. For instance, humans have gone from cave drawings to Web sites; from petroglyphics to blogging; from conversations to instant messaging; and from story telling to e-books. As such, technology has played a key role in shaping how humans communicate and understand one another. Three different, yet interwoven methods of communication have occurred through history, from speaking to print to PowerPoint presentations. We label these three methods the oral mode, or orality, the literate mode or literacy, and electracy. This newest mode involves the use of computer or electronic forms of text and images.

Offline and Online

> ***"A 1996 poll of U.S. teachers found that they ranked computer skills and media technology as more 'essential' than the study of European history, biology, chemistry, and physics; than dealing with social problems such as drugs and family breakdown; than learning practical job skills; and than reading modern American writers such as Steinbeck and Hemmingway or classic ones such as Plato and Shakespeare."***
>
> —ATLANTIC MONTHLY, JULY 1997

I³ *Write down any ideas that come to you after reading this quote.*

I believe there are two very different approaches to using technology—offline and online. An offline approach involves computers and their peripherals, whereas an online includes access to a network, such as the Internet. Both can be used very powerfully in the classroom, however, educators must be intelligent and informed in order to identify the best one to meet their goals.

Offline: What Are the Five Most Essential Pieces of Technology in the Classroom?

There is substantial evidence to suggest that the computer also offers the advantage of making work more stimulating, thereby motivating the individual. The search for information is made considerably easier, thus making one's workload less tedious, and perhaps more interesting. It is possible the difference in types of computer software can be used to motivate various kinds of students. Poorly motivated students may be so due to lack of understanding or interest. If appropriate software is used, they may be enticed with the sheer novelty, the implied prestige of using a computer, and the benefits of drill and practice of tutorials they are able to work through at their own pace. On the other hand, highly motivated students or students who know how to use computers well can be directed to enrichment coursework, which is mind-provoking, features games and avenues of learning how to create through the medium of the computer.

1. Computers

Computers are an essential aspect of our lives. It seems only natural to make these available and possibly a daily part of student's lives since they will be interacting with computers for the remainder of their lives. School districts differ on how they approach placing computers in schools. Two main models are either a computer lab in which teachers take their students to work on computers or placing several computers in the classroom in which they are accessible to teachers and students on a daily basis. Either of these approaches can work effectively or can be doomed to failure if used improperly.

2. Projector

A Liquid Crystal Display (LCD) projector is a must in the classroom. Either mounted on the ceiling or on a mobile cart from the media center, access to this equipment on a regular basis will enable the teacher to plan and provide technology-oriented opportunities. The brighter the projection, the better since students may tend to fall asleep in the dark. However, many classrooms are difficult to make dark and as such, it may be difficult to see a projector with low lumens (the amount of light falling on a surface of one square foot). The lower the lumen, the lower the cost and chances are schools with tight budgets will be purchasing lower lumen projectors. If this is the case, you might wish to request a room, which you can darken, or at least one that is available that you can move when using a projector. The best approach is to try to purchase a projector with higher lumens, typically 4,000 lumens will be sufficient. Although you will have less projectors, since you can see the ones you do have, chances are you will use them more frequently.

3. High-speed Internet Access

Access is and will be the key for using technology in the classroom, especially when the Internet becomes a standard part of teaching. Similar to the philosophy of the projector, even though it may cost more, gaining access to high-speed networking will enable teachers and students to search, research and present more information in a timely manner. If the speed is sluggish or does not work consistently, people will tend not to use it, so all the money spent may not be used at all in the classroom. There are a variety of methods to gain access to high-speed Internet, contacting your school district is the best step, as they will most likely have a company they are working with to provide the district services.

© 2004 SMART Technologies, Inc.
Used with permission.

4. Smart Board®

Relatively new to the technology scene are Smart Boards®. Smart Boards® resemble white boards, however, they also enable the user to collect written information electronically and control the computer as one big touch pad. The Smart Board® interactive whiteboard transforms your classroom space into an interactive working and learning environment. With the combined power of a projector, computer and whiteboard you can do everything you do on your computer and more. Simply touch the Smart Board, to highlight key points, access applications and Web sites, and write notes in electronic ink. Then, save all your work to one file that you can print, email, or post to a Web site. This approach allows teachers to save their work and their student's work as well. Teachers can collect the work electronically and store on a CD or DVD for their principals, students or parents. Also, this allows the teacher more flexibility in walking around the room and working with their students instead of being tethered to the computer.

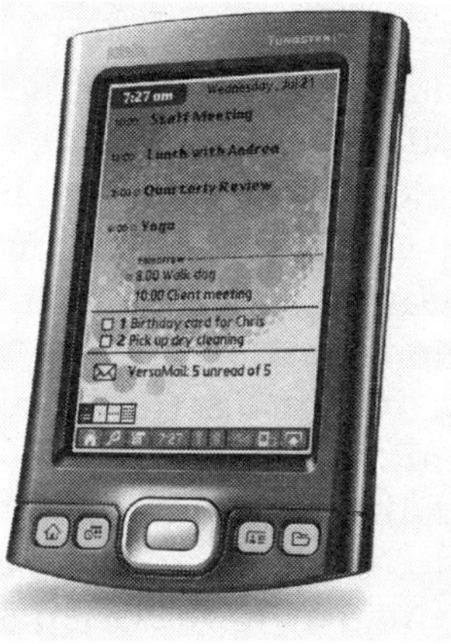

5. Handheld Computers

As mentioned in an earlier section, handheld computers hold great potential for teaching and learning. Handheld computers can be transformed into data collection devices by adding probes for pH, temperature, conductivity, and basic chemical analysis. In addition, these devices can be converted into graphing calculators for math, downloading electronic books for language arts, and taking digital photos and voice recordings for social science projects. They have wireless capabilities, so students can pair up, work with them on an in-class project and then send their data to the teacher's computer to develop a database from which to interpret and analyze the data. Among all of the devices currently available for integrating technology into the classroom, the handheld computers seem to offer the most direct advantages and applications. Even when considering cost, the handheld is at an advantage, since it can perform the same functions as a laptop computer at a much lower cost.

Online: Integrating the Internet

"A library is where you go to find facts. The web is more like a garage sale: it's possible you'll find what you want, but only with a lot of digging, searching, and wading through things that smell funny."

—Unknown

I³ *Write down any ideas that come to you after reading this quote.*

____

____

What Is the Internet?

I³ *Please go out and search the Internet and gather the history. Believe me, there are plenty of sites, so this will not be difficult. Try to review several sites to compare data.*

____

____

____

____

____

____

There are several reasons why educators, administrators, and parents should support the use of the Internet in schools, e.g., equity, an infinite resource, students as active participants, self-motivation, student inquiry, and assessing and improving student progress. Online education provides the flexibility and efficiency of computer-assisted instruction as well as the individual attention of instructor-guided instruction (Huang, 1997). Berge (1997) discusses the advantages of online instruction in terms of meaningfulness, open communication, organized essential ideas, learning aids, modeling, active appropriate practice, pleasant conditions, and consistency. Results also show that online use can increase student performance (Follansbee, 1997). Technology can help some people to participate more easily in education, to learn more effectively, and to enjoy learning more (Palmieri, 1997). Palmieri also realizes that technology will continue to be important in education because it will allow learners to access knowledge in their homes, in their workplaces, (informal settings), at times in which they want to learn. Determining the benefits and pitfalls for education requires extensive research and evaluation of the Internet and its alternatives. Keep in mind, there are some people that believe using technology really "gets their goat." Ideally, you will want to offer technology as a tool for instruction, but also have a traditional contingency plan for those who may have anxieties using it, in order to avoid the "cold shoulder."

BTW

Getting one's goat refers to an old English belief that keeping a goat in the barn would have a calming effect on the cows, hence producing more milk. When one wanted to antagonize/terrorize one's enemy, you would abscond with their goat rendering their milk cows less- to non-productive.

BTW

When guests would over stay their welcome as house guests, the hosts would (instead of feeding them good, warm meals) give their too-long staying guests the worst part of the animal, not warmed, but the COLD SHOULDER.

The Internet has seen unprecedented growth when compared to other inventions and the amount of years that it took to reach mass use.

Date	Invention	Years to Mass Use
1873	Electricity	46
1876	Telephone	35
1886	Gas Automobile	55
1906	Radio	22
1926	Television	26
1975	Personal Computer	16
1983	Mobile Phone	13
1994	The World Wide Web	4

Mark Milion, League for Innovation, *Newsweek,* 1998.

The following table from Internet World Statistics demonstrates how quickly the web has grown, although the point of it truly being a WORLD web is yet to be seen as only about a tenth of the population has access. This access is in the developed countries, primarily the United States.

Date	Number of Users (millions)	World Population (%)
December, 1995	16	0.4
December, 1996	36	0.9
December, 1997	70	1.7
December, 1998	147	3.6
December, 1999	248	4.1
March, 2000	304	5.0
July, 2000	359	5.9
December, 2000	451	7.4
March, 2001	458	7.6
June, 2001	479	7.9
August, 2001	513	8.6
April, 2002	558	8.6
July, 2002	569	9.1
September, 2002	587	9.4
March, 2003	608	9.7
September, 2003	677	10.6
October, 2003	682	10.7
December, 2003	719	11.1
February, 2004	745	11.5
May, 2004	757	11.7
June, 2004	785	12.2

www.InternetWorldStats.com

The following table puts the data into global perspective.

World Regions	Population (2004 Est.)	Internet Usage (Year 2000)	Internet Usage, Latest Data	User Growth (2000–2004)	Penetration (% Population)	% of Table
Africa	905,954,600	4,514,400	12,253,300	171.4%	1.4%	1.6%
Asia	3,654,644,200	114,303,000	243,664,549	113.2%	6.7%	31.0%
Europe	728,857,380	100,993,093	217,852,995	115.7%	29.9%	27.7%
Middle East	259,166,000	5,272,300	16,831,400	219.2%	6.5%	2.1%
North America	326,695,500	108,096,800	227,944,619	110.9%	69.8%	29.0%
Latin America/Caribbean	546,100,900	18,068,919	51,181,736	183.3%	9.4%	6.5%
Oceania	31,892,487	7,619,500	15,981,423	109.7%	50.1%	2.0%
WORLD TOTAL	6,453,311,067	358,871,012	785,710,022	118.9%	12.2%	100.0%

NOTES: (1) Internet Usage and Population Stats were updated on May 24, 2004. (2) Click on each World Region for detailed regional data. (3) Demographic (population) numbers are based on data contained in the web site *gazetteer.de*. (4) The most recent usage information comes from data published by *Nielsen//NetRatings, International Telecommunications Union,* local NIC's, local ISP's and other reliable sources. (5) Data from this site may be cited, giving the due credit and establishing a link back to *InternetWorldStats.com*.

I³ *Review the data and try to make some interpretations, generalizations, and predictions about the Internet in general and how it relates to education.*

____

____

____

____

____

____

How Can I Secure Technology for My Classroom?

Probably the last thing you want to do if you wish to add more technology in your classroom is to wait for the administration to bring it by. Administrators typically mean well, however, they are not able to anticipate and predict your needs, so it will depend on your motivation as to the amount and type of technology that ends up in your classroom. You could develop a detailed proposal for your school administration, which might result in additions to your classroom. However, the following approaches may prove more fruitful.

Grants

Most agencies love education and teachers, so they may offer special funds for teaching. There are federal, state, and local grants for various areas of teaching, especially in the areas of critical needs. Each grant has its own proposal guidelines and process, however, developing a good generic proposal may be worth your time as you can cater it to each grant as you identify your needs and how they align with what the grant can offer. Searching the Web for these grants is a good first step. However, keep an eye on your local mail, school bulletin boards, newspapers, and general networking.

Partnering

Anytime you can partner with another group, either another school, business, or higher education, and this will typically position yourself better to secure funding. Many grants and initiatives require collaboration as part of their criteria.

Universities

Try not to lose contact with your professors, especially those who were easy to communicate with and/or worked on grants themselves. Many times, they need to partner with teachers in schools or they need someone to perform literature reviews or other work on grant projects during the summer that can provide income for you as well as potentially place hardware in your classroom. Professor's gain grants to research the effects of teaching tools in the classroom, as mentioned earlier for action research. You may wish to volunteer you and your class as a place to conduct the research in return for technology.

Corporations

Many times corporations and businesses have designated an outreach source of funds so that the consumer views their company as community friendly. Contact businesses and ask if they can assist with funds to purchase technology. Some may offer used equipment, however use caution if accepting these. Sometimes, they can be more work than is worth the time. It may take a few phone calls or emails, but if you wait until the technology is dropped off at your door, chances are slim that this will occur.

Municipal Agencies

Local municipal, utility, and other government agencies often have budgets for assisting education. Contact them in the same way that you did corporations and ask if they have any resources for education.

New and Useful Technology for the Classroom

Flash USB Drive

Flash USB (universal serial board) storage drives are relatively new and can be a real assistant to a teacher. These small, relatively cheap devices allow teachers to transport large files from one system to another, such as from a home computer to a classroom computer without software or peripherals, such as a CD burner. Flash drives currently offer up to 2 gigabytes (yes, that was Gb, not Mb) of storage, the equivalent of 10 yards of books on a shelf, a symphony in high-fidelity sound, or a broadcast quality movie, in a drive the size of a pack of gum. Flash drives are solid-state memory devices that are versatile, compact, and easy to use. A flash drive works a lot like a portable hard drive—just plug the USB flash drive into your computer's USB port and drag and drop your files. No cables, adapters or software are required. Flash drives offer the freedom to add and delete files up to 100,000 times and are suitable for storing digital content for up to 10 years.

As a plus, there are flash drives that double as an MP3 music player. So, you can store music files on your drive and listen to them using earphones. You can transform or "rip" your CD songs into MP3 format and move them on and off your Flash MP3 USB drive. This is an easy way to add music to your classroom as well with a simple set of inexpensive speakers, which plug directly into the Flash MP3 USB drive.

Tablet Personal Computers

Tablet PCs are the newest generation of mobile computers. Tablet PCs provide all the power of a standard Microsoft Windows-based notebook plus additional features that improve mobility including pen-input, light form-factors, and handwriting and speech recognition. The tables offer pen-writing capabilities that allow users to save notes in their own handwriting, or to convert them into typed text for use in other applications. The pen used to operate the PC can also handle common mouse and keyboard tasks like opening applications, selecting text, and displaying menus. Today, Tablet PCs come in two primary form factors: convertible notebooks and slate design.

Document Cameras

Document cameras are wonderful tools that allow you to show detailed drawings, 3-D renderings, photographs, and practically any object. When using a document camera in the classroom to demonstrate something like an intricate biology specimen or how to use a graphing calculator you have the power to focus the audience's attention on nearly anything. No more transparencies or oversized sketches taped to a wall. Think of a document camera as a twenty-first century overhead projector. However, unlike traditional overhead projectors, document cameras use a high-resolution video camera for display. Also, these are relatively low-cost and very small and portable. In addition, these are great teaching tools that allow students to present their group work or activities, which have been completed in class.

Blogging

A web log or blog is a web page made up of brief, frequently updated entries that are arranged chronologically like a journal. The purposes of blogs vary greatly from links and commentary about other sites, to news, to journals, photographs, poetry, and mini-essays. Blog posts are similar to instant messages to the Web. Blogs are also excellent communication tools. They help small groups communicate in a way that is simpler and easier to follow than email or discussion forums. Oravec (2002) suggests that educators can use weblogs to encourage students to access the Internet for useful information; weblogs can also help students organize the resources they locate. Weblogs are increasingly being used in education by researchers, teachers, and students. Duber (2002) in his article on Weblogs identifies SchoolBlog (*http://www.schoolblogs.com/*), a free blogging package and community with the primary aim of providing a forum for children to publish and interact with others over the Web. Schoolblogs indicates that teachers and students are motivated to share information because they have ownership of it.

Electronic Portfolios

Electronic portfolios are selective and purposeful collections of student work created by using various forms of technology. E-portfolios focus on the students' reflections on their own work and how they have processed what they have learned. They are records of learning, growth, and change in development. They can provide meaningful documentation of students' abilities inside and outside of the classroom. E-portfolios provide information for students, parents, teachers, and members of the community about what students have learned or are able to do. The E-portfolios can also be used in an interview process or to assist in-service teachers with developing lessons. Electronic portfolios can include varied media such as text, graphics, video and audio. The format of E-portfolios varies greatly and can be anything from an organized series of electronic files to a Web site. Many of the course management companies are now offering students the accessibility to create and manage their E-portfolios through the university.

Adaptive or Assistive Technology

Adaptive technology describes the use of hardware and software to assist individuals who have difficulty accessing information systems using conventional methods. It allows individuals with disabilities the same access to information and production as their peers who are not disabled. One example of such technology is computer generated voice output of scanned printed material used by a student with a print impairment, such as dyslexia or blindness. Another example is mini keyboards that can be used by people with a small range of hand movement, and screen readers can be used by people who are blind.

Distance Learning

Distance learning means many different things to different people. Generally, it encompasses learning that takes place at locations remote from the point of instruction. Distance learning may take the form of an instructor-led course delivered to multiple remote locations. Distance learning may also be training applications delivered via computer networks to students at any network node. Web-based training is one distance learning method in that the training application resides on a Web server while students may use the training from any location that can access the server. There are also hybrids of distance learning, where students may meet once or twice, or even half of the meetings. In addition, there is using technology to enhance or supplement learning, which is at times categorized as distance learning. Distance learning can be very productive for some students, however, the student typically needs to be self-regulating as a major difference is the interaction between the student and teacher.

Final Note on Technology

Top Ten List That Maybe You Have Had Way Too Much Technology

10. You just tried to enter your password on the microwave.
9. You have a list of 15 phone numbers to reach your family of three.
8. You call your son's beeper to let him know it's time to eat. He emails you back from his bedroom, "What's for dinner?"
7. Your daughter sells Girl Scout Cookies via her Web site.
6. You chat several times a day with a stranger from South Africa, but you haven't spoken with your next-door neighbor yet this year.
5. Your grandmother clogs up your e-mail inbox asking you to send her a JPEG file of your newborn so she can create a screen saver.
4. Every commercial on television has a Web site address at the bottom of the screen.
3. Your reason for not staying in touch with family is that they do not have email addresses.
2. You turn off your modem and get this awful feeling, as if you just pulled the plug on a loved one.
1. You wake up at 2 A.M. to go to the bathroom and check your email on your way back to bed.

$\mathbf{I}^3$ *Can you relate to any of these items? Which ones? Do you believe any of these are detrimental? To society? To education? How and why?*

What Did You LEARN?

References

Berge, Z. (1997). Characteristics of online teaching in post-secondary, formal education, *Educational Technology, 37(3),* 35–47.

Duber, J. (2002). Mad blogs and englishmen. *TESL-EJ, 6(2),* 77.

Follansbee, S. (1997). Can online communications improve student performance? Results of a controlled study. *ERS Spectrum, 15(1),* 15–26.

Forman, D. C. (1987). The use of multimedia technology for training in business and industry, *Multimedia Monitor, 13,* 22–27.

Huang, A. H. (1997). Challenges and opportunities of online education. *Journal of Educational Technology Systems, 25(3),* 229–247.

Internet World Statistics (*http://www.internetworldstats.com/stats.htm*)

Oravec, J. 2002. Bookmarking the world: Weblog applications in education. *Journal of Adolescent & Adult Literacy, 45(7),* 616–621.

Palmieri, P. (1997). Technology in education: do we need it? *ARIS Bulletin, 8(2),* 1–5.

PowerPoint Outline to Assist In-Class Note-Taking

A. **Introduction**

B. **Why Use Technology?**

C. **Technology Literacy**

D. **Offline—What Are the Five Most Essential Pieces of Technology in the Classroom?**

E. **Online—Appropriate Web Site Integration**

F. **How Can I Secure Technology for My Classroom?**

G. **New and Useful Technology for the Classroom**

H. **Adaptive or Assistive Technology**

I. **Distance Learning**

11

Assessment and Measurement

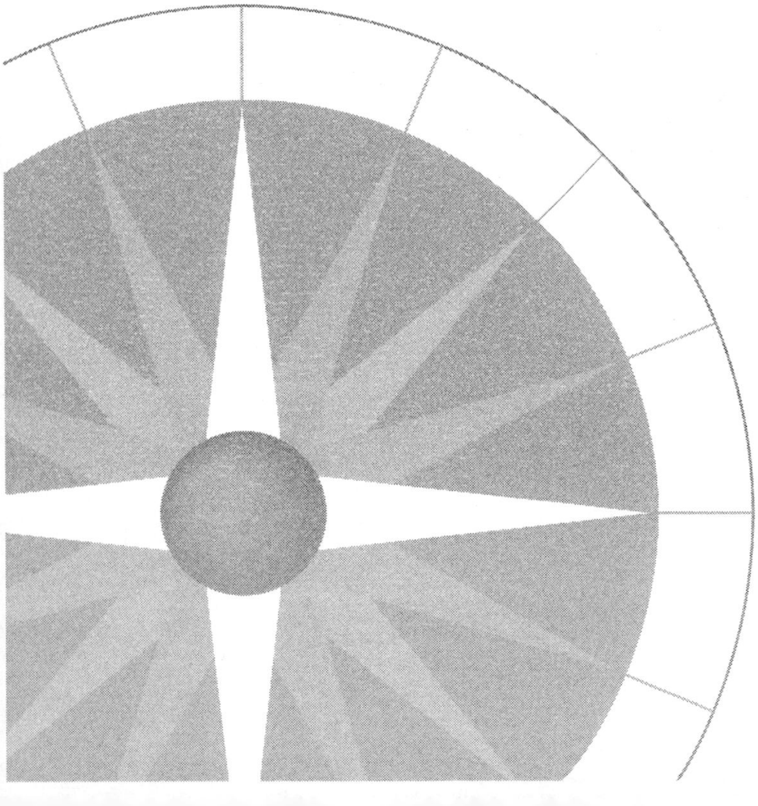

Guest Editorial: David Fenner, PhD, Associate Professor of Philosophy/College of Arts and Sciences, UNF

Why I Hate Grades

Problems with grading are legion. Part of the trouble must be that the practices and procedures of grading students in college or university classrooms are generally practices the instructors inherit through a system of teaching apprenticeship. One grades like the professor for whom she was a graduate assistant. Or one grades like he recalls being graded in college. Or one grades like one's peers. In whichever case, the grading practices are inherited. Instructors, astute, critical, analytic instructors are not offered the opportunity, in all disciplines except perhaps pedagogy, to confront the reasons that might be offered for certain grading practices, so that they might make a conscious, informed, thoughtful decision about how they will evaluate their students. One must believe that this is a correct etiology of the disease; it is too fantastic to think for a moment that any instructors might have undergone a careful study of grading and evaluation and subsequently settled on the sorts of practices now widespread in America's colleges and universities.

The following questions require answers. How should one grade? What should one grade? Why should one grade? Can one grade meaningfully? In this short paper, however, I will only concentrate on the third question, the "why" question.

Why Should One Grade?

"Why should one grade?" questions the motivation of the instructor to grade—not to grade at all, that can be pragmatically established on the grounds of a teacher retaining employment at a university—but to grade in the ways that the teacher might. For instance, one may assign grades on the basis of encouraging students to do better. That is, one may assign grades on the basis of psychologically motivating the students toward learning qua learning.

Consider two such stories. First, consider the case where the instructor's first examination of the term is especially difficult, and that subsequently assigned grades are more or less on the low side. Such an instructor initially may be assigning low grades with a view to assigning higher ones later to convince students that they are, through steady work, getting better. Second, consider the case where a teacher tells students on the first day of class that they all have As. She then offers them the requirements for retaining their As. Here, the student is given an initial boost, through the teacher's communication of the idea "I believe in you; I believe that you are an A student." The student, then, if the strategy is psychologically worthy, will go on to do those things that are necessary for retention of the A. This, of course, later may cause problems for the teacher, especially if her supervisors are inclined to suggest that the teacher grade-inflates or is an "easy grader." But pragmatic difficulties aside, the psychology might be sound.

Consider another teleological story for the assignment of grades. This one not psychologically motivating students to learn, but rooted in the real world appraisal of results. If an instructor is interested in her students not merely as they are her students, but as persons for whom this course and others are bridges to further goals and accomplishments, that instructor may well take the student's future into account in the assignment of a grade to that student. Suppose that a student declares an interest in becoming a physician in the inner cities or in a third world country. This is an admirable goal, and one obviously motivated by altruism. Her instructor might, in view of this goal, assign her a better grade than she might otherwise be assigned—especially if that instructor knows that she is taking 18 semester hours, 15 of which are senior level pre-med courses, working to put herself through college, and that this course is a freshman level course widely out of her field of interest. Understand that all such empirical information is relevant given the instructor's interest in the student as a person whose life extends outside her particular classroom. Indeed, the instructor might assign her an A in order to strengthen her chances of entering med school and fulfilling her noble goal. If it is the case that instructors do care about their students, and see them as persons with lives outside the classroom, as persons who have goals and aspiration at least noble in their own eyes, then the instructor might uniformly assign higher grades then she might otherwise do. The logical result is that regardless of class performance, we help our students in practical endeavors and practical matters by assigning them, each and every one, As.

It is that teacher who rejects the practical world, the world of results, who assigns grades on merit alone. But this is also frequently the teacher who uses pre-set scales, demanding that only excellent work receive a grade of excellent, an A. And it is precisely she that is most called upon to offer a justification for her standards of grading. How will she respond?

Finally, what of the defense of grading which holds that the purpose of grading is only for use as a predictory device. Through grading our students, we make predictions about how they will do in future pursuits, especially future scholastic, instructor and, for want of a better word, cerebral pursuits? Grading is a matter of bring the inductive practices of science to students. We predict which pursuits are most appropriate for a given student in future based on the evidence of the past. Problems of induction aside, this rationale suffers from having to fix at exactly what point the induction is well enough confirmed so that additional prediction-making is unwarranted. Certainly predictions of future success are irrelevant on the eve of one's doctoral dissertation; certainly they are irrelevant in passing from master degree to doctoral. They seem a bit irrelevant in passing from college to graduate school. While they seem most relevant in the primary grades, and perhaps somewhat relevant in secondary education, it is difficult to imagine needing still further and further evidence that one will succeed in future when one is in those final stages of formal education.

Why should one grade?

1. One may assign grades on the basis of psychologically motivating the students toward learning qua learning. Two problems, however, present themselves:
   a. assigning grades for the psychological value of those assignments smacks of covert manipulation and coercion of students;
   b. the possibility of grade inflation is quite present; if grades are inflated, it undermines the very idea of assigning grades in a responsible way.
2. The logical result of assigning grades so that students have a better shot at grad school or employment, and so on, is that regardless of class performance, we help our students in practical endeavors and practical matters by assigning them, each and every one, As.
3. If grading is a mechanism by which one may predict future success (in whichever venues), it makes little sense to continue this predictory practice in the latter stages of one's formal education. Yet it is just at the highest levels that grading takes on its greatest power; a low grade in doctoral work can spell the end of a career and the waste of seven years of work.

The answer? Perhaps the answer is to lay down grading in favor of whatever mechanism might accomplish the purposes hiding behind the grading. Is the purpose of grading to psychologically motivate the student toward greater learning by virtue of having students develop in themselves greater learning skills? If this is the purpose, then why not use, say, negative reinforcement: instead of a low grade, the student might receive a strong electric shock. Perhaps positive reinforcement is the key: instead of a high grade, the student might receive a check, perhaps a tuition rebate. I would think that pain and pleasure of a more immediate, more straightforward sort would be not only more effective in motivating students toward developing learning skills, and thereby learning more and learning better, I would think that such methods would be a good deal more honest, for both the instructor and the student.

I am not advocating moving to such a position. I only mean to point out that in this day and age grades have taken on the ethos of being rewards and punishments—and certainly understandably so when they have such life-impacting importance. I do not want to shock students, have them beaten up, or pass out checks or candy or toasters. Moreover, I am not sure than any such methods would be meaningful given the evidence that a certain student will learn just exactly as her genes and environment allow her to.

The upshot then must be a move to grade-less education, where evaluative techniques and subsequent judgments are used only in the most pragmatic manners and only on the most pragmatic of justifications. Anything more is too ambitious and ultimately dishonest.

My best students—those that demonstrate a true competence for the methods and content of the discipline, those that eagerly embrace the offering of new ideas and new challenges, those that see greater criticism as a chance for greater improvement, those that seek out new learning experiences—these students work not because I hold grades over their heads. My best students work for the sheer joy of the work. I can point to student after student who now pursues such experiences for their own sakes. But these students are at a point that has taken a fair amount of evolution: they had to overcome years and years of hearing about, and feeling the effects of, the importance and efficacy of "good grades." It is time for the institutions, which purport to develop and foster this spirit in students to evolve to a similar level (Fenner, 1999).

KWL

What Do You KNOW? **(prior knowledge)**

What Do You WANT to Know? **(objectives and goals)**

"The value of achievement lies in the achieving."

—Albert Einstein

I³ *Write down any ideas that come to you after reading this quote.*

"I prefer the company of peasants because they have not been educated sufficiently to reason incorrectly."

—Michel de Montaigne (1533–1592)

I³ *Write down any ideas that come to you after reading this quote.*

I³ *How can you justify that both of these quotes may have merit?*

First of all, let us assess how well you listen, by taking this listening quiz. Have someone read the following items to you and write down your responses (answers are located at the end of the chapter).

1. Is there a Fourth of July in England?
2. How many birth days does the average person have?
3. Some months have 31 days; how many have 28?
4. If there are 3 apples and you take away 2, how many do you have?
5. How many members of each animal did Moses take on the ark?
6. A clerk in the butcher shop is 5′ 10″ tall. What does he weigh?

What Is Assessment, Measurement, and Evaluation?

"Examinations are formidable even to the best prepared, for the greatest fool may ask more than the wisest man can answer"

—Charles Caleb Colton (1820)

I³ *Write down any ideas that come to you after reading this quote.*

- Assessment is a vehicle for gathering information about students' achievement or behavior.
- Measurement is the assignment of marks based on an explicit set of rules.
- Evaluation is the process of making judgments about the level of students' understanding or performance.

Why Do We Need So Much Measurement?

First of all, assessing student skills acts as a basis for further instruction. Through appropriate assessment, a teacher can understand misconceptions, misunderstandings, and incomplete comprehension. Assessment also helps us determine whether national and/or state curriculum standards are met by students and schools. Finally, assessment helps us determining the effectiveness of teaching and possibly how we can modify for better instruction.

Brief History of Assessment

Assessment has been around and documented in the Bible, Chinese civil service, and of course, the famous Greek teaching of Socrates. More recent assessment philosophies were developed in 1850 by Horace Mann in Boston, Massachusetts; Joe Rice in 1890, evaluating schools and using the data to propose restructuring; Robert Thorndike, considered the "father of testing" developed achievement testing as early as 1905 and Frenchman Binet proposed the infamous Stanford-Binet intelligence testing.

Early trends in testing continued in 1923 as the Stanford Achievement Test was developed and the Scholastic Aptitude Test (SAT) followed 2 years later. Dewey's Progressive Education movement led to Eight-Year Study in the same time period, which led to Ralph Tyler use of objective instruments to evaluate education in 1930. By the 1930s more than half of the United States had statewide testing assisted by IBM machine scoring. In the 1940s, the National Council on Measure in Education was formed, quickly followed by the Educational Testing Service (ETS), which is still used today. All of these events culminated in the 1965 Elementary and Secondary Education Act (ESEA), which was described in an earlier chapter, which mandated norm-referenced tests. Remember, the No Child Left Behind (NCLB) Act is a reauthorization of the ESEA, which should help you make connections between historical assessment and today's accountability movement. The accountability movement began in the 1970s when James Popham, modern-day father of assessment opposed norm-reference tests in favor of criterion reference. The Florida Comprehensive Assessment Test is a criterion referenced test.

Standardized Tests

"The fact is, when we say 'All students can learn,' we should mean it and measure it."

—Lisa Keegan, Superintendent of Public Instruction, State of Arizona

I³ *Write down any ideas that come to you after reading this quote.*

____

____

One of the most famous standardized tests is the Scholastic Aptitude Test or SAT, which is taken in secondary schools to provide entry information for post-secondary acceptance. Between the inception of 1930 and 1964, SAT scores continued to increase. However, after 1964 the scores began to fall and continued to fall for the next 15 years.

I³ *Why would SAT scores fall within this period? Provide a few plausible explanations, variables or possible factors that you believe could have contributed to this decline.*

(Note: if you are struggling with this, consider demographic changes, less-demanding curricula diminishing educational standards, social changes, or lower abilities of teachers.)

Norm-Reference Tests

The persons performance is compared to his/her peers, thus depends on where the person stands relative to those in the norm group. Norm-referenced tests assess a student's score is in relation to students in a similar group. Norm-referenced measurements do not tell what a student can or cannot do but tell if a student's performance relative to peers. Examples include the Scholastic Aptitude Test and the Graduate Record Exam.

Criterion Reference Tests

The persons performance is compared to set criteria or standards, thus depends on how they responded to each item and whether it was correct or incorrect. Criterion-referenced tests assess a student's score is in relation to an absolute standard without comparison to other's performance. Criterion-referenced tests have specified criteria against which a person's performance can be measured. Examples include Florida Writes! criteria for content mastery, grading rubrics, and minimum level skills test.

Lake Wobegon

The mythical Minnesota town immortalized by Garrison Keillor in the *Prairie Home Companion* radio series as a place where "All women are strong, all men are good-looking and all the children are above average!" This has come to be known as the Lake Wobegon Effect, where data or perceptions are believed, making it possible for more than half of the population to be above the 50th percentile. Think about this for a moment.

I³ *Where is the flaw in the Lake Wobegon Effect?*

Test Preparation

"I love criticism just so long as it's unqualified praise."

—Noel Coward (1899–1973)

I³ *Write down any ideas that come to you after reading this quote.*

____

____

When creating your own test, be certain to clarify your instructional objectives and align your teaching with the assessment. Next, systematically examine course content and decide what is most important. Be certain to use all levels of questioning. In order to ensure this, it may be best to initially use Bloom's Level of Taxonomy. Blooms developed six levels of questioning from lower to higher order, which include knowledge, comprehension, application, analysis, synthesis, and evaluation. In order to ensure you are addressing a certain level, you may wish to use the following prompts to develop questions.

I. **Knowledge** (factual, testing recall)—*low level.* Who, What, Why, When, Where, How, How Much, Describe, Define, Match, Select, Which One, Choose, Omit.

II. **Comprehension** (translate, interpret, and extrapolate)—*medium level.* State in Your Own Words; What Does This Mean; Give an Example; State in One Word; What Exceptions are There; What are They Saying; Show in a Graph or Table; Classify, Infer, Indicate, Outline, Summarize.

III. **Application** (to situations that are new)—*low-medium level.* Predict, Choose, Select, Explain, Identify, Tell.

IV. **Analysis** (breaking down into parts)—*medium level.* Distinguish, What Assumptions; What Conclusions, Make a Distinction, What is the Premise; What ideas Apply; What is the Function of; What Statement is Relevant; State the Point of View; What Ideas Justify the Conclusion; What is the Theme; What is the Relationship Between.

V. **Synthesis** (combining elements into a pattern)—*medium-high level.* Create, How Would you Test; Propose an Alternative; Solve the Following; Plan; Design; Compose; Formulate a Theory, Develop.

VI. **Evaluation** (according to criteria and state reasons)—*high level.* Appraise, Judge, Criticize, Defend, Compare.

Guidelines for Test Development

1. Test for important ideas, not trivial
2. Write items as simple as possible (KISS)
3. Make items grade-level and ability appropriate
4. Objectively scored items have only one answer
5. Avoid using interrelated items
6. Avoid irrelevant clues
7. Avoid using direct quotations from text
8. Have colleague review your items
9. Avoid trick questions

10. Response options as short as possible and distracters are the same length.
11. Avoid the use of ALL, NONE, NEVER, ALWAYS, NONE OF THE ABOVE or ALL OF THE ABOVE.
12. Avoid including clues in the stem
13. Avoid "C" as a common response

Test Score Pollution

Test score pollution is typically caused by extraneous variables. These variables typically include test-taking skills, test wiseness, response sets, anxiety and motivation, administrative factors, coaching, and practice and test bias.

Item Analysis

After the test is administered and graded, it is best to determine how effective each test item was at measuring. Two popular methods are using a Discrimination Index and Item Difficulty analysis. To do this, rank order from high to low. Set aside the upper and lower 30%. For each item, count the number of students who selected each alternative. Compute the *difficulty level* (% of students who got the item correct). Compute *discrimination index* (how well each option distinguishes between high/low scores). Evaluate the efficiency of each option. Figure the percentage of students who responded correctly to an item. The index should be between 20% to 80%. For example, if 8/10 were correct on an item in the upper group and 2/10 in the lower, then there would be a total of 10/20 correct responses or a difficulty level of 50%, which is ideal. This indicator tells how well that item distinguishes between students who did well and who did poorly. To do this, subtract number of students who got the item right in low-scoring group from the number of students who got the item right in high scoring group, divide by the group size.

For the same example: (8 – 2)/10 = .60; A value > .4 is a very good item; .3–.39 is good; .2–.29 is reasonable; .1–.19 is marginal; and less than .1 you should consider discarding.

Normal Curved, Central Tendency, and Dispersion

> ***"Science is made up of facts as a house is with stones. But a collection of facts is no more a science, than a heap of stones is a house."***
>
> —Poincaire, French philosopher

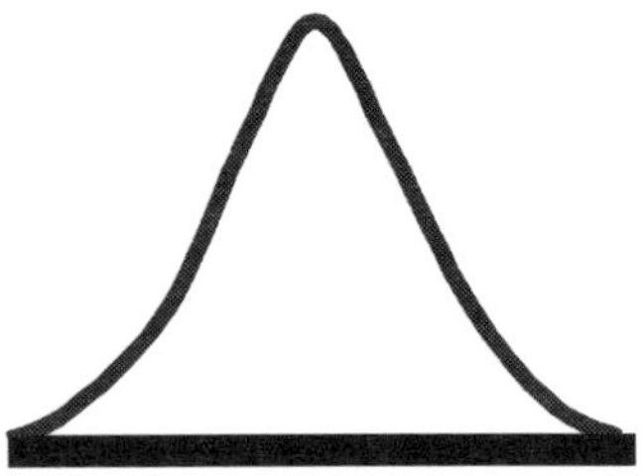

A normal curve is a general distribution of data that contains a few points at one end, a few at the other and most of the points in the middle. Many natural systems resemble a normal or bell curve. There are also parameters, such as human weight, strength, height, and so on. However, many things, such as students scores on a test are not bell shaped, but they are skewed. A skewed data set may represent an event when most students did particularly well or poorly on an assessment. Examining these trends assist the teacher to determine the effectiveness of instruction and follow-up procedures. In the case of poor scores, it may be possible that instruction was inadequate, the testing instrument was too difficult, items were confusing, students prepared poorly, or insufficient time was allowed for completion.

Central tendency is the description of how close the scores are to the center of the distribution. There are three primary means for describing central tendency, although one major one is used. The mean or arithmetic average is used most frequently and it is the sum of scores divided by the number of scores. It is generally the most stable descriptor. The median is the value in the middle when all scores are ordered from lowest to highest and the mode is the score that occurs most frequently. Two graphical examples are shown to assist in your understanding of these terms.

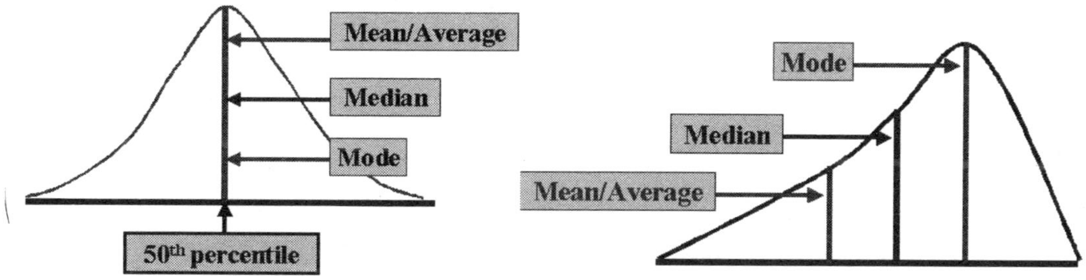

Dispersion is the amount a data point is away from the central tendency value. This can also be measured by what is called a deviation or standard deviation (SD) or the variance from the mean. The SD provides a number that indicates how far each score typically deviates from the mean and is less influenced by extreme scores. The variance is the standard deviation squared. For all normal curves, about 34% of the scores fall in the part of the curve that is between the mean and one SD from the mean; thus, about 68% of the scores fall between –1.0 and +1.0 SD. The graph below presents a summary of this information along with an example of intelligent quotient or IQ scores.

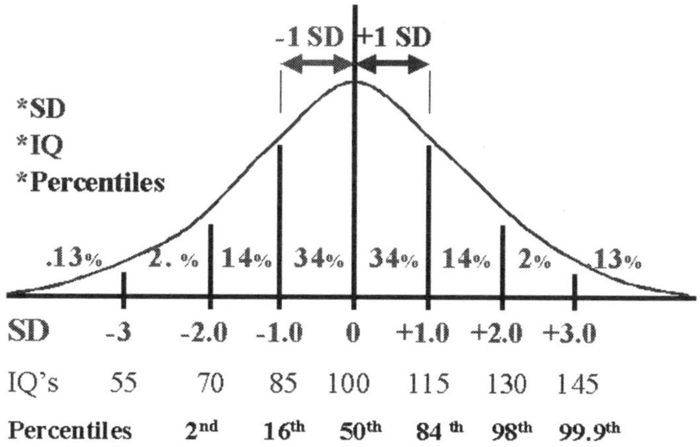

Correlation

It is important to not only be able to calculate scores, averages, and observe trends, but also to correlate these scores to one another as well as other variables that might affect student achievement and instructional strategies. Correlation is a measure of the association between multiple scores and it is helpful to develop what is termed a correlation coefficient, *r*, which has values from –1 to +1, inclusive. A +1 indicates a very strong positive relationship and a –1 indicates the opposite. Questions which might address relationships would be "Do people who are good at science tend to have a lower level of English"? Or "does student achievement tend to be lower in urban than in rural schools"?

Reliability

Reliability is the degree of consistency with which the measurement provides information about the examinee. Reliability is how well a test agrees with itself, or how stable and dependable is it measuring same thing with similar results. Hence, there is no measuring tape made of rubber, which would move and change each time something is measured. We often speak of a test as being reliable or not, does it test the students consistently. There are several methods used to determine test reliability, including test-retest, parallel form, internal consistency and inter-rater. You will learn much more about these in a later course dedicated to Assessment and Measurement.

Validity

> ***"There may often be excuse for doing things poorly in this world, but there is never any excuse for calling a poorly done thing well done."***
>
> —W. E. B. DuBois (1868–1963)

I³ *Write down any ideas that come to you after reading this quote.*

____

____

Validity is the degree to which a test measures that which it is intended to measure. It is determining whether interpretation of test scores and inferences drawn from test scores are appropriate and adequate. The degree to which the individual differences of test scores represent true differences in what is being measured and not from some other factor. Basically, this should be addressed so that you make certain you are testing what you intend to test. For example that you find a way to test mathematical skills and not the students English ability to read the math word problems. Therefore, we typically do not speak of a test as valid, but are the test scores valid with reference to their intended purpose.

There are three basic types of validity: content, criterion, and construct. Content validity is the extent to which the test's items represent the entire body of content that the test measures. Criterion is the extent to which one can infer from an individual's score on a test how well she or he will perform some other external task that is supposedly measured by the test. Construct is an unobservable, postulated attribute of individuals that we create to help us explain behavior.

Alternative/Authentic Assessment

Authentic assessment is a direct or performance assessment. It provides alternatives to traditional answer-select and refers to direct examination of student performance to life outside school. It is based on different view of learning and competence that assumes knowledge is a function of the context learned and used. It is not enough for students to learn science concepts—we want them to learn how to THINK! Also, it has a direct alignment between what is taught and assessed. It refers to students to actually performing, demonstrating, constructing, or developing a product or solution under defined conditions. There are various types of this assessment, which include portfolios, on-demand tasks, projects, demonstrations, and teacher observations. Factors that favor authentic assessment are demands for accountability; use of test scores to make high-stake decisions; negative consequences of high-stakes testing programs; increasing criticisms of standardized tests; and changing views of aptitude, learning, and knowledge.

I^3 *So what do you think of assessment now?*

KWL

What Did You LEARN?

Answers to the Listening Quiz

1. Is there a fourth of July in England? *Yes, July 4th comes after the third*
2. How many birth days does the average person have? *A person has just one birthday*
3. Some months have 31 days; how many have 28? *All of the months have 31 days*
4. If there are 3 apples and you take away 2, how many do you have? *2—You took them*
5. How many members of each animal did Moses take on the ark? *Moses did not take any animals, Noah did*
6. A clerk in the butcher shop is 5′ 10″ tall. What does he weigh? *A butcher weighs meat*

Reference

Fenner, D. E. W. (Ed.) (1999). The problem with grading. In Fenner, D. E. W. (Ed.) *Ethics in Education.* New York: Garland Press, pp. 243–257.

CHAPTER 11—ASSESSMENT AND MEASUREMENT

PowerPoint Outline to Assist In-Class Note-Taking

A. What Is Assessment, Measurement, and Evaluation?

B. Standardized Tests

a. Norm Reference Tests

b. Criterion Reference Tests

C. Lake Wobegon

D. Test Preparation

E. Test Score Pollution

F. Item Analysis

G. Normal Curved, Central Tendency, and Dispersion

H. Correlation

I. Reliability

J. Validity

K. Alternative/Authentic Assessment

12

Are You Ready to Teach?

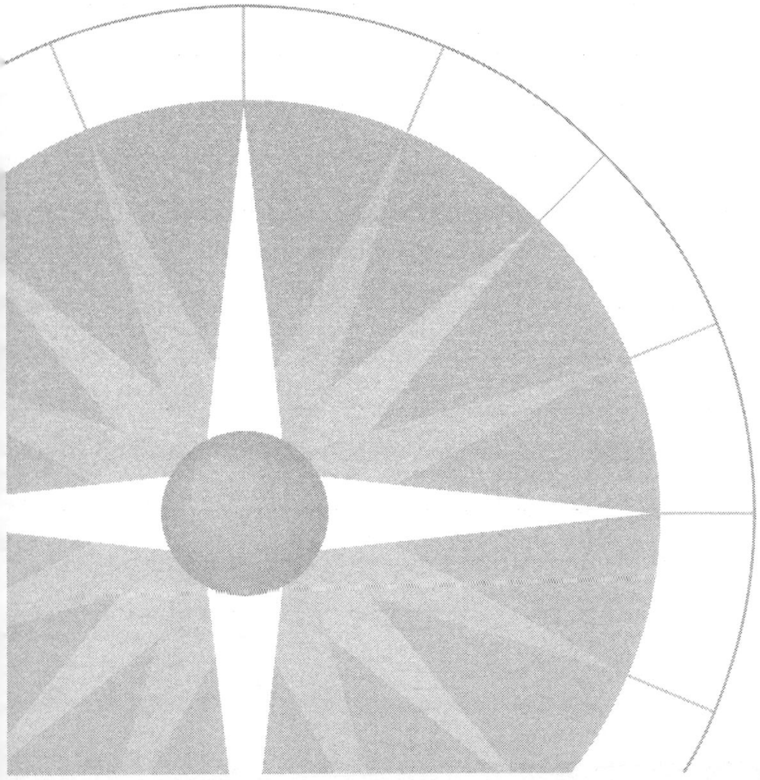

Guest Editorial: Gordon Rakita, PhD, Assistant Professor of Anthropology/College of Arts and Sciences, UNF

I have been asked to write about the question "Are you ready to teach?" Having gotten this far in this textbook and accompanying course, I suspect most of you already have a fairly good answer to that question. Or if not, you are at least prepared to ask and answer that question of yourself. And I imagine that for many of you, the answer is "yes." You can probably point to many things that have prepared you to teach or that indicate your readiness to be a teacher. Certainly completing this class is one such validation of your training and preparation.

I should like to preface my comments with a short exposition (or assertion, admission, confession; whichever way you want to see it) about who I am and my expertise. I have only a limited experience in the teaching field. I am a bioarchaeologist, which is a fancy way of saying I study human skeletons from prehistoric sites. I am especially interested in studying how people buried their dead in times long past. So I am perhaps more comfortable dealing with people who are quite dead. Training in bioarchaeology is no more or less rigorous than many other fields. I spent a good portion of my robustly healthy youth scratching in the dirt uncovering skeletons, or in the laboratory analyzing those skeletons, or in front of a computer writing about those skeletons. But I also spent an even larger percentage of that youth taking graduate courses in the methods and theories of archaeology and biological anthropology. In between I worked as a research assistant for the leading bioarchaeologist in the country. In all, the process of scoring a plum job teaching anthropology at an accredited university took me somewhere close to a decade; at the end of which my robust health had faded into simple health that I aid with the judicious ingestion of appropriate levels of caffeine and alcohol. I often like to quote the movie archaeologist, Indiana Jones, "It's not the years, it's the mileage."

My employment in the university (or *academe* to use the more pompous term), has been and promises to be a wonderful experience. Here, I am given a private office and ample laboratory space. I have insightful colleagues whom I learn from each day. I am given time to do my own research on whatever topics I might wish to pursue. And I *get to teach.* Actually, I don't so much get to teach as the university *demands* it of me. Indeed, the faculty handbook that I was presented with upon my arrival states that "Teaching is the primary mission of the University." All of this is fine by me because I love to teach. But am I ready to teach? Or was I ready to teach when my appointment here started? I certainly had had some experience teaching. I had served as a teaching assistant in undergraduate and graduate school. I had even taught some courses. But scan back through my short autobiography above. Had I been trained in pedagogical techniques? I had not. Did I take coursework in theories of teaching and learning? I had not. Was I ever certified by a city, state, or federal governing body? I had not. Now I could try to argue that I had learned my pedagogical skills on the streets, in the trenches, walking the walk not just talking the talk, and out there actually doing. I surely did learn things about teaching that way. But the reality is I have no formal training in teaching. From a very reasonable perspective, I was not and am not ready to teach.

Of course, whether one is ready to teach or not is a question that can be asked at a variety of levels (or scales of analysis, to use the parlance of my field). Are you ready to begin a career teaching? Are you ready to teach the course you have been assigned this fall or spring? Are you ready to teach the upcoming unit on differential equations, bone histology, phonics, or whatever? Or are you simply ready to teach today's class? I find I ask this last question of myself often in the 10 minutes before I go to class. Sometime my answer involves cursing at my computer when it chooses exactly that moment to crash while burning my lecture presentation to a CD. On better days, my answer involves going over in my mind the examples, concepts, questions, and pedagological tricks that I plan to use. Both sorts of answers are useful in their own way, and I hope you'll find yourself answer in the vein of the latter more often than the former. "Are you ready to teach?" is an excellent question to ask yourself at whatever scale of analysis. It helps you make sure you are ready to teach. But I would also like to suggest what I think is an equally good question to ask—*Are you ready to learn?*

That's right—*Learn!* I may have a fairly brief history as a teacher, but I think you'll agree that I have considerable experience being a student. And what I've observed is that teachers who are constantly and perpetually willing to learn make far better teachers than those who are not. Well, you might ask, "What is there to learn?" You've taken all the courses in your topical area and know the stuff like the back of your hand, right? You've been certified to teach in your area, right? What more is there? Plenty!

Part of my job is to teach about the evolution of the human species. When I was taught human evolution (some 12 years ago) I could count on my fingers the number of species of fossil hominids that were known. Nowadays, there are dozens and dozens of species. I needed to keep up, and to learn not just a few new species names, but how they all fit into the grand picture of human evolution. I need to learn not just the facts, but the concepts. And I need to know them well enough to be able to teach them to others.

When I began teaching, Microsoft's PowerPoint didn't exist. Neither did BlackBoard, MP3s, PDAs, or even the Internet as we know it today. I've had to learn these new ways of presenting ideas and information to students. I've also had to learn which are effective (and in which circumstances) and which are not. It's not just the big things either, this year our campus audio-visual department has moved to padlocking the media podiums in the large classrooms. I have no idea what the combination is for the lock in the room I'll be teaching in, but I'll learn.

I've had to learn all those pedagological theories and methods that they didn't teach me in graduate school. I still wouldn't know Piaget from Vygotsky, but I'm getting better. I'm cognizant now that different students learn in different ways. I think about authentic assessment techniques, even if I'm still struggling to implement them.

Perhaps most importantly, I'm learning from my students. They are the clearest guide to what's working and what's not working in the classroom. Are my assessments inauthentic? My students will let me know. Is that new set of PowerPoint slides a clear exposition of the ideas I wish to convey, or am I spending too much class time clarifying my points? Is there a flaw in the logic of an argument I present? You better believe my students will set me straight. And if I don't improve, if I don't progress, if I don't *learn* just as fast as they do—they'll send me packing.

So think about whether you're ready to teach. By all means take time to consider that question. But give me someone who's ready to learn—from their mistakes, from others, from their students, on their own—and I'll show you a great teacher in the making. Being ready to teach makes you a teacher. Being ready to learn makes you an even better teacher.

KWL

What Do You KNOW? **(prior knowledge)**

What Do You WANT to Know? **(objectives and goals)**

> ***"I believe that every teacher should realize the dignity of his calling; that he is a social servant set apart for the maintenance of proper social order and the securing of the right social growth."***
>
> —JOHN DEWEY

I^3 *Write down any ideas that come to you after reading this quote.*

"Great minds discuss ideas; Average minds discuss events; Small minds discuss people."

—ELEANOR ROOSEVELT

I^3 *Write down any ideas that come to you after reading this quote.*

____

____

I^3 *How can you justify that both of these quotes may have merit?*

____

____

Hopefully, you have many concerns about being ready to teach. This is normal and a healthy perspective.

You may be wondering,

"How good of a teacher will I be?"

"Will I be able to keep my student's attention?"

"Can I develop effective lesson plans?"

"How will I teach everything and prepare my students for standardized test?"

"How will I gain students respect and still be liked?"

These are good questions and if you continue to ask good questions, chances are resolutions will be found.

I^3 *Write down other good questions that you might have at this point about your preparedness to teach.*

____

____

____

Am I as Smart as I Am Supposed to Be?

Actually a past student had asked me this question and I thought it was one of the most honest and insightful questions I had ever heard. After a great deal of thought, I have realized that a student will be as smart as they are suppose to be if, and only if they can answer the following one hundred questions accurately. Care to give them a try?

Are These the Top 100 Important Questions in Life?

1. Name three people who have been part of your dream.
2. Tell me something amazing.
3. Name one learning theory and define.

4. Tell me one objective from the syllabus.
5. Who is your hero?
6. Write a commercial slogan that best describes you.
7. If you were an animal, what animal would you be and why?
8. Define success.
9. What are your goals for this course (please do not say an "A")?
10. If you were Gilligan, name three people that you would like to have on the deserted island.
11. Again, you are Gilligan, name three things that you would like to have.
12. What is the most important concept that you learned during our last session.
13. What is that song that is in your head right now?
14. Write a question that you have over and over.
15. How has your behavior been conditioned over your life?
16. So, if a tree falls in the woods and no one is there to hear it, does it make a sound?
17. What makes the world go round?
18. What is life?
19. What's it all about?
20. Who do you trust?
21. Has there been a teacher in your past that has really impacted you? (Name three major characteristics that they possessed.)
22. What is the CPT, who developed it and why should you use it?
23. What is LP gas and why is it L?
24. What is your favorite TV sit-com? Drama?
25. What is your favorite color? Why?
26. Describe the last novel you read.
27. What museum did you visit last (if not, aquarium or zoo)?
28. How does determining the role of socialization in schools address one of our objectives?
29. Describe your most comfortable environment in detail.
30. If you were king of curriculum, what three topics would you teach?
31. If (hypothetically) your mother were to call me, what would it be in reference to?
32. On your last vacation, did you do anything educational? If not, what will you be doing educational on your next vacation?
33. What is an ed voucher?
34. What is technology?
35. In 5 years, you would like to be living in (rural area, suburbs, etc.)?
36. In 5 years, the kind of place you would like to live in?
37. In 5 years, you would like to be working as a what?
38. In your spare time (those few precious minutes), what do you enjoy doing?
39. Define your style: observer, leader, follower, assertive, passive, aggressive, or other.
40. How important is a mentor within your career? How will you choose a good mentor?
41. A meteorite is heading toward earth, you have 24 hours before it hits and all life is destroyed. What do you do?
42. What is morality? What is ethics?
43. If you had a digital camera, what would you use it for?
44. What is your current ISP? Do you connect by DSL, ISDN, modem, or Broadband?
45. When is the last time you went fishing and what did you catch?
46. When is the last time you picnicked and where?
47. What is Ritalin?
48. What is your favorite city and why?
49. What is your favorite musician and song?

50. What is your favorite work of art?
51. Who is your favorite scientist and why?
52. Who is your favorite philosopher and why?
53. What is your favorite movie and why?
54. Do you believe that others think as you do?
55. Are you any different that the person next to you?
56. Describe one or two of the most important accomplishments.
57. How would you describe your learning style?
58. How do you handle criticism? Can you give me an example?
59. On your first job interview for a teaching position, the principal asks, "Why should I hire you?" What do you say?
60. Describe yourself using three adjectives.
61. If you were a road sign, what would you say?
62. If you could travel anywhere in the world, where would you go and why?
63. You were abducted by aliens. What were they like and what did they do/say to you?
64. You have multiple personalities. Describe a few of them.
65. If you were some ice cream, what flavor would you be?
66. What would your autobiography be called and why?
67. If you could be a superhero, who would you be and what powers would you have?
68. Which is better: shampoo or conditioner?
69. What's your worst injury ever? Describe what happened.
70. How many hours per week do you watch TV?
71. If you could get a tattoo, would you? What would it look like and where would you want it?
72. Pop? Soda? Soda pop? Does it really matter?
73. If you got stuck on a deserted island, what movie, CD, and person could you not live without?
74. Do you brush your teeth before or after eating breakfast and why?
75. Which TV show or movie best describes your life?
76. List the 10 largest cities in the United States.
77. List five of those cities and its correlating population.
78. How does the dominant industrial factory model of management, education, and leadership continue to manifest itself and why has it become outmodeled and obsolete?
79. How do *you* judge when pasta is done?
80. How do we reconcile the paradox of having a nineteenth century education system that is trying to serve the needs of the twenty-first century?
81. What value does the brick-and-mortar world play in preparing us for the future?
82. What did you last learn and how do you measure it?
83. When did you last observe an educator learning?
84. If we cannot manage change, how do we stay ahead of it?
85. If you could be a character in a movie, who would you be and tell me why you want to be that character?
86. What was the last thing that made you laugh with a good belly laugh—not just a chuckle?
87. Have you ever worn your pajamas outside of the house? If yes, what were you doing? If no, why not?
88. Pick an animal that reminds you of yourself in some way (don't say why, let me try and guess).
89. Have you ever played the Hokey-Pokey?
90. Do you step on bugs that cross your path or let them pass?
91. What is your worst fear?
92. What is your greatest accomplishment so far in life?

93. If you rented a movie and were late returning it and then you died, would someone you know or a family member have to pay the late fee?
94. Before you were the age of seven, what did you want to be when you grew up?
95. Do you like any unusual foods that your friends would say "yuck" to if offered?
96. What was the most interesting book you've ever read?
97. Have you ever walked in your sleep?
98. Who would you like to be if you could not be you?
99. Have you ever eaten honey straight from the comb?
100. Have you ever ridden a motorcycle?

First Teaching Position

What's the best advice for a first year teacher?

Some will tell you to stay away from the teacher's lounge, for it is where all the gossip and cynicism lies. Others will suggest you find a way to survive, stay afloat, and take short-cuts. In actuality, if you took your collegiate experience seriously and consciously attended to your coursework and field experiences, you will have the foundation and skills to step into the classroom. After the first 5 minutes, you will realize that it takes much more to make through the next five minutes, let alone an entire day. If you were smart enough to build relationships with colleagues, professors, and other support persons, then you will most likely be able to survive the first few days. However, it will require more than that to make teaching a career. Through the milieu of trials and tribulations, there is only one thing that will ensure your success—passion. If you have passion and truly love teaching, you will be able to not only make it through the first day, but you will find a way to enjoy it.

State Certification Requirements (FTCE, 2004)

Most states have professional certification licenses to teach in that state. To obtain one of these, you must typically earn an undergraduate degree from an accredited college and successful pass their state teacher certification exam. In the state of Florida this is called the Florida Teacher Certification Exam or FTCE. The FTCE is composed of three tests: professional education, general knowledge, and subject area exams. Depending upon your background, you may need to take one, two, or three of the tests.

1. **Professional Education**—Candidates applying for a professional certificate may need to take the Professional Education Test. See your official statement of status of eligibility.
   - This multiple-choice test assesses general knowledge of pedagogy and professional practices and consists of approximately 120 items.
   - A revised, updated version of the Professional Education Test was administered for the first time in July 2003.
   - The revised *Competencies and Skills,* Eighth Edition may be accessed online.
2. **Subject Area Exam**—These are exams for degreed academic and some vocational subject areas. These exams measure content area knowledge, usually in a multiple-choice format. English 6–12, Middle Grades English 5–9, French K–12, German K–12, and Spanish K–12 also require an essay. Spanish K–12 and French K–12 are administered in a language lab, and German K–12 has an interview. Speech 6–12 has a videotaped portion. Candidates applying for a Professional Certificate and those adding a subject area to a Professional Certificate must pass a subject area exam in the field(s) in which they seek certification.

3. **General Knowledge Test**—Prior to July 1, 2002, the required basic skills test for teacher certification was the CLAST. Beginning July 1, 2002, the required basic skills test for teacher certification is the General Knowledge Test for which you can register using the application in the registration bulletin. The General Knowledge Test is a basic skills achievement test containing four subtests: mathematics (multiple-choice, items), reading (multiple-choice passage-based items), English language skills (multiple-choice items), and essay.

National Board Teacher Certification (NBTC, 2004)

After teaching for at least 3 years, you can consider applying to be a National Board Certified Teacher. The National Board Certification® measures a teacher's practice against high and rigorous standards. The process is an extensive series of performance-based assessments that includes teaching Portfolios, student work samples, videotapes, and thorough analyses of the candidates' classroom teaching and student learning. Teachers also complete a series of written exercises that probe the depth of their subject-matter knowledge, as well as their understanding of how to teach those subjects to their students.

National Board Certification is voluntary and open to all people who have a baccalaureate degree and three years of classroom experience in either a public or private school. It is valid for 10 years, after which a teacher must seek renewal. The fee for National Board Certification is $2,300.

Your First Job and What You can Expect as a Beginning Teacher

"In the time of your life, live."

—William Saroyan

I^3 *Write down any ideas that come to you after reading this quote.*

____

____

"If you have a job without aggravations, you don't have a job."

—Malcolm S. Forbes

I^3 *Write down any ideas that come to you after reading this quote.*

____

____

I^3 *How can you justify that both of these quotes may have merit?*

____

____

Your first professional job should be an exciting event, although very possibly very stressful. Of course, this is normal and will subside, however, I encourage you to embrace this time and uncertainty, for it may be an event that could never occur again in your lifetime.

“Life is a series of moments; to live each one is to succeed.”

—CORITA KENT

If life is truly a series of moments, then one should capitalize on those moments, even the ones, which are not thought of as “good moments.”

As a beginning teacher, you can expect chaos, uncertainty, confusion, and pain. But you can also expect moments of joy, satisfaction, and exhilaration. The better questions are what do you do in these cases and how can you create more of the latter experiences. First of all, you need to realize they will not create themselves. The young teacher who is under the impression that life will thrust its jewels on them may find somewhat different from the world. We have all seen our share of motivational statements even before you picked up this book, and they are fairly simple in their approach. YOU are the one who make their time and especially their moments as a beginning teacher either fruitful or full of something else. Please do not underestimate the power of your initial indoctrination to the world of education. Far too often, it only takes a few months to convince young teachers that this profession may not be for them. Or even worse, they begin their steady slid into the cynical world of becoming a negative, bitter veteran teacher, whom I am guessing we have all had the displeasure of interacting with at some point of our educational career.

The First Day—Relationships with Students, Colleagues, Administrators, and Parents

“Try not to mess up. This will satisfy a few people, and amaze everyone else.”

—FORREST GUMP

I^3 *Write down any ideas that come to you after reading this quote.*

____

____

“I don’t know the key to success, but the key to failure is trying to please everybody.”

—BILL COSBY

I^3 *Write down any ideas that come to you after reading this quote.*

____

____

I^3 *How can you justify that both of these quotes may have merit?*

____

____

You may hear many “rules of thumb” for approaching your first day as a teacher and developing appropriate relationships with students, colleagues, administrators, and parents. Many say, “don’t smile until Christmas,” meaning that students may react a certain way if you address the objectives of the course first and "being a friend" later. Rules of thumb are nice, but the bottom line is that all of your students (and colleagues and administrators and parents) are unique fragile organic masses, which we call human beings. As such, you will need to use all of the education you acquired in your pre-service teacher program, including understanding how people learn and behave to address each person individually and with respect to how they react. This may sound like an oversimplification and impossible, however, the theories and models that you will be provided with in you program of study will provide you with the tools needed to address practically every situation that you will encounter in teaching.

Job Options

"It is not the man who has too little, but the man who craves more, who is poor."

—Lucius Annaeus Seneca

"In a consumer society, there are inevitably two kinds of slaves: the prisoners of addiction, and the prisoners of envy."

—Ivan Illych

"A man's treatment of money is the most decisive test of his character—how he makes it and how he spends it."

—James Moffatt

"Money may buy you a mattress to sleep on, but it won't buy you a good night's sleep."

—Zig Ziglar

"A man is rich in proportion to the number of things which he can afford to let alone."

—Henry David Thoreau

I^3 *Think about these quotes (there are several, hopefully one will speak to you). After carefully considering these, share a few statements on how these relate or could help you gain perspective of your options and their outcomes?*

____

____

____

____

____

There are many options for those possessing an undergraduate degree in the field of education. Even though there are sever shortages for classroom teachers, some students may prefer to consider other educational avenues, such as informal education opportunities in museums, zoological parks, aquariums, science and nature centers, and so on. In addition, there are possibilities writing and editing curriculum at textbook companies as well as educational software companies.

If any of these alternative educational environments seem interesting to you, the best approach is to visit them frequently, ask questions and possibly even volunteer as a docent, who is typically a volunteer guide, who conducts visitors through museums and delivers a commentary on the exhibitions. These informal settings require staff with an educational background to provide signage, talks, guidance, and possibly arrange the exhibits in a way that people can best understand them.

There are also many leadership possibilities and venturing into another specific field such as business can be attractive to those who would like to teach, but found that the traditional forum of a public K–12 school system is not where their strengths reside.

Education Issues for the Twenty-First Century

"The most powerful force in the world? Compound interest."

—Albert Einstein

I³ *Write down any ideas that come to you after reading this quote.*

____

____

"I am interested in why the apple falls. The company wants me to catch it and make applesauce."

—H. J. Shaw

I³ *Write down any ideas that come to you after reading this quote.*

____

____

"When you come to a fork in the road, take it."

—Yogi Berra

I³ *Write down any ideas that come to you after reading this quote.*

____

____

"A fish could not discover water, nor Native Americans find a 'scenic vista.'"

—Michael Phillips

I³ *Write down any ideas that come to you after reading this quote.*

____

____

"History never repeats itself. Man always does."

—VOLTAIRE

I³ *Write down any ideas that come to you after reading this quote.*

____

____

____

I³ *Can you prepare a global statement summarizing (synthesizing) these statements?*

____

____

____

There are many perspectives on the issues for the future of education, some indicate that technology is either overemphasized or understated; others are concerned about literacy and still others believe we are losing the science and technology race, which we had secured by through our NASA program. The first step to answering these questions is to understand the issues and be able to connect them to our society nationally and as a global unit. This is a major reason why you, as a teacher candidate are taking general education courses and why you will want to share information with your students and help them become a literate citizen.

What Is (Y)Our Vision for the Future of Education?

"A hundred years from now it will not matter what my bank account was, the sort of house I lived in, or the kind of car I drove. . . . but the world may be different because I was important in the life of a child."

—SIMONE WEIL

I³ *Write down any ideas that come to you after reading this quote.*

____

____

"This time, like all times, is a very good one, if we but know what to do with it."

—RALPH WALDO EMERSON

I³ *Write down any ideas that come to you after reading this quote.*

____

____

"Time is but a stream I go a-fishing in."

—Henry David Thoreau

I³ *Write down any ideas that come to you after reading this quote.*

___

___

"Only those who will risk going too far can possibly find out how far one can go."

—T. S. Eliot

I³ *Write down any ideas that come to you after reading this quote.*

___

___

"You make a living by what you get. You make a life by what you give."

—Winston Churchill

I³ *Write down any ideas that come to you after reading this quote.*

___

___

I³ *Can you prepare a global statement summarizing (synthesizing) these statements?*

___

___

In the year 2000, the "top issue in the nation (of the United States)" was education (the second-ranked issue was the economy/jobs/taxes from a survey of 1,000 adults by Reuters, June 2000). So it is no surprise to anyone that many people, even outside the world of education have been, currently are and most likely will be in the future very concerned with education. One might wonder with all of this concern, why very little has been done to reform the educational system and address all of the issues and needs that we have identified throughout this book.

I³ *Please take a moment and try to come up with a few thoughts to this question: Why haven't we addressed these weaknesses throughout the past several decades?*

___

___

___

___

___

What Is YOUR Educational Philosophy?

I^3 *Please share your current educational philosophy. You will be asked to share this throughout your teacher candidate program and ultimately when you intern. You may not have a clear vision of this now, but it will be interesting to look back on this when you are about to graduate and view the difference in your thoughts.*

Priorities

"I've had a lot of problems in my life and most of them never happened."

—Mark Twain

I^3 *Write down any ideas that come to you after reading this quote.*

"The three moments in a man's life: when he buys a house, a car, and a new color TV. That's what America is all about."

—Archie Bunker

I^3 *Write down any ideas that come to you after reading this quote.*

"The problem with the rat race is that even if you win, you're still a rat."

—Lily Tomlin

I^3 *Write down any ideas that come to you after reading this quote.*

I^3 *Are these quotes humorous? Do they still have relevance? Why/why not?*

A philosophy professor stood before his class and had some items in front of him. When class began, wordlessly he picked up a large empty mayonnaise jar and proceeded to fill it with rocks, rocks about 2 inches in diameter. He then asked the students if the jar was full. They agreed that it was. So the professor then picked up a box of pebbles and poured them into the jar. He shook the jar lightly. The pebbles, of course, rolled into the open areas between the rocks. He then asked the students again if the jar was full. They agreed it was. The students laughed. The professor picked up a box of sand and poured it into the jar. Of course, the sand filled up everything else. "Now," said the professor, "I want you to recognize that this is like your life. The rocks are the important things—your family, your partner, your health, your children—anything that is so important to you that if it were lost, you would be nearly destroyed. The pebbles are the other things that matter like your job, your house, your car. The sand is everything else—the small stuff. If you put the sand into the jar first, there is no room for the pebbles or the rocks. The same goes for your life. If you spend all your energy and time on the small stuff, you will never have room for the things that are important to you. Pay attention to the things that are critical to your happiness. Play with your children. Take time to get medical checkups. Take your partner out dancing. There will always be time to go to work, clean the house, give a dinner party, and fix the disposal. Take care of the rocks first—the things that really matter. Set your priorities. The rest is just sand."

I^3 *What does this mean to you? What are your priorities? How do you determine your priorities? Do you believe these will change? How and why?*

I^3 *So what do you think—are you ready to teach?*

What Did You LEARN?

References

Florida Teachers Certification Exam. (2004). Web site. Retrieved July 2004 from *http://www.firn.edu/doe/sas/ftce/ftcedesc.htm*

National Board Certification Program. (2004). Web site. Retrieved July 2004 from *http://www.nbpts.org/about/index.cfm*

CHAPTER 12—ARE YOU READY TO TEACH?

PowerPoint Outline to Assist In-Class Note-Taking

A. Am I as Smart as I Am Supposed to Be?

B. First Teaching Position

a. What's the best advice for a first-year teacher?

C. State Certification Requirements

a. FTCE

b. NCATE

c. National Board Certification and Alternative Certification

D. Your First Job and What You Can Expect as a Beginning Teacher

E. The First Day—Relationships with Students, Colleagues, Administrators and Parents

F. Essential Instructor Goals

G. Job Options

H. Education Issues for the Twenty-First Century

I. What Is (Y)Our Vision for the Future of Education?

a. What Is YOUR Educational Philosophy?

b. Priorities

EPILOGUE

Author Editorial: Jace Hargis, PhD, Director, Faculty Enhancement and Assistant Professor of Education/UNF

What is an epilogue anyway? An epilogue is the closing part of a discourse, in which the principal matters are recapitulated; a conclusion. The intentions of this epilogue are more to guide you to a culminating perspective. I hope to provide some thoughts that will enable to you place the information in this book into perspective and as always "keep you thinking."

You may have thought that I have already said plenty in this book and what other opinions could I have to share. I will not attempt to repeat any of the "very important" information that I am certain you have read, understood, used, and incorporated into your working schema. However, I would like to provide a brief insight of advice. Typically, I do not give advice unless I am asked for it, so you can feel free to skip over this section if you believe that you cannot benefit from advice of someone such as myself. However, my advice is short, simple and to the point.

The Need to Fail

I believe we need to fail. This may sound odd coming from an educator who many perceive as the keeper and promoter of success and that failure or a failing grade is the worst thing that could ever happen to someone. If I could change one major societal perspective, it would be how we view failure. People need to fail, they need to be provided opportunities to fail multiple times and given a supportive structure in which to learn from these events (some crazy people call this structure a school, imagine that?). We have all heard amazing human-interest stories about those who have failed and then gone on to accomplish great things. How about those who have failed and failed again and then possibly failed again, never even coming remotely close to success? Were their failures any less valuable than those who made it into the newspaper? I would propose that their failures are even more important to them as well as to those who are aware of their failures.

So, the bottom line is that I believe we all should have and maintain a healthy **need to fail!**

Supportive Statements on Failure

"I have missed more than 9000 shots in my career. I have lost almost 300 games. On 26 occasions I have been entrusted to take the game winning shot and missed. And I have failed over and over and over again in my life. And that is why, I succeed."

—Michael Jordan

I am going to throw out the names of some people. Each of them shifted career goals at some point in their lives. Let me tell you what would have happened if each one had committed irreversibly to an earlier dream, had "taken charge" and "refused to fail."

- John Wooden would have become a civil engineer.
- Rod Serling would have been a P.E. coach.
- Reggie Jackson would have stayed in football.
- Rush Limbaugh would still be a PR man for a baseball team.
- Boris Yeltsin would have been a construction supervisor.

"The silliest question that intelligent people ask is 'Where do you want to be in five years?' Thank goodness I haven't had a job interview in forty years—I hate that where-do-you-want-to-be question. I plan to be a different person in the future. I don't know who I want to be five years from now, much less where."

—Dale Dauten

Wrap Up

Now for those who have mastered the long term memory, you will know this, but for those still working on this phenomenon, feel free to review an earlier chapter.

"Don't recite other people's opinions. I hate quotations. Tell me what you know."

—Ralph Waldo Emerson

I^3 *Remember this quote earlier in this book. Now that it is presented in its complete form, please share your thoughts and possibly look back on your earlier thoughts and try to make sense of the differences.*

So, Am I Really Ready to Teach?

Of course not. Chances are, this is your first educational course and one course does not a teacher make. However, hopefully, you are well on your way and more importantly, you have identified critical elements, which you will attend to over the next several years. The more important, pertinent question is am I ready to fail?

For now, take this first year teacher test. ***(Answers are at the end of the chapter)***

1. How do you put a giraffe into a refrigerator?

   ____

2. How do you put an elephant into a refrigerator?

   ____

3. The lion king is hosting an animal conference. All the animals attend except one. Which animal does not attend?

   ____

4. There is a river where the crocodiles live. How do you manage to cross it?

   ____

Here is another quick assessment called the "Gossip Test." Your answers to these may help you gain some insight as to how you process.

1. Most of the time, I let the cat out of the bag when someone is expecting me to keep a secret.
2. I enjoy telling stories about other people's misfortune.
3. I often times see the negative in people.
4. I rarely talk about myself, because I'm usually talking about others.
5. I've embellished stories to make them sound more interesting.
6. I see the weeds more than the flowers when I'm looking at others.
7. I sometimes find myself telling secrets and breaking confidentialities.
8. I like to snoop out personal information about people.
9. I've started a story like this: "I'll tell you this it you promise not to tell anyone . . ."
10. I tend to tell stories about others because it makes me feel important or accepted.

Final Advice (Schmich, 1997)

1. Don't worry about the future—or worry, but realize that worrying is as effective as trying to solve an algebra equation by chewing bubble gum. The real troubles in your life are apt to be things that never crossed your mind.
2. Do one thing every day that scares you—it will keep you alive!
3. Remember the compliments you receive, forget the insults—if you succeed, tell me how.
4. Travel—live in New York City, but leave before it makes you hard and live in northern California, but leave before it makes you soft.
5. Advice is a form of nostalgia. Dispensing it is a way of fishing the past from the disposal, wiping it off, painting over the ugly parts and recycling it for more than its worth.

Answers to Management Quiz

1. Open the refrigerator, take out the giraffe, put in the elephant, and close the door—tests your logic skills.
2. The Elephant. He/she is still in the refrigerator—tests your memory skills.
3. Open the refrigerator, put the giraffe in, close the door—tests whether you are doing simple things in a complicated way.
4. Simply swim through it. The crocodiles are at the animal conference—tests your comprehensive skills.